Asceticism in Ancient India and Ancient Greece

A Comparative Study

ANITA GOSWAMI

ANAMIKA PUBLISHERS & DISTRIBUTORS (P) LTD.
4697/3, 21A, Ansari Road, Daryaganj, New Delhi-110 002
Phones: 011-23281655, 011-43708938
e-mail: anamikapublishers@yahoo.co.in

Edition 2026

ISBN 978-81-7975-712-3

PRINTED IN INDIA

Published by Anamika Publishers & Distributors (P) Ltd., 4697/3, 21A, Ansari Road, Daryaganj, New Delhi 110002. Typset by Shivani Computer, Delhi 110093 and Printed at Nagri Printers, Delhi.

CONTENTS

ACKNOWLEDGEMENT

I take this opportunity of expressing my heart-felt reverence and gratitude to my esteemed teacher and supervisor Prof. Udai Prakash Arora, who inspired in me a passion for history, and without whose sagacious, ready and ungrudging assistance, this thesis would have remained merely a dream. His guidance served me as a beacon light in my efforts to make my way through the dark hours of my undertaking. I am grateful to Prof. Atul Kumar Sinha (Deptt. of Ancient History and Culture, University Campus, Bareilly), who encouraged me much in the pursuit of my research. I owe my gratitude also to Dr. R.P. Yadav, Dr. Abhay Singh, Dr. Shyam Bihari Lal, Dr. Vijay Bahadur Yadav (Deptt. of Ancient History and Culture, University Campus, Bareilly) for rendering me valuable help during the course of my research. I also express my reverence and gratitude to Mrs. Gita Arora for encouraging and inspiring me in various ways to bring this thesis to completion.

I am also thankful to Dr. Pankaj Sharma, Dr. Anup Ranjan Mishra and Dr. Aparna Mathur (Deptt. of Ancient History and Culture, University Campus, Bareilly) for giving me their kind guidance, suggessions and support while doing my thesis.

I am greatly indebted to Indian Council for Historical Research, New Delhi for granting me Junior Research Fellowship for this research work.

First of all I would like to pay my highly gratitude to my loving kids Amitansh and Divyangna for their innocent support to me. I would like to feel heartly thankful for my better half my husband for their innenre support and encouragement for make this dream come true in the form of book. I am also thankful lovable support of my in law Mr. Shiv Kumar Giri and Mrs. Kamla Devi for helping me in all the manners.

My friends who always encouraged me for future and given me support to fulfill my dreams and to do my thesis, also deserve my thanks specially to Rashmi, Puja, Parul, Mahendra, Vikas, Prashant, Mahima & Renu.

My parents Mrs. Malti Goswami and Mr. Rajju Giri Goswami not merely permitted me to undertake this work but also encouraged and inspired me much during the course of my research. I am thankful to my elder brother Mr. Yogesh for guiding me and giving me support all the time. I also thanks to Neetu, Rajeev, Vivek, Rishabh and Neeraj Bhabhi. I pay my tribute to my very respectable and loving elder sister Late Mrs. Seema who always supported and encouraged me to do hard work, she will always remain in my heart and encourage me in future. It would have been impossible to complete this work without my family's care, support and active cooperation.

For the collection of materials, I also owe my gratitude to the library staff of Indian Council for Historical Research, New Delhi, Central Library, Rohilkhand University Campus, Bareilly for rendering me valuable help.

I am specially thankful to Mr. Pankaj for publishing my thesis into book form and make my dream come true. I am thankful to Anamika Publshers & Distributer for printing this book in superb manner.

In the end I owe my deepest gratitude to the various scholars of history whose works have been of immense help in pursuit of my research.

ANITA GOSWAMI

ASCETICISM : ITS ORIGIN, DEVELOPMENT, MEANING AND FORMS

According to Encyclopedia of Religion the word asceticism is taken from the Greek noun askesis, meaning "exercise, practice, training." The Greek athlete, for example, subjected himself to systematic exercise or training in order to attain a goal of physical fitness. In time, however, the word began to assume philosophical, spiritual, and ethical implications: one could "exercise" and "train" not only the body in the pursuit of physical goal but also systematically and rigorously—the will, the mind, and the soul as to attain a more virtuous life or a higher spiritual state.[1]

For Louis Dumont, the French sociologist, the renouncer, as he calls him the ascetic or samnyasin, as he is known in Brahamanic tradition, is the only class of preson that is an individual[2]. Only the samnyasin, as long as he has renounced society, is an individual;..... As La Vallee Poussin has said "The renouncer is not sceptical, he freely admits all the traditional and popular mythology... his aspiration is direct beyond the worlds, it is something hypercosmical (lokattara).. It is really too adventurous to say that the agent of development in Indian religion and speculation, the "creator of values", has been the renouncer... Not only the founding of sects and their maintenance, but the major idea, the "inventions" are due to renouncer whose unique position gave him a sort of monopoly of putting everything in question."[3]

Sannyasin is one who has relinquished all worldly attachments and values and has chosen a life of religious contemplation or asceticism. It was customary, when economically practicable, for the head of a family 'when he had seen his eldest son's son' to spend his closing years as a recluse. The term was later applied generally to religious mendicants, and particularly to Saiva itinerant devotees.[4]

Asceticism has two aspects one is negative and other one is positive. Negative is its renunciation or repression of desire identified as dangerous or wicked, which sometimes extends to intentional self-injury of the body. Positives are its prescriptions for physical and mental self-discipline, designed not only to promote renunciations but also to produce pious works of mystic experience. As a method of purely external purification—indifferent to the inward state of the practitioner's soul—asceticism can be found as part of the most ancient primitive religions. Typically it is associated with ritual injunctions: avoidance of acts disturbing to the gods; performance of purificatory ceremonies prior to worship. In ancient India the practice of asceticism included a variety of physical austerities, sexual abstinence and mental contemplation—all hopefully leading to the ultimate ecstasy of mystic experience.

Asceticism has been a persistent feature of ancient Indian civilization. While the European scholars were studying Indian religious and philosophical thoughts they took great interest in asceticism. But these scholars have presented different views with regard to the origin. Some scholars like Hardy[5] and Kern[6] traced the origin of the ascetic to the Vedic Brahmachari; Max Muller[7] and Jacobi[8] ascribed it to Brahmana parivrajaka; while others like Keith[9], Griswold[10] and Griffith[11] thought that the Sramana (Acetic) was the descendent of the vedic Muni or the pre-vedic Yogi as suggested by Marshall[12].

The Western scholars did not examine the reasons and responsibilities of motives underlying the ascetic institution. They explain 'when' rather than how various factors and forces of time were responsible to that state of mind of withdrawal from the society. They focused on *human agents* in place of ideas responsible for driving them to the ascetic life. Durga

Bhagvat[13] gives a corrective by examining certain traits which gradually developed Indian monachism. She traces the origin of asceticism to the Brahmanas[14] but does not deal with the idea which led a person to choose a life of asceticism. The 'ascetic' philosophy of *Upanisads* and epics were not included. She follows Sayana and accepts the Rgvedic Muni of the *Muni-Sukta* as a seer (rishi). On the other hand, we have evidence to prove that he is like a shaman of a primitive tribal society and thus the ascetic institution should be reasonably traced to him.

Indian scholars like Barua, Das, Sharma and Ghurye have also examined the problem of asceticism. Barua refers to the wanderers as the sophist movement.[15] Das traces the origin to the vedic Muni[16] and thus follows the line of Keith and others. Sharma opines that Samnyasa was originally the doctrine of the dissenters from the orthodox ritualism of the ancient Aryans. According to him, " the institution of Samnyasa arose out of the recognition of the transitoriness of all worldly objects.[17] Ghurye traces the ascetic origins to the Rgvedic Munis who are 'some kind of ascetics'[18]. Though he traces the development of traits like celebacy, austerity, concentration and ecstasy[19] which form the main content of asceticism, he does not explain how these constitute 'a whole complex' of it. As a result he touches only the fringes of the problem.

Sramana or Parivrajaka was a common name which we can give to ascetics of all community whether Brahmanic, Buddhist or Jaina. Attempts are also made by scholars like Dutt a[20] Upadhye[21] and Deo[22] to trace the origin of the *sramanas.* Dutta traces the origin of the Sramanas to 'a class of men answering to the Brahmanas in Aryan society'[23] According to Deo: 'Sramanism was the outcome of the blending of all elements—indigenous and borrowed'[24]. It seems probable that the philosophy of the Upanisads idealized a condition of life that already existed and was in practice, filling it with a spiritual content and idealistic purpose.[25]

Before 1920 or thereabouts many scholars were disposed to look upon the addition of the fourth or the ascetic stages as

Post-Buddhist.[26] After the discovery of the Indus valley civilization there has been a tendency to look upon asceticism as a continuation by Indian civilization and a loan from the culture that existed in India before the coming of the Aryans[27].

Most of the Western and Eastern scholars hold the view that Aryans had came in India from outside. Some Indian scholars have recently maintained that the Aryans were indigenous to India.[28] The Aryans were quick in adopting the culture with the multitude of indigenous elements. It was thus abvious that the Aryans were influenced by and borrowed many beliefs and practices of the indigenous people who had been till then believed to be not so civilized.

These indigenous people were Dravidians who led the Aryan conquerors to borrow elements of their culture. Radhakrishnan tells about the interchange of the culture between Dravidians and Aryans with each other.[29] Suniti Kumar Chatterjee holds the view that three-fourths of Indian culture is non Aryan[30]. It seems clear that the Dravidians lent their beliefs to conquering Aryans and in turn imbibed their cultures.

The above views indicate the non-Aryan influence on the earliest Vedic thought. This becomes obvious if we try to explain the existence of the ascetic beliefs and practices in the Rgveda. In Rgveda the society likes to live life in pleasure and material prosperity. There is no evidence of an ascetic so we can say that it has been derived from the Dravidians.[31] This makes Oldenberg to believe that 'the practice of *tapas* which lies in the midst of the Vedic ritual is a relic of bygone days'.[32] J. Van Troy who calls *tapas* 'a-non Rgvedic practice' holds a similar view. He says: 'the word *tapas* come to be used for a practice already existing with all its basic characteristics before it was assumed in Rgvedic society'.[33] This practice was a trait associated with the medicine man called the *shaman*, by the primitive peoples. According to Schweitzer, the Ṛgvedic Muni was the shaman and medicine man later called the Yogin.[34] So we could associate the origin of ascetic (*Ṣṛamaṇ*) or the yogi to the primitive *shaman* or the medicine man.

In the Rgveda both 'munis' and 'yatis' are referred to. The word 'muni', which occurs many times, regularly means some kind of ascetic. Indra is declared to be their friend. In one passage of Rgveda, these 'munis' are described as vatarasana, kesin, and as wearing yellow and soiled garments. There is no controversy about 'Kesin', which means long-haired. These attributes of long hair and yellow soiled garments are typically of ascetics in the full-fledged system of asceticism.[35] The Rgvedic hymn about 'Kesin' described him as a powerful being:

> The Kesin bears fire, he bears water, the Kesin upholds earth and heaven, the kesin sees all visions of luster, the kesin is called the light.
> Munis with the wind for their girdle wear soiled yellow robe; they go long the course of the wind where the Devas have gone before.
> "Maddened by austerities we have ascend on the wind, and only these bodies of ours are what your mortals ever see"
> The Muni through the mid-air flies while he looks at varied forms and he is every Deva a comrade in doing good[36].

Vedic man's idea of the ascetic as magical being is evident in this hymn.[37]

With the discovering of the Indus valley civilization and its critical study, there came about a change in the opinion about yatis Ramaprasad Chanda[38] propounded the view that the Indus valley civilization cultivated 'Yoga' and meditative technique alongwith its cult of Siva as Pasupati and Yogi. Ascetic and Yogic cult was in his opinion a contribution of the Indus valley civilization. D.R. Bhandarkar[39] distinguished the 'yatis' from the 'munis' and considered the former as Asuras and the latter as Aryans of the Indra Cult.

Here we may say that the Rgvedic Indo-Aryans had developed among them a class of ascetics who were not only naked and credited with miraculous powers, but were also, as we have tried to establish, in the habit of demonstrating their achievement of power in holding their penis in tumescence without excitement. There is no reason to think that they might not have had another class of ascetics who made the male organ their object of worship. And they were the 'yatis'.

In the same way as in the *Ṛigveda* is extolled the keśin, there is a hymn in *Atharvaveda* in which the *brahmacarin* is extolled in very similar words.

> The Brahmacarin, born before the sacred knowledge, robed in libation, stood up with his *tapas*: through him were manifested the sacred love, highest Brahman and all Devas with immortality.
> The Brahmacarin, bright with the blaze of the sacrificial wood, comes, clad in black buck-skin, consecrated, long bearded; and he forthwith goes from the eastern to the northern sea, and grasps the worlds together, constantly drawing them near.[40]

Here the ascetic motif is even more evident. *Tapas* in fact means heat especially the internal heat produced in the body by austerity which is a magical force whose power can even dominate the Gods and move the whole universe as we shall see below. Tapas is the force utilized by the Gods themselves to create the world:

> When Prajapati was creating beings, death surpassed him he practised austerities for a thousand years, striving for leaving, evil behind. While he was practising austerities, sparks came out of his pores: those sparks are stars: there are as many stars in heaven as he has pores.[41]

As we see, the concept of asceticism is central to that of magical power and creative power, and it is this *tapas* which gives prestige and importance to the ascetic in the Indian tradition. Asceticism is mentioned several time in the older Upanishads—it could even be said that Upanisadic literature is a creation of ascetic hermits. And in that sense the opinion of Dumont is correct, in India the creator of values is the anchorite. The Upanisads are part of the Araṇykās, the forest books, that is to say, the books composed in the forest by men retired in the forest, that is *vānaprasthās*. These maintain certain sacrificial rituals and give the sacrifices a mystical interpretation. They live as hermits sometimes together with other ascetics, and they develop the theories of the fundamental identity of *atman* and *Brahman*, that is to say the theories of bondage and liberation, *samsara* and *mokṣā*.

Asceticism is a complex of a number of traits the principal ones may be distinguished as celibacy, austerity, concentration and ecstasy. To take the last first, it should be noted that the Vedic Aryans were fond of an intoxicating drink called Soma. They could describe themselves as having become immortal and as having discovered the gods.[42] In some passages[43] 'Muni' is described as in ecstatic trance. During its continuance the 'muni' is described as having attained the fellowship of the deities of the air and as being able to travel with them in their course because of his miraculous powers. The following observation of Albert Schweitzer[44] brings out the significance of *Rgveda* passages like the one referred to above for the history and development of asceticism. " In these hymns we encounter men who know they are uplifted above this world. They are the shamans and medicine men—later called Yogins—who get themselves into a state of ecstasy through drinking the intoxicating Soma by mortification of the flesh. This consciousness of being uplifted above the world which is experienced in ecstasy is the condition determining Indian world and life negation (Samnyasa)... They regard this state of being uplifted above the world as something that only came under consideration for themselves because they possessed the capacity of attaining to community with the gods."

The second element of the ascetic complex is austerity, 'tapas' etymologically means heat and significantly its practice is described in Sanskrit in terms of the root, 'tap' to get heated. In Vedic cosmogony '*tapas*' plays an important role and in Rgvedic passages it figures in connection with the creative activity of Prajapati as well as a power by itself. In the*Chandogya-Upanisad* (11, 23) three factors of Dharma are specified. Yojna or sacrifice is the first of them. Yojna is here identified with '*tapas*'. In the same upanisad (VIII, 5), in another context where Brahmacarya, life-long celibacy is propounded, at least two kinds of practices of austerity are specified and identified with Brahmacarya. It is asserted that what is known as "mauna", silence is brahmacarya itself. Keeping silence is well-known to be one kind of austerity. Fasting is thus another kind of austerity. In the *Brahadaranyaka Upanisad*[45] (IV, 4, 22) it is stated that Brahmins described to know the Brahman is accordance with the Vedic injunctions through sacrifice, through alms and gifts, and through the austerity of fasting. Knowing him one becomes as 'muni'.

The Prasna Upanisad[46] declares that self-realization is achieved through austerity (tapas), celibacy, faith and knowledge (vidyā).

It is next to impossible to determine how early in the history of Vedic culture yogic technique came to be formulated and practiced. Prana, Apāna and Vyāna are three kinds of breaths which along with seven others from the ten vital energies. The specification of not only the breaths but also of their number in the Atharvaveda inclines us to the view that some kind of breath-control was known and practiced in the early Vedic period.

We may conclude from these informations that yoga in its more or less developed form was not only known but was enjoined to be practised as a necessary element in one's spiritual endeavour. Even some of the esoteric aspects of what later come to be known as Hathayoga, like the importance of the coronal artery were also known and their role in the spiritual endeavour was appreciated.

Celibacy is another trait of the complex of asceticism. Asceticism, in general, has expected an even insisted that its aspirants should take to it before they have tasted sex in ordinary course and settled down as married men and women.

It is only in Indian civilization, which is undoubtedly the mother of asceticism and of monastic order, that asceticism is laid down as the last stage in an individual's life. Celibacy cannot form a rational and cogent element in the theory of four Asramas. Āśceticism or Samnyāsa is entered into not only after sex is satisfied but also after its urge has subsided. The question of celibacy in the samnyasa Asrama or the fourth stage has no practical significance. It is only when ascetic life is undertaken in youthful years, whether one is married or unmarried, that the problem of celibacy assumes practical significance.

Vardhamana Mahavira, the first historical personage to have renounced the worldly life in pursuit of spiritual endeavour, was a Naisthika Brahmacari. He took to ascetic life without ever becoming a householder. Buddha, the second historical personage to renounce the world and to take to ascetic life, did so sometime after a son was born to him. In the *Bṛhadāraṇyak Upanisad* [47] we see that Yajnavalkya when about to become a *parivrajaka* (a-wandering ascetic) tells his wife Maitreyi that he was going to leave home and that he wanted to divide whatever wealth he had between her and her co-wife Katyayani. This shows that a parivrajaka had even then to leave home and wife and to give up all belongings. In *Brahadaranyaka Upanisad* [48] Yajnavalkya proclaims that for Brahma realization wise men straight way take to the life of mendicants, without becoming householders, as the right path for self-realization,[49] it means that 'naisthika Brahmacarya' or asceticism from before the time of sex-indulgence was looked upon as the proper course of spiritual endeavour.

It should be clear from all these facts that, first of all, sacrifice came to be realized as inadequate for spiritual benefit. Austerity, '*Tapas*', and its allies, the yogic practices, were thought to be more efficacious than sacrifice in the search for Brahma. 'Brahmacarya', not only as an aspect of austerity but owing to its detachment from life, also as an opportunity for the persistent persuit of knowledge, came to replace mere physical penance as a mode of spiritual endeavour. The need for moral qualities in this endeavour could not long remain undiscovered. In the last two passages quoted, we therefore find the moral qualities of faith and truth given equal weight along with austerity, knowledge and Brahmacarya. 'Naisthika Brahmacarya' thus is a fairly ancient institution, and is the form of asceticism earliest known and practiced.

It has been debated, as we have sated above, whether samnyas , asceticism, as the fourth stage of life is at all ancient. Sharma [50] came to the conclusion that the first three Asramas are ancient and that the fourth Āśrama came to be recognized to accomodate the dissenters, who had lost faith in sacrifice even before the rise of Buddhism. P.V. Kane [51] concludes that the fourth Āśrama, though later in origin than the other three, is pre-Buddhist. By implication all the four Āśramas may be taken to have been formulated before, though they are specifically named for the first time in the *Jabala Upanisad* (4). In the *Muṇḍka Upaniṣad* (1 1 1, 2,6) final salvation is declared to be achieved by yatis of pure spirit, who have cultivated Vedanta knowledge and practised Saṃnyāsa. We may conclude that asceticism or Saṃnyāsa had come to be recognized as a necessary step in the endeavour of self-realization and that it had come to be treated as the fourth and final stage in the orthodox scheme of individual life.

We know for a fact that a slightly junior contemporary of Mahavira, Maskarin, known in Buddhist and Jain literature as Mokkhali or Mankhali ,[52] was the leader of an ascetic sect called Ajivakas, who were bitterly apposed to Mahavira's sect. There is good reason to think that there were ascetic predeccessors of Mahavira, at least some of whom have been canonized as Tirthamkaras by Jains. According to Jain tradition, Mahavira himself was the twenty-fourth Tirthamakara or prophet, and the first was one king Rsabha was afterwards renounced his kingdom[53]. The *Bhagavata Purana* (II, 7,10,) further states that Rsabha was initiated into asceticism directly as a Paramahamsa, the highest stage in asceticism. In the same Purana, he figures as an incarnation of Vishnu[54] . If this tradition about Rsabha's Paramahamas-initiation may be accepted as correct, then the existence of the Paramahamsa order of asceticism is attested at a very ancient date. Allowing twenty years for a generation Rsabha may be taken to have lived about 900 B.C.

In Upanisads we come to know about some Paramahamsa who were well-known as ascetics they are Uddālaka Āruṇi, Śvetaketu, Nachiketa, etc. Here we should like to refer to the puranic tradition about Dhaumya and his family, so instructive in our quest of ascetic origins. Besides the two Brahamrealizing Paramahamsas, Uddālaka Āruṇi and Svetaketu, there are only three other Paramahamsas in that list about whom some information is available, namely Jadabharata, Durvasa and Dattatreya.

In the Rgvedic Muni, we seem to have the familiar figure of the shaman of the primitive society. The descriptions of his abondoning the body, divining the thoughts of others, flying in the air, roaming at will indifferent regions suggest that he was as an ascetic who has acquired magical powers (siddhis) very similar to the primitive medicine man. The prescriptions of the *Attharvaveda* which have a whole collection of magic, indicate that some classes of Aryan society believed in magic practices. The vedic hymns were used as having a peculiar magic property; it was thought that if correctly used in sacrifices they brought about desired results. Sacrifice was invested with magic.

The *rata* and *satya* were believed to have sprung in the beginning of creation from *tapas*; similarly the primeval principle descried as neither *sat* nor *asat*. Just as this mysterious principle controlling the whole universe could be known through sacrifice, so it came to be believed that the ascetic was able to control nature and gods by the force of his*tapas* and also obtain supernatural powers. Thus originated *tapas* from the acquisition of magical powers or siddhis. At the same time at the idea to achieve ajas seems to have been dominant with many ascetics an essential condition for the attainment of celibacy and the highest spirituality.

Let us analyse the influences which were on men or conditions working upon man and inducing him to adopt the ascetic mode of living. These spring from man's environment, its effect upon him and his power to react to it. Broadly speaking, these may be enumerated as physical conditions which influence him from without and internal states like sorrow, frustration, pessimism, pleasure, intellectual craving, spiritual urge etc., which work within him and his attempt to satisfy them, pacify them or overcome them. The factors have to be assessed in the context of the social, religious and economic conditions prevalent in ancient India.

There are some reasons which we may draw for a man to be an ascetic : A troubles, to propitiate the Unseen Powers. A longing on the part of the intensely religious to follow in the footsteps of their *master*, almost invariably an ascetic. A wish to work out one's own *future* salvation, or emancipation, by conquering the evil inherent in human nature, i.e. the flesh. A yearning to prepare one self by purification of mind and body for entering into *present* communion with the Divine Being. Despair arising from disillusionment and from defeat in the battle of life. And lastly, mere vanity, stimulated by the admiration which the multitude bestow upon the ascetic.

It is an interesting question whether the physical climate of India has affected the course of asceticism. Brunton writes : "A fiercely hot and depressingly humid country whose climate causes everyone to shun physical effort, led man naturally to search for part of his satisfaction in contmeplative thought and inward life.[55] Oman also observes that the hot and extreme type of climate prompts and favours this thoughtful, sobre and philosophical bent of mind.[56]

A different view has been suggested by Basham : "The climate of India produced in its people a kind of alternating rhythm of reaction between a sensuous appreciation of the delights of the world and an austere rejection of even the simplest comforts.[57] So it can be said that climate seems to have influenced their religious expression and it was one of the important factors shaping the religious thought of the people in ancient India.

Western scholars state this pessimistic note about Indians when they say: 'By the Indians, life has ever been regarded as essentially evil and relief from burden and sorrow from existence as the chief and final aim.'[58] What are the forces responsible for pessimism? Bloomfield observes : 'India herself, through her climate, her nature and her economic conditions, furnishes reasonable ground for pessimism.[59] Behind the growth of pessimism and asceticism lay, according to Basham, a deep psychological uneasiness and a deep feeling of insecurity.

Climate as a factor leading to pessimism and asceticism is examined. It is found to be an important factor hoping the religious temperament of the people of ancient India. It is to the intellectual craving for a higher life, the spiritual urge for self-realisation that the ideal of renunciation is to be traced. However, the idea where it first appears in the *Brhadaranyaka Upanisad* is made both the cause and effect of self-realisation. But soon after, with the Vedic outlook turning into a pessimistic one, the idea develops. As the Aryan mind reflected on the finite and limited character of human existence, it was overcome by fear. When the fear became conscious of itself due to suffering and *Karma* theory, it turned into anguish. To be free from it demanded destruction of desire as also extinction of the bondage of *Karma* which seemed perpetual. This led to all worldly objects being considered transitory and the human body an abode of evil. Pleasures were short-lived and hence to be rejected. But this was not enough. *Tapas* was insufficient to lead to the knowledge of the self. *Karma* theory operated to create more *Karma* and add to the sense of pessimism. A deep psychological uneasiness and a deep feeling of insecurity as also frustration and suffering, brought in their wake increasing pessimism. It was an unhappy and unsatisfying world to be escaped from at all costs. As the material life believed to be evil and deceptive it was a hindrance to a life of the spirit and the release from the eternal cycle of birth and death lay in the total destruction of desire, turning away from the world was the next logical step. It was thus thought necessary to break away from all the ties of this earth which bound man to the world, its desires and temptations. We thus find in the age of the Upanisads the ideal of renunciation taking a firm shape.

This ideal of renunciation came to be practised as the result of many forces like : intellectual craving for a higher life and thirst for spiritual wisdom; the fear of present ills and the unending cycle of births and rebirths, the inadequacyof *tapas* for self-realisation, the emergence of anti-hedomistic tendency, the impermanence of the world and a mood of psychological uneasiness and insecurity—all resulting into a pessimistic view of life.

Viewed cross-culturally, the variety of ascetic forms is limited. Virtually universal are (i) fasting, (ii) sexual contenence, (iii) poverty, under which may be included begging, (iv) seclusion or isolation, and (v) self-inflicted pain, either physical or mental. More difficult to define, but perhaps also more significant, is what may be termed an "inner asceticism" consisting essentially of spiritual rather than physical discipline. Such asceticism involves not detachment from or renunciation of any specific worldly pleasure but rather detachment from or renunciation of the world per se. It is reflected in the biblical attitude of being "in the world, but not of it," or in the *Bhagvadgita's* "renunciation in action, rather than renunciation of action". It appears in almost every major religion yet has no equivalent in primitive thought. In addition to the universal forms indicated, specific not must also be made of that set of practices or techniques (e.g. specific postures, chanting, breathing techniques) that make up the yogic and meditative complex indigenous to the Indian subcontinent. Yoga, although an asceticism of the body, is an inner asceticism as well.

All theistic traditions virtually develop a mystical movement wherein the individual, through an ascetic program, seeks a personal union with the deity. This desire for personal experience of the deity may be seen as a reaction against doctrinal abstraction or ethical formalism. Even theistic traditions such as Judaism, Christianity, and Islam, in which the gap between creator and creature is perceived to be unbridgeable, have produced ascetics in pursuit of such mystic union. So virtually all mystics in a theistic tradition therefore, make it clear that the state of apparent union with the deity is only momentary and, at best, a foretaste of that salvation yet to come.

In non-theistic traditions this thirst for the ultimate through mystical experience takes on varied forms. The Hindu yogin employs the sophisticated techniques of yoga to realize that his atman, or permanent self, is one with brahman, the unchanging foundation of all. The *Yoga Sutra* of Patanjali (first century CE) describes breathing and meditative techniques, which, when coupled with sexual continence, fasting, bodily postures, and other disciplines, permit the individual to move "inward and downward" untill its true essence is "perceived". Similarly, the meditative techniques of Zen Buddhism permit the practitioner to realize the Buddha nature within himself.

According to the Hindu philosopher Samkara(788 - 820 CE), the body and personality with which we habitually identify ourselves are revealed to be no more than maya or illusion. The Jain monk, through the most rigorous of ascetic techniques involving total passivity and detachment from the world, seeks to purity and eventually liberate his true self (jiva) from the material defilements that most actions produce. An ascetic life of monastic simplicity and celibacy, an ascetic program of detachment, and a meditative effort to cultivate a selfless state lead the Thervada monk to realization of nirvana- "extinction" or "liberation".

Awareness of one's atman in Hinduism of or one's purusa in Samkhya (i.e., a philosophical system associated with tratidional Yoga) or of one's Buddha nature in Zen is englightenment or salvation. Unlike the theistic religions, nontheistic systems frequently affirm that salvation is attainable here on earth. One become, "Liberated in life" as in tantrism, or one realizes, as in Zen, that one was never bound.

In both theistic and non-theistic systems asceticism may be seen as a meritorious form of behaviour, a good work, or a laudable course of action left to ensure or facilitate a preferred condition after death. Self-denial is considered to be a way of earning, pasthoumous reward. In non-theistic traditions ascetic works are more appropriate. Through self-denial for example, one can burnout bad Karman (the effect of past deeds) and improve one's future state in the on going round of transmigration.

In both theistic and non-theistic systems, acts of self-denial–particularly self-inflicted pain-may serve as a form of penance of previous misdeeds. The objectives of self-flagellation is merely forgiveness, in theistic systems asceticism as a form of penance has enjoyed a less problematic rationale than has asceticism as a way of achieving salvation itself. This is particularly true when ascetic acts are seen as an expression of repentance rather than a means of earning it.

Most evident in Catholicism, but confined neither to it nor to theistic traditions in general, is the use of asceticism, particularly self-inflicted pain, as a means of experiencing or re-experiencing the sufferings of either a deity or a human paradigm (i.e., a model individual).

Non-theistic Jainism produced ascetics whose acts of selfdenial took as their model the activities of Jain saints (tirthankaras) such as Parsva or Mahavira. The Hindu hero Bhism was so pierced by arrows during the great battle described in the *Bhagavadgita* that, supported by their shafts, he lay parallel to the ground. This event forms the model for the well-known bed of nails employed by some Indian holy men. In Catholic Christianity the imitation of Christ's suffering is raised to a level of mystical significance suffering not only as Christ suffered but with him has became a means of mystical union with the deity. In this regard, suffering became virtually an end in itself, taking on soteriological significance.

Viewed cross-culturally, a given ascetic form differnt, even opposite objectives. In primitive society, for example, self-flagellation or scourging indeed primarily to drive away demonic powers that have attached themselves to the individual. In Chrisitianity, however, the same activity—one prevalent in Italy, the Phinland and Maxico- was intended to produce pain, thereby bringing the ascetic into mystical union with the suffering Christ. Likewise, fasting in Christianity often has sought to produce pain, either as penance or, again, as a way of identifying with the suffering deity.

In Yoga, however, the purpose of fasting is quite different. The objective is not to cause but to alleviate discomfort. Fasting is therefore a teachnique through which the yogin becomes oblivious of his body and is thus able to direct all his mental energies toward meditation. Similarly, the many other forms of self-discipline found in Yoga—the postures and sexual continence, for instance are to be seen less as privation that as techniques to redirect energies towards a meditative end.

Yoga itself, however, as an ascetic form, has different objectives. In most of Upanisadic Hinduism its purpose is to realize the unity of one's permanent self, or atman, with the unchanging foundation of the universe, or brahman. In Thervada Buddhism its goal is to realize that there is no permanent self, while in the Samkhya system it seeks to realize that the true self is ideally in a state of total isolation from the phenomenal world of flux.

In virtually, every religious tradition, meditation or contemplation takes place in some degree of seclusion. Anthony (d. 356 CE) and other Christian saints lived for prolonged periods alone in the African desert. The early Buddhists likened themselves to rhinos who wondered alone, far from the haunts of men, and Taoist recluses sought to commune with nature beyond the reach of civilization and its distractions, but again, the goals of such secluded exercises are varried. The Taoist seeks harmony with nature and therewith serenity and joy. The Theravada Buddhism seeks to realize that nature is transient and thus the source of sorrow. Saint Anthony, somewhat like a Tibetan Buddhist, went forth to confront demonic powers in their own ominous haunts.[60]

Sarokin has examined the elements which according to him constitute the highest mentality in Hindu and Buddhist systems[61]. It's fulfillment through a complete mastery of all sensate needs, even to the point of aninhilation of personality, can be achieved through asceticism which presents several aspects and they became afterwards more or less a feature common to all religions.

In the stage of samnyasa we see that asceticism presents several aspects viz. fasting or at least reducing the intake of food, abstention from meat and drink and pleasures of sense, total absence of sexual gratification and suppression of the sexual emotion, vow of silence, sleeping on bare ground, nakedness or making use of minimum clothing, contempt for the world and its riches.[62]

The Hindu Scriptures however do not enjoin self-infliction of pain or flagellation that was indulged in by monks in the early centuries of Christianity. It is the fashion to assert that Indians[63] have the highest regard for asceticism and that the men whose memories they cherish as ideals of human conduct are ascetics.

The concept of Indian asceticism had four dimensions : *Tapas, Vairagya, Samnyasa* and *Yoga.*

Tapas or austerity had two aspects. In its negative aspect it was self-mortification or self-torture. In its positive aspect it was self-control through self-training or self-discipline. *Vairagya* was an essential condition to cultivate non-attachment to worldly pleasures and interests leading to renunciation, *tyaga* or *samnyasa.* It was a worthy path towards the attainment of self-perfection or preparation for a spiritual life even when leading a worldly life. All schools of thought including Brahmanism, Buddhism and Jainism viewed extinction of desire (*trsna*) as an essential state or discipline leading to the path of emancipation. *Samnyasa* was an unsocial, resourceless and detached existence when all earthly ties were broken and all worldly desires given up for the final quest of the Atman. *Yoga* was an art of medition which was closely connected with *tapas* for achievement of physical and mental powers. When Yoga was accepted as a system of philosophy, certain basic rules of ascetic practices and behaviour viz. observance of *Ahimsa, Satya, Asteya, Brahmacarya,* and *Aparigraha* came to be included in it. They formed a standard of holiness to be observed by Hindu *Samnyasis,* Buddhist *Bhikkhus* and Jaina *Samanas*. Yoga became a technique of intellectual illumination and a means of spiritual enlightenment.[64]

In this way the above study shows the necessity of *Tapas, Vairagya, Samnyasa* and *Yoga* as specific forms of processes and disciplines of Indian asceticism. The concept of these four disciplines and therefore of asceticism itself, have changed from time to time. Asceticism as a socio-religious institution was a barometer of social changes and needs of ancient India.

In Greece, the word Asceticism shows the meaning as training. The 'athlete' was one trained, and one might be an 'athlete' in virtue. So very early the ascetic became the spiritual athlete of church History. Two quite different conceptions mingle in the history of aseticism. One of these preserves the original meaning of discipline of the body for some ultimate purpose, as when William James urges sacrifice to God and duty as a means of training the will. The other conception distrusts the body altogether. Asceticism has then as its function not the training but the destroying of the body or the negation of its importance.

The best known type of Greek asceticism is purely philosophical, associated with no prescribed form of physical or mental discipline. On the other hand as a practical discipline, asceticism in India developed into a complex and difficult art, known in its systematic form as yoga. In Greece, the body-soul dualism of Plato led naturally to the conclusion that the soul's welfare demanded subjugation of bodily appetites. Plato's attitude toward the body perhaps was influenced by Orphic beliefs that purity of soul brought escape from reincarnation. Thus he suggests, through the mouth of Socrates, that "those who have indulged in gluttony and violence and drunkenness, and have taken no pains to avoid them, are likely to pass into the bodies of asses and other beasts of that sort." "Desire of the corporeal" cause such souls to wander about untill they again become imprisoned in a mortal frame.[65] " Each pleasure or pain nails [the soul] as with a nail to the body and rivets it on and makes it corporeal, so that it fancies the things are true which the body says are true."[66] Escape from constant rebirth is only possible through "beholding that which is true and divine and not a matter of opinion," i.e. through philosophy.[67]

The Greeks accepted certain notions of ritual purity or pollution from a very early period. To make contact with the Gods, i.e. to enter a temple or perform a sacrifice, anyone desiring to do so had first to free himself of pollution. Exceptional purity was required of priests and priestesses—i.e. those persons who entered the temple regularly and handled sacred objects. According to the views of different cults the sources of ritual pollution varied widely; most were prohibition of a fairly primitive kind. The list of animals which might not be sacrificed, or of food which might not be eaten by the devotees of one or another deity, is a long one. There was a list of metals which could not be brought near to certain shrines ; contact with murderers, corpses, insane persons, menstruating women or women in childbirth was taken as widely polluting. The god would take offense and withhold worshipper blessings only till the worshipper observed the prohibitions. There are many ways by which the pollution could be removed but only through specified procedures (depending on the cause) : by washings or fermigations (freequently with sulphur), or by contact with pure things like laurel or olive branches, or by pig's blood (which was allegedly capable of trapping demons).[68] Similar concepts of ritual pollution and cleansing; although differing in specific methods and in the items forbidden; may be found in the ritualistic portions of the Indian Vedas or the Laws of Manu.

Both in ancient India and in classical Greece an act widely regarded as polluting was sexual intercourse. It was demanded in many Greek cults that the participants in divine worship be chaste. Thus in some cases virgins and youths performed cult ceremonies, or priests and worshippers had to abstain from sexual activity for a specified time-period before and during worship services. Chaste priests and priestesses served the great virgin goddesses, Athena and Artemis. Participants in the Elusinian mysteries were required to avoid sexual acts during the process of initiation.[69] The Pythagorean brotherhood permitted sexual relations only for purposes of procreation.[70] But on the whole, continence plays a much smaller role in Greek than in Indian religion of the same period. Judging from the references to saints and sages in early Indian literature, Indian holy men frequently practiced a severe asceticism which included life-long sexual abstinence. By contrast, the Greek type of religious chastity was usually temporary in nature. None of the Greek cults regarded permanent celibacy as an ideal mode of existence. From the remotest times, both in India and Greece, the opinion was widespread that the sexual act is polluting even in wedlock, and that sexual intercourse constitutes an impediment to holiness.[71]

The prohibition of meat-eating is another typical feature of classical Greek asceticism. The Orphics, for example, were known for their strict abstention from flesh; Plato says this was because they considered it "unholy to eat [meat] or to stain with blood the altars of the Gods."[72] Aristophanes in his drama *The Frogs* says that—Orpheos was famous for teaching mankind not to kill—he does not specify animals, though this is probably what he means[73]. Euripides' play Hippolytos a father taunts his son with the 'lifeless food' he eats since taking Orpheos for his 'King[74] clearly the prohibition was so common.

In Greek religion, the animal-sacrifice was sometimes a important part of their acts. In this ritual ordinarily meat-eating was inseparable from the sacrifice. Refusal to touch meat thus carried political as well as religious overtones. An ancient myth explained the meaning of sacrifice : when the God Prometheos taught mankind the use of fire, he reserved cooked meat to human beings, but left flavours and odours as the food of the Gods. Animal sacrifice, which produced the odours of cooked meat, thus supplied the Gods with nourishment and established direct communication between them and humankind.[75]

From ancient sources whether the Pythagoreans forbade meat-eating absolutely is not clear. Some ancient authorities claim that Pythagoras himself abstained from meat-eating,[76] though others say that he did not forbid the tasting of sacrificial meat.[77] According to Plato, the Pythagoreans explained their abstention from meat on the ground that animals and human beings have the same type of souls, and that it is impious to act unjustly toward one's own kindred.[78] Pythagoras' near contemporary, Empedokles, took approximately the same line; he abhorred animal sacrifice on the ground that one might thereby slay a close relative.[79]

According to Aristoxenos, the Pythagoreans permitted the eating of goat-meat and pork and forbade only mutton and ox-meat.[80] These exclusions had a certain rationale that the sheep and the plow-ox are human kinds close companions and essential to civilized life. By contrast, the pig roots out planted seeds; The goat eats vines and destroys grapes. Greek myths made plain these distinctions in declaring the pig to be the enemy of Demeter, Goddess of agriculture, and the goat the enemy of Dionysos, God of vegetation and wine.[81]

The existence of two opposed attitudes toward meat-eating within the same Pythagorean order might also reflect a division between "ascetic" and "political" Pythagoreans. Clearly, men who totally rejected the central ritual of Greek religious life were unlikely to be effective politically. Perhaps for this reason the "politicals" compromised on the matter of meat-eating, refusing to touch only those animals already recognized by Greek myth as harmful to civilized life. Within the same brotherhood, however, other members may have renounced civic participation in order to follow more consistently their ascetic proclivities.[82] Some such explanation could account for the contradiction in the ancient sources as to whether the

Pythagoreans were or were not complete vegetarians.

The injunction against eating beans is another curious dietary regulation which appears both in India and in Greece at an early date. In India beans were felt to be unclean, unholy, unworthy of the sacred ceremony.[83] In classical Greece the same prohibition is linked to the name of Pythagoras,[84] from whom the philosopher Empedokles (early 5th Cen. B.C.) perhaps learned it. One of Empedokles' poems includes the lines : "O wretches, utter wretches, from beans withhold your hands."[85] Initiation into the Eleusinian mysteries, which honoured the Goddess Demeter, required abstinence from all types of fish, fowl and beans.[86] Herodotas observed during his travels (5th Cen. B.C.) that beans were forbidden to the priests of Egypt.[87]

Classical and Hellenistic authors cite a wide variety of reasons for the prohibition of beans, all of which assume some connection between that vegetable and the forces of nature. For example, beans were thought to be full of life-force, or to arise from the same primal matter as human beings, or if buried in the earth or in dung to assume human shape, or being flatulent, to possess animal properties. The Pythagoreans actually claimed that bean-eating was equivalent to cannibalism of one's own parents. Thus the bean evidently represented rottenness and decay, sexuality and death—all qualities which distinguish human beings from Gods. Avoidance of beans was apparently also liked to the belief in metempsychosis, inasmuch as the same people who held that doctrine also forbade bean-eating—namely the Orphics, Pythagoreans and Empedokles.

The meaning of the Greeks' sexual and dietary prohibitions—which dated back to very ancient times—was by the classical period already obscure. Undoubtedly many of the taboos were linked to fears of the demons and wicked spirits which cause ritual pollution, disease and other calamities. These prohibition were hardly explainable on rational grounds alone. The efforts made during the classical and Hellenistic period to justify the taboos philosophically, far from elucidating their original meaning, testify merely to the Greek's inability to ignore them.

In any event, the motivations behind classical Greek asceticism almost certainly have nothing to do with any wish to renounce the world as such or to mortify the flesh in the interest of holiness. Such impulses were common to Indian ascetics and later to Christian anchorites and monks, but—despite Plato's advice to cultivate soul over body—foreign to the Greek lifestyle in classical age.

Geographical and racial factors in the development have exposed the population of Persia, India and Egypt to a long succession of oppressive tyrannies by physically superior, but often mentally and spiritually inferior, races (Mangol, Muhammadan, English). For the religions of despondency or even despair the Orient has hence became the breeding-ground. Although fasting and mortification are forbidden in the Avesta, and a great many of the alleged evidences for a primitive asceticism are evidences that in Persia will not stand a critical investigation, yet Mani and the very prohibitions of asceticism are evidences that in Persia as well as in India and Egypt spiritual suffering gave rise to a pantheistic worldview, with despair and asceticism as characteristic features. This asceticism has many forms which are those of world-flight, the hermit life, the mortification of the body by unnatural inhabitions of all its desires. The most imperative of these was the sexual impulse, and hence, as it was also linked with the continuance of a hated existance, the mortification of this impulse became primary. It was a little bit different from Indian asceticism. As Indian religion became fully self-conscious in Buddhism and Jainism, it deliberately opposed the ascetic to the legal, and the life of contemplation to rituals and sacrifice, and democracy to caste-aristocracy.

All early religions resort to various forms of self-inflicted privation or suffering to appease the assumed wrath of Gods or demons. Famine is anticipated by fasting, and wounding the body becomes a surrogatum for the punishment the offended powers would otherwise inflict with more fatal results. The motive in these cases is, however, not strictly speaking ascetic.

In Judaism the spiritual life is not being trained, nor is the body being destroyed as thing evil in itself. So we may say that Judaism was a non-ascetic religion. It may seem ascetic at first sight that some of the directions about the relations of sex but the purpose was not ascetic, but had to do with the conception of a physical uncleanness before Jahweh. We find no trace of ascetcism proper in the gradual evolution of the Jewish ritual, infact this magical conception of impurity led to washings, lustrations, certain sexual inhibitions. The dualistic asceticism of the Orient seems to leave no trace upon the canonical books. For spiritual discipline the Jew turned to the study of the Torah[88] or submitted with great ease to the burden of a legal system. In all ages, however, the mystic world-view that lends itself to asceticism is sooner or later at war with any developed legalism, and likewise a developed legalism works inevitably against the mystic-ascetic type of religious thought. The evidences cited by Zockler for an undeveloped asceticism[89] will not bear critical examination. The Nazirite vows have no real marks of strict asceticism.[90] In them the spiritual or ethical training was wholly lacking (of the story of Samos), and they had no marks of any desire to destroy the body. The abstinence from wine is a survival of nomad morality protesting against the agricultural stage. Jahweh as the storm-god of the desert had those who even in the midst of an agricultural economic stage were His earnest champions and the maintainers of more primitive types of conduct. Thus the forms were given in which asceticism might begin to develop, as perhaps in John the Baptist, although even here again we deal with other spiritual phenomena; and only when the influence of the Orient and Greece can be historically traced in Judaism do we find undoubted evidences of the ascetic ideal. The fasts, feasts and ceremonial regulations of Jewish religion proceeded upon a supposition which excludes Oriental asceticism, for the nation is holy to Jahweh, and the body can and must be kept ceremonically holy. These boundations are for all ; but priests and Nazerites, who come into closest contact with Jahweh, must be especially holy, i.e. ritually clean. The religions of the Orient centre in the negation of the body; Judaism insists upon its physical and ceremonial cleanness. It gives an entirely different character to the thought of the relation of the physical to the spiritual. So that we may put even more strongly than Zockler his closing words : 'Only the closing period of the pre-Christian Jewish history gives us real historical parallels and anticipations of monasticism and add that only in this period does ascetic practice proper have any place at all.

The distinction between fasts that have as their object the training of spiritual life and those intended to propitiate an offended God must be constantly borne in mind. The first type is ascetic, the second has no necessary ascetic motive underlying it. The national fasts of Judaism, connected also as they generally were with times of special rejoicing, were intended to ward off the displeasure of the worshipped God. The non-ethical quality of these very fasts led to their entire rejection by the ethical prophets. As custom hardened into a formulated legalism, neither world-flight nor spiritual discipline can be recognized as a formative motive. The mingling however, of Oriental and Greek elements with Judaism began early. The influence was probably wide-spread, but it reached its climax in the work of Philo at Alexandria. Here we find all the familiar marks of the Neo-Platonic teaching of a later day. God is not dragged down by the material; the highest life is that of contemplation; and abstraction from the body is the essential thing in religion. Holiness is also a negative thing. The dualism between God and nature is spanned by the Logos. The dualism between the flesh and the spirit is resolved in the contemplative life, where the spirit frees itself from the flesh and rises to the vision of God. The Essences[91] are, as we have seen, doubtfully to be considered as an ascetic development. The communism is the simple agricultural communism that marked all Israelitish life in early times. The marriage customs are hidden is evident by inaccurate estimates of them, and the asceticism reported by Philo may well be imported from his pre-conceptions into their practice. It is difficult to believe that a sect that in so many ways suggests a recurrence to primitive type should become a medium for carrying a Greek culture. John the Baptist is the reversion to the semi-nomad prophetic type. He proclaims no asceticism, but faithfulness to everyday duty. Only when Plotinus and Porphyry and Iamblichus leave the assumptions of the Old Testament, and by symbolic interpretation read Greek and Oriental thought into Judaism, do we get a system of contemplative asceticism well-developed. This asceticism is not a Jewish product and has left little trace upon jewish life, but it has profoundly influenced the Christian development.

Very early in its history the transformation of Christianity from a life to a philosophy of life began. The marks of this change are already upon several of the New Testament books where the influence of Philo and Alexandrian Judaism is marked. Thus Judaism with which the Christian Church found herself dealing was often not that of the Old Testament, but a Hellenistic Judaism whose thought was based no longer on the ethical monotheism of 8th cent prophecy, but on Greek dualism. This distorted the whole conception of the relation of the body to the purpose of the kingdom; but the distortion was not realized because the faith in a catastrophic introduction of a new age seemed in itself to minimize the importance of existing world. Upon this distortion grew up the conception of world flight; and the asceticism of the purest Oriental character was linked with the life of the Church. The so-called therapeutre, described as a Jewish monastic order, probably never existed, but the invention reflects the ideals of the highest holiness of certain circles profoundly influenced by Hellenized Christianity. As might be expected, it was in the Oriental Churches that the most negative type of asceticism flourished. Egypt become the home of men and women fleeing from the world to find in ascetic solitude the holiness they longed for. The attitude of St. Paul to marriage had nothing fundamentally ascetic in the Oriental sense. In opposition to Marcion, however, Tertullian protests[91], and he was not the only one to do so, against the rising tide of ascetic denial of marriage, urging that Christian liberty must be preserved. Thus in Egypt and Africa world-flight and ascetic fasting and an un-Christian and un-Pauline celibacy came more and more to mark the ecclesiastical development. It culminated in the world-flight of Paul of Thebes, whose retreat to the desert was, however, only the logic of the transposition of Christian values effected by Cyprian and Origen. Manichaeism and Gnosticism had really conquered, and opposed with true instinct by the Church, had yet forced upon the Church the dualistic Oriental conception of life. And logic went to the fullest extent in the hermit seclusion and the absolute isolation of the individual, as in the case of Antony and Simeon Stylites. The grouping of the priests of the workship of Serapis is sometimes regarded as the model for what now sprang up as a modification of this hermit isolation. The monastery was at first a mere group of hermits gathered about some conspicous example, or banded together for mutual protection. To such groups Pachomius (285-345) gave a set of rules, and monastic asceticism was formally foisted upon the early Catholic Church. Then, as persecution began lessen, and martyrdom become rare and rarer, the enthusiasm that found vent in this last evidence of zeal and sincerity began to express itself in ascetic practices. The spiritual athlete proved his constancy by self-inflicted depriavations

It may be said that the negative, contemplative, mystic type of asceticism had its largest development in the Oriental Greek Church. From the time of Pachomius and Antony the contemplative withdrawal from life into the desert was indeed bound up with extraordinary limitation of diet, etc. but the life of contemplation was the end sought by these fastings. The bodily exercises remain in the late conception of Greek asceticism a means to the contemplative self-abstraction. This is seen clearly in the rules of Pachomius and their subsequent development. The influence of Origen and of the Neo-Platonic conceptions on the Oriental Church, as it ceased to be intellectually quick, was to emphasize dogma and details of ritual on the basis of an extreme literalism in the use of Scripture. This ritual development was excessive, and the monastery reflected the most primitive type, an aggregate of hermit cells. It was only when, in 1988, the Russian organization education called out the best in the monastic development that it exhibited any signs of life and growth. Yet asceticism in the true sense of the term was overlaid by formalism and ritual. The negative conception of holiness was even forgotten amidst the mass of superstitious externalism.

The primary interest of the Christian Church as an Imperial organization was neither in dogma nor in the negative conception of holiness fundamental in ascetic monasticism. Her interest was in the re-organization of the Empire in the service of an Imperial ecclesiasticism. Under the leadership of Rome, asceticism became a handmaid of inestimable value. It was the great monk-pope Gregory VII, who forced on the whole of the clergy the ascetic celibacy as an ideal, and in him were united the two contradictory ideals, the ruling of the world by an institution whose ideal was world-flight. The missionary activity of the monastery in Northern Europe had changed its character, and while bringing a mass of evils connected with the holding of property, it was at the same time the barer of order and culture, and even of literature, to the relatively barbarous North. It had, however, of necessity drifted away from the ideals of Oriental asceticism. The new reformed monastic orders looked with suspicion on the agricultural and literary work which marked the less ascetic monastic institutions, and exalted more and more the life of contemplation and ascetic negation. From this period onwards extreme forms of ascetic life—scourging, wearing of chains and haircloth garments, no longer as survivals of primitive life, but planned to inflict plain and discomfort—as well as extreme seclusion, became the accepted means for the attainment of perfection; and the ideal of perfection was world-flight and the negation of desire. At the same time, the linking of these ideals with Churchly ambitions gave peculiar form to the ascetic conception. Everywhere the monastic reform set before itself the same ends:

> "The revival of monastic institutions, the recovery of lost lands, and the acquirement of new possessions, the establishment of old ecclesiastical laws, the acquirement of a better class of novitiate, introduction of stricter discipline and cultivation piety, as described in the older stories of monastery life, and especially in the writings of Gregory, the Great (590-604), penance and self-inflicted pain of all kinds, contemplation in solitude, humility to the point of self-renunciation, constant employment of confession and the sacrament, homage of the saints and relics, pilgrimages, search for the miraculous, pessimistic judgement of the world, longings for death, and generally an abnormal raising of the emotional life, increased sensitiveness, and, above all, a high estimate of the "grace of tears".[92]

Each new attempt at monastic reform of necessity but revived this negative idea of holiness, and hence it is no accident that the circumstances which originally produced the pacimistic world-flight religious type in the Western Church. The times of revived asceticism are periods of national disorder and social disruption. It is impossible for any religious development to be wholly without the note of service and self-sacrifice for others, yet this sinks more and more into the background the more self-consistent the pursuit of the ascetic ideal becomes. To save one's own soul by retirement from the dangers of life is the chief goal, and the selfishness of this goal is only partly hidden by the fact that service on behalf of others may become a means to this end. Even the asceticism that marked the great monastic revival under St. Francis of Assisi (1182-1226) made the great services rendered by the order often a source of real corruption. The complete impossibility of making the negative monastic asceticism a universal demand upon all Christians, while still maintaining Imperial world ambitions, has always led in the Western Church to compromises with the lay world. Hence each revival of the extreme emphasis has also led to 'lay-brotherhoods', to modified vows for those who cannot atogether flee the world, and to an extention of ascetic symbolism. The ascetic symbolism plays, therefore, a larger and larger part in penance, fasts, prayers, vigils, etc., in which the elemental of pain and bodily deprivation is reduced to a minimum, and the ascetic element is represented by symbols, 'half-fasts', fish and eggs, instead of meat, beads, told, and masses said by proxy, etc. Against these compromises protests were constantly being raised by those who seriously held the monastic ascetic type of Christian ideal (Bernard of Cluny); but more and more as the Imperial organizing force of a centralized Vatican made its way, these compromises received the sanction of the Church. The goal of Jesuit order set before itself was world-conquest rather than world-flight, and thus again is clearly seen the old struggle between two distinct ideals of holiness, while both are maintained within the great historic communion of the Roman Church. The triumps of the Jesuit policies since the great Jansenist controversy have therefore steadily relegated asceticism to a secondary and disciplinary place, and its recent history shows no new development within the Roman communion, while it still maintains its place as one of historic legitimacy.

There is no room for Oriental asceticism based upon world-flight in a true protestantism. The only place asceticism can properly have is as a training for the life of service, and it is only a matter of loving expediency whether the Protestant shall prepare himself for service by fasting, deprivation and negation of legitimate desires, or by the simple and faithful discharge of daily duty. In the Mathew tradition Jesus certainly anticipated fasting; but in actual facts His disciples did not emphasize it during His lifetime, as is seen also in the Mark tradition and St. Paul's doctrine of Christian freedom, permitting, indeed, any act that may prove for spiritual edification, excludes any emphasis upon such practice are necessary. Hence the reformers admit fasts. All the ascetic practices have dropped away, or been actually condemned by both Lutheran and Reformed Churches. In the form of world-flight Protestantism has overcome asceticism. Only in the forms of a legalism can be trace remains of the Catholic conception of a negative holiness, and even the legalism that forbids dancing, theatre-going , wine-drinking and card-playing does : So now on the basis of the expediency of the Christian life, or on the ground of inherent immorality in the practices, thus removing the discussion of them from the sphere of asceticism. It is therefore a source of confusion to confound these two separate motives. With protestantism, therefore, Oriental asceticism may be said to have been theoretically overcome.

Besides Indian culture, Christian culture is the only one which has recognized asceticism as a legitimate mode of life. Christian asceticism is known to have begun in Egypt about the 3rd or the 4th century A.D., and is associated with St. Anthony. About the end of the 3rd century it is believed that Anthony's life as a solitary ascetic was brought to an end by a number of disciples gathering round him. St. Anthony thus becomes the father of Christian monasticism. It was this type of monastic life that prevailed in Egypt upto the middle of the 5th century A.D. All later Christian asceticism and monasticism is traceable to it. The earliest of the ascetic and monastic orders in Western Christianity was the work of St. Benedict about the begining of the 6th century A.D. He "effected a permanently working adaptation of the monastic ideal and life to the conditions of Western races." The life to be led did not involve great austerity through it was self-denying and hard. The whole day a monk was occupied with the public celebration of the canonical office, reading and work.[93]

For about 600 years, c. 550-c. 1150, in Italy and other European Countries monastic life based on the code of St. Benedict was the only type of religious life. This monastic influence continued to dominate the Church until the emergence of the Universities and the foundation of the Orders of Mendicant Friars in the second half of the 12th century, The lose connection in general between the Universities of Christianity is testified to by the fact that they established chairs in theology which came to be held by mendicant Friars. Even more significant than this general connection is the direct papal support given to the University of Paris as the centre of orthodox theological teaching.[94]

It is well-known that the Protestant reformation of Christianity not only protested against asceticism but also led to the despoilation of the monasteries. Protestant Christianity having rejected ascetic and monastic life altogether has acclaimed only one ideal type, namely, that of the householder, or the non-monk. Catholic Christianity, however , has continued to own and encourage the monkish type inspite of various vicissitudes and difficulties. The vitality of ascetic ideal type as an integral part of Catholic culture cannot be better demonstrated than by the fact that within twenty years of Martin Luther's burning of the papal bull of excommunication was founded the most significant and perhaps the latest of the regular ascetic Orders. And that is the Society of Jesus, popularly known as the Jesuits. The wide ramifications, both in the sphere of work and in the extent of territory, which this ascetic order has made, need not be entered into here. Their great significance is brought out by the fact that "the Jesuit has not home the whole world is his parish. Mobility and cosmopolitanism are the very essence of the Society."[95] Catholic Christian culture has continued to be served by two ideal types— the ascetic and the non-ascetic. The ascetic ideal type has exerted not only to spiritualize the other type but also to do selfless service in the cause of society.

The Christian ascetic ideal, which has now remained as an ideal of Catholic Christianity alone and whose development has been more or less parallel with that of Indian Asceticism, was first developed in Egypt. Its Egyptian development was in its turn, inspired by Buddhist asceticism.[96] Flinders Petrie, the great Egyptologist , in his excavation of Memphis, the capital of ancient Egypt, discovered in the Persian strata of that city pottery- heads and figures of Indian type along with Scythian and Tibetan ones, Pondering over Indian infilteration at Memphis through its Persian conquest, he observes: "The importance of the Indian colony in Memphis under the Persian empire lies in its bearing on its importation of Indian thought, and the rise of the ascetic movement before Christ-which culminated in western monachicism." This influence of Indian culture, according to him, culminated in Western monachicism through the medium of the "Communal form of asceticism" which had already come into existence in Egypt by 340 B.C. Rev. Frank Knight further specifies the Indian influence as having been associated with Buddhism and having been disseminated throughout Egypt by the end of the 5th century B.C. Commenting on the significance of this influence he observes : "the consequences were remarkable. Monasteries or groups of ascetic devotees living together in a communal form and ordering their lives on rules laid down by Indians were established in Egypt by B.C. 340. It is in many ways probable that Greek stoicism was not an idigenous Hellenic product, but merely infiltration via Egypt of beliefs derived from the Buddhist priests of India."

REFERENCES

1. *The Encyclopedia of Religion,* Ed. Mircea Eliade, Vol. I, New York, 1987, p. 441.
2. Benjamin Preciado-Solis, "Some Problems Concerning the Origin of Samnyasa" *ABORI, op. cit.,* p. 359
3. Dumont Leuis, "Renuciation in Indian Religions", in *Religion, Politics and History in India*, Nouton, The Hague, 1970, pp. 45-66.
4. Margaret and James Stutley, *A Dictionary of Hinduism*, London, 1977.
5. *Eastern Monachism,* p. 74.
6. *Manual of Buddhism,* p. 73.
7. Hibbert Lectures, p. 351.
8. Jaina Sutras, I pp. xxiv - xxxii.
9. Vedic Index, II, p. 164
10. *Rigvedic India*, pp. 338-39.
11. *Samveda*, p. 50
12. *Mohanjodaro and Ancient Indus Civilization*, I, p. 44.

13. 'Origin of Indian Monachism', *J.B.U.*, Vol. VIII, 1939, pp. 104-30.
14. *Bhagvat, op. cit.* p. 29.
15. Barua, *A History of Pre-Buddhistic Indian Philosophy*, p. 130.
16. Das, *Rigvedic India*, p. 11.
17. Sharma, *Contributions to the History of Brahmanical Asceticism (Samnyasa)*, p.11f.
18. Ghurye, *op. cit.*, p. 12.
19. *Ibid*, pp. 17ff.
20. Dutta, *Early Buddhist Monachism. p. 54-55.*
21. Upadhye, *Provacansara*, Preface.
22. Deo, *History of Jaina Monachism*, p. 56.
23. Dutta, *op. cit.*, pp. 54-55.
24. Deo, *History of Jaina Monachism*, p. 56.
25. *Buddhist Monks and Monasteries in India*, p. 45.
26. Ghurye, *op. cit.*, p. 22.
27. Chanda, R. , *Memoirs, Archaeological Survey of India*, xxxxi, pp. 31-34.
28. Majumdar ed., *The Vedic age*, pp. 215-217.
29. *Hindu View of Life*, pp. 37-38, 41.
30. Bhattacharya, Art : The Background of Buddhist Philosophy, *Indo-Asian Culture*, July 1952, p. 66.
31. Geden, *ERE.*, II, p. 88, Also Bouquet, *Hinduism*, p. 33; Brandon, Man and his Destiny in the Great Religions, p. 301.
32. Ancient India, its Language and Religions, p. 83.
33. The Origin of Asceticism and of the Asrama Dharma, *Bharti*, VIII, pt. I, pp. 6-10.
34. Indian Thought and its Development, p. 22.
35. Ghurye, *op. cit.* p. 11.
36. *Rigveda*, 10.136. Tr. A.C. Bose, *Hymns from the Vedas*, Bombay, 1966.
37. *ABORI*, *op. cit.*, pp. 363-364.
38. Chanda R., *op. cit.*, p. 32.
39. Bhandarkar, D. R., *loc. cit.*, p.18; Vedic Index, II, pp. 185, 447.
40. *Atharva Veda*, 11. 5. 5-6 Tr. A.C. Bose, *Ibid*.
41. *Satapatha Brahmana*, 10.4.4.1.2. Tr. J. Eggeling, *Sacred Books of the East*.
42. Macdonell, pp. 108-09; Keith. I, p. 168; *Vedic Index*, II, 479.
43. R.V., X, 136; VII, 56, 8.
44. Indian Thought and its Development, 1936, p. 22
45. *Br. Upanisad*, IV, 4, 22.
46. *Prashna Upanisad*, I, 1, 2, 4, 9.
47. *Br. Upanisad*, II. 4.1.
48. *Br. Upanisad*, IV, 2, 1; 4, 22, III, 5.
49. Kane, P.V., *History of Dharmashastra*, Vol. II, Part II, p. 931.
50. Sharma, *op. cit.*, p.20.

51. Kane, P.V., *op. cit.*, Vol. II, part 1, p. 422.
52. Cambridge History of India, Vol. I, pp. 158-159.
53. *Cambridge History of India*, Vol.1, p. 153.
54. Bhandarkar, R.G., p. 42.
55. *Indian Philosophy and Modern Culture*, p.11.
56. Oman, Mystics, *Ascetics and Saints of India*, London, p. 13.
57. Basham, A.L., *The Wonder that was India*, pp. 3-4, 9.
58. ERE., Vol. VIII, p. 803.
59. Bloomfield, *Religion of the Vedas*, p. 264.
60. *The Encyclopedia of Religion*, ed. Mircea Eliade, 1987, Vol.1, p. 443.
61. Sorokin, *Social and Cultural Dynamics,* Vol. 1., pp. 119-120.
62. Kane, P.V., *op. cit.*, p. 975.
63. Oman, J.C., *Mystics; Ascetics and Saints of India*, 1903, p. 271; 'it is the ascetic profession that time out of mind has been a pre-eminent dignity in the eyes of the Indian people.'
64. Bhagat, M.G., *op.cit.*, p. 61.
65. "Phaedo" 81e, in *Plato* (Loeb) I, 285.
66. "Phaedo" 83d, (Loeb) I, 291.
67. "Phaedo" 84a, (Loeb) I, 291-93.
68. Swain, Joseph Ward , *The Hellenic Origins of Christian Asceticism,* New York, 1916, pp. 8, 11.
69. Lohse, Bernard, *Askese and Monchtum in der Antike und in der alten kirche,* Munich , 1969, pp. 25-26, 31; Swain, *Hellenic Origins*, pp. 9, 24.
70. Detienne, Marcel, *Les Jordins d' Adonis,* Paris, 1972, pp. 230-31.
71. Lohse, *Askase und Monchtum,* p. 25; Swain, *Hellenic Origins*, p. 12.
72. "Laws" 782c, in *Plato* (Loeb) IX, 493.
73. "The Frogs" 1032, in *Aristophanes* (Loeb), 11, 393.
74. "Hippolytus" 953, in *Euripides* (Loeb), IV, 237.
75. Detienne, *Adonis*, pp. 85-87; *Dario Sabbatucci, Saggio sul Misticismo greco*, Rome, 1965, pp. 75, 79.
76. Eudoxus, cited by Porphyry, *Life of Pythagoras*, 7; Onesicritus, cited by Strabo, XV, 716; Guthrie, *Greek Philosophy*, p. 187.
77. Porphyry, *On Abstinence from Animal Food*, 11.28, 1.26, trans. Thomas Taylor, ed. Esme Wynne-Tyson, London, 1965, pp. 82, 37.
78. *Ibid*, III. 26, p. 139.
79. Empedocles, *fragment*, 137, p. 260.
80. *Diogenes*, VIII. 20 (Loeb) II, 339; Detienne, *Adonis*, p. 381.
81. Detienne, *Adonis,* pp. 100-104
82. Detienne, *Adonis,* pp. 108-109.
83. *Maitrayani Samhita* I 4.10-s *Kathakam* XXXII.7. *[Yajurveda]; Taittiriya Samhita* V.1.8.1; all cited by Schroeder, *Pythagoras*, pp. 35-36.
84. Zeller, *Greek Philosophy*, p. 344 n 4.

85. Aulus Gellius IV. 11, in *The Attic Nights* (Loeb) I, 347-49.
86. Lohse, Askese and Monchtum, pp. 30-31.
87. *Herodotus*, 11.37 (Loeb) I, 321.
88. *ERE*, James Hastings, p. 803.
89. Zockler, *Askese und Monchtum*, pp. 113-120.
90. 'Nazirite' in Hastings' DB.
91. By Conybear in Hastings' DB.
92. Muller, K., *Kirchengesch*, pp. 885-386.
93. *Encyclopaedia Britannica*, XV, p. 687; Compton Piers : *The Great Religious Orders*, 1931, p. vi; Coulton, G.C., *Five Centuries of Regions*, 23-36, Vol-I, p.16.
94. Ghurye, G.S., *Indian Sadhus*, 1953, p. 7.
95. *Encyclopaedia Britannica*, XIII, pp. 9-10.
96. Flinders-Petrie, *Memphis and its Foreigners in Scientific American Supplement*, 1904, p. 300; *Memphis*, I, p.17; Frank Knight, G.A., *Nile and Jordan*, 1921, p. 368.

CULTURAL AND HISTORICAL CONTACTS : ANCIENT INDIA & ANCIENT GREECE

In ancient times, in the case of two countries situated at such a long geographical distance, the possibility of exchange of ideas can be considered only when it is demonstrated that there was an actual contact between the two countries. The facility is provided by political or trade relations. It is not necessary that one of these countries should exercise political control over the other. A third country, having contacts with the two, can serve as the meeting ground for them. Thus, though there are stray indications for India's contact with the West even in the first half of the first millennium B.C.[1], the first clear opportunity for the Greeks and Indians to meet was provided by the widely extensive Achaemenid empire. It had political and trade connections both with Greece and India, which possibly served as the vehicle for cultural exchange as well. It is not unlikely that at the Achaemenid court, some Greeks had an occasion to hear about India and its culture. The first Greek who is known to have visited India, was Skylax of Caryandra, an admiral whom Darius commissioned to explore the route of India upto the mouth of Indus. But the extensive accounts prepared by him are lost. The way Herodotus and Ktesias refer to India rules out the possibility of any intimate understanding of India on the part of the contemporary Greeks before their times[2], thus, it will be difficult to argue for the Greek philosophy in this early period containing elements of Indian philosophy[3].

It was the Macedonian invasion which brought India to the full gaze of the Greek world. Alexander had revolutionary ideas about the fusion of all mankind into one harmonious world and due to him intercourse between East and West, previously a tickle now swelled into a flood[4]. Alexander is known to have established Greek colonies in India. He opened a sea-route and three land-routes between the two countries. Under the Hellenistic kingdoms and the Mauryas in India the contact grew in both intensity and volume. During the period of Indo-Bacterian kings, the Scythians the Indo-Parthians and the Kusanas, despite the political changes and disturbances occurring from time to time, the cultural exchange between the two countries become livelier[5]. The discovery of the Monsoon facilitated voyages to India. Thus, we see that from the time of Alexander to the period of the Guptas the political and trade contacts made it possible for people and ideas to travel from one area to the other.

The period prior to Alexander the great, direct evidence of Indian-Greek contacts is almost non-existant, though this naturally does not mean that no such contacts, took place. Some interesting resemblances can be cited between Indian and Greak ideas of this period : especially with respect to soul-wandering and notions of the world essence. No doubt Indian influence on Greek ascetic practice is an ever present possibility, if only because itinerent Indian holy men might at almost any time have wandered westward, providing visible comparisons are thus in order between Indian and Greek asceticism in the classical period. Finally, some similarities occur between the respective Indian and Greek cosmological ideas concerning the succession of world-ages.

A new historical era—the Hellenistic began as Alexander led his army of Macedonians and Greek into Asia, accompanied by various Greek literary men who recorded their observations of the countries through which they passed. Subsequently, other Hellenistic writers reported upon the Indian trade which moved from Alexandria in Egypt via the Red Sea and the Indian ocean, particularly after the first century B.C. when sailors discovered how to utilize the monsoon to shorten the voyage. Indian envoys appeared at the courts of various Roman emperors.

Unquestionably Indo-Greek contacts did take place; the difficulty lies in finding and interpreting their consequences.

The cultural contacts between India and Greece representing the Asiatic and the Western consciousness respectively occur since remote antiquity despite geographical and linguistic barriers. The striking analogies between Sanskrit and Greek languages and Vedic and Greek deities in their names and functions led early European Indologists to believe in their common Indo-European origin. They discovered the closest equivalents of the Greek inflections in Sanskrit and made attempts to reconstruct the Indo-European lexicon. Panini's Grammer formed the main basis for the Indo-European comparative Grammer.

Before Alexander, Greek knowledge of India was acquired on the whole by way of Persia. King Cyrus, founder of the Persian empire and of the Achaemenid dynasty (reigned 559-530 B.C.), added to his territories the region called Gandhara, directly south of the Hindu Kush mountains. About 518-515 B.C. Dareios-I extended this conquest southward as far as the Indus river[6]. Thereby the Indus became the easternmost boundary of the vast Persian colosus, which sprawled across all of western Asia to include, after 546 B.C., most of the Greek cities on the coast of Asia Minor. Communications between the extremities of the huge polity were now unimbeded by political frontiers. Moreover, Persian policies served inadvertently to promote that mixture of nationalities which so frequently provides intellectual stimulus. Many Greeks served as officials or mercenaries in the various Achaemenid provinces, on occasion Greek physicians were employed at the Persian royal court[7]. Conversely, Indian troops formed a contingent of the Persian army which invaded Greece in 480 B.C., and of the army which opposed Alexander at Gaugamela in 331 B.C.[8]. Unquestionably the requirements of war, administration and commerce in the far-flung Persian empire produced numerous encounters between Indians and Greeks. Most of these, no doubt, were inconsequential; but even genuine exchange of ideas will ordinarily have left no trace for posterity.

It was with the emergence of Achaimenian empire of which the Greeks living in Ionia and the Indians of North-Western region were integral parts. We have the first definite proof of interaction between Indians and the Greeks. Xenophon reported that the Bactrians and Indians were brought under the rule of Achaemeneans by the emperor Cyrus, who had brought in his control all the nations from Syria to Erythraean Sea[9].

Greeks had become well-known in North-Western region is attested by the grammarian Panini a native of Salatura near Taksasila. He mentioned them as Yavanas, derived from the Persian Youna used for the Greek inhabitants of Ionia[10].

There were not only soldiers, traders, sailors and persons in administrative services, who came into contact with one another but also philosophers and ascetic wanderers. Aristoxenos, the musicians, disciple of Aristoteles reports a widely believed anecdote of his days which tell us about the visit of a group of Indian philosophers to Greece during the 4th century B.C. In Athens they met Socrates and asked him the object of his philosophy, 'An enquiry into the human affairs,' he told them the Indian burst into laughter, 'How', asked the leading sage, 'Can a man understand human affairs if he is ignorant of divine affairs'[11].

Thus from 6th century B.C. to 4th century B.C., the Persian Empire made possible the inter exchange of ideas between diverse types of peoples. In the domain of philosophy, the results of these contacts were spectacular, Greek philosophy was born not in Athens, the intellectual capital of classical Greece, but on the coast of Asia Minor in Ionia, where the Achaemenian empire had provided an opportunity to Ionian Greeks to come into contact with developed civilizations of the Orient. The Ionian philosophers like the sages of the Upanisads had concluded that a single substance (arche: Brahman) lies at the basis of all existence. Furthermore, the identification of the element fire with changeability occurs both in Herakleitos and

Buddhist thought.

Like Vaisesikas and many others in India the thinkers like Leukippos and Demokritos had also developed atomism in Greece. Infact atomism of India is earlier than that of Demokritos for at first it was taught by some Pakudha Katyayana, an older contemporary of Buddha.

It is generally believed that the Nature Science was first born and developed in Greece. But according to Prof. Chattopadhyaya it was Uddalaka Aruni of Pancala and not Thales of Miletas who can be declared as the earliest Nature Scientist. Uddalaka Aruni, who could not be presumably later than the 8th or 7th century B.C. proceeded to sketch a view of the evolution of everything in nature ultimately from the primeval being or sat with a dynamism or motion inherent in it[12].

The doctrine of metempsychosis inquestionably provides more specific analogies, causing scholars to speculate that the idea as occurred in Greece was ultimately derived from India. After Alexander, India came to be known as the land of philosophers, it was also recognised as the source of Pythagoreanism[13]. Schroeder made an indepth study to show the Indian origin of all the doctrines ascribed to Pythagoras. These includes the theory of the transmigration of souls. The doctrine of the five elements, the character of his religio-philosophical fraternity, his mystical speculation, vegetarianism, the prohibition of eating beans and the pythagorean theorem[14].

The Indian animal fables also seem to have reached Greece through Persia. The more well-known of the Greek animal fables are attributed to the Ionian slave-Aesop. They were quite popular in 5th century B.C. and Socrates, Herodotos and Aristophanes have referred to them. In Aesop's fables, 'The Ass in a lion's Skin', the skin in which the ass is disguised is blown off by the winds. In the Jataka version, the ass disguised in a lion skin is betrayed by his own cry. The Jataka story of the Swan who dropped the Tortoise, appears in Aesop as "The Eagle who Dropped the Tortoise". Like these there are numerous similar fables of Greek and Indian stock. Some Greek tales similar to Indians also occur in Herodotos[15]. There is a great possibility that the fables contained in the Jatakas and the Panchatantra are much older than their most ancient versions. The oral tradition upon which these stories were inevitably based must have been considerably older. When one notices in these fables the cycle of rebirth, their didactic nature, the animals (peacock, lion, tiger, monkey) native to India and the frequency with which the same fables occur in Indian sources as compared to only once or twice in Greek texts, the theory of Indian origin of Greek fables is strengthened. In fact, on account of the presence of parallels with European tales in most parts of India and of still other parallels in the old literary collections, a whole generation of scholars was led to regard India as the great homeland of most of the European folk stories[16].

The inter exchange in the field of medicine would have also become probably possible as a result of the communication between the Indian and Greek doctors of the Persian Empire.

While all these things were going on, India does not appear to be well-known in the West during the first phase of Indo-Greek contacts. Interest in marvels (fabulous races and animals, miraculous objects), idealization of the land (fertility of soil, abundance of gold, favourite climate, excellent products, largest in size and population) and idealization of the people (most just, long lived, free from diseases, truth loving) alongwith some geographical misconceptions (India is joined to Ethiopia, India's location at the Eastern end of the world, continuous desert or ocean beyond the Indian satrapy) are the dominant trends, which we notice in the Greek writings of this period. These trends continue to remain during the entire period of Graeco-Roman history and also during middle ages of Europe.

But amidst marvels and exaggerations in early Greek accounts on India, there are also reports which have unveild the unknown chapter of Indian History. Thus, Herodotos' reports of the inclusion of Indus region in the Achaemenian empire, payment of highest tribute in the form of gold dust, description of North-Western horses. Cotton as wool bearing tree, Indian soldiers with iron tipped arrows in Xerxes' army and mercenaries in Merdonios' army reveal valuable Historical informations. His description of gold digging ants has genuine Indian tradition and is described in the Mahabharata. Ktesias' description of the use of Indian elephants in war and demolishing walls, talking parrots and monkeys were based on facts. His report of the high quality of Indian steel sword, ivory, cotton, purple dye, pepper, wine, perfume, gold, silver, precious-stones throw light on the development of North-Western urbanism. Corroborated with archaeological evidences these accounts lead us to believe that the North-Western urbanization was an indigenous evolution[17].

A new era in the history of India's relationship to the Greek world begins with the career of Alexander, called "Great" on account of his unprecedented military achievements. He was bent upon spreading Greek culture in the countries he conquered, independently of whether he subsequently succeeded or not in doing so in India. The army of Alexander consisted of not only generals and soldiers but also historians, technicians, geographers, philosophers, artists, engineers, topographers etc. Two at least of Alexander's companions were the philosophers Anaxarchos and Onesicritos. As a disciple of Diogenes Onesicritos' interest in India was mainly in its philosophical ideas. Aristoboulos of Cassandra was interested in geography and engineering. Ptolemaios wrote a purely military account. Some of these authors had personally accompanied the expedition : the best known of these are Kallisthenes, Aristobulos, Nearchos the admiral, Onesikritos his chief pilot, and Ptolemaios the general and later king of Egypt. Among three main authors of Alexander's companions Onesikritos is said to have reported on exaggerated account of India: Nearchos was moderate : and Aristoboulos the most restrained. Each one had his own motive and the subjective element was dominant in him.

Alexander's companions have left a good deal of

information on political condition of this North-West region in the 4th century B.C. For ascertaining the nature of republic developed in ancient India this material is very significant. The Indian sources do not have enough informations about the North-West region. Thus what is missing in Indian sources, is compensated by the Greeks.

According to Onesikritos, Alexander had reports that Indian gymnosophists went naked bore hardships cheerfully, and were held in great honour. Onesikritos was deputed to contact them outside the city of Taksasila. He saw fifteen ascetics standing, sitting or laying naked in different postures and motionless till evening. Onesikritos invited them to have an audience with Alexander, but with one exception, they declared saying that whoever wished to learn about their doctrines should come to them. The two gymnosophists with whom Onesikritos had conversation, were Kalanos and Dandamis. Kalanos laughed at the dress of Onesikritos. After the discourse Kalanos had asked the heavenly dressed Onesikritos, if he wished to hear him, he should strip off his clothes and lie down on the stone like Kalanos[18].

Onesikritos may have wished to flatter Alexander[19]. Thus, he claims that the leader of the ascetics, named Dandamis, praised Alexander for his interest in philosophy—an interest he said he had never before observed in a warrior-King Dandamis also asserted that such a king should persuade or force all his subjects to practice (ascetic) self-control. Onesikritos interpreted his statement, Cynic fashion, to mean that the Indian believed that the best doctrine was "that which removes pleasure and pain from the soul"[20]. Obviously the Indian holy man impressed the Greeks favourably by his overt indifference to worldly power and goods. Ordered to appear before Alexander upon the promise of gifts if he complied but punishment if he did not, Dandamis replied that he desired nothing at all and did not fear the king's power. Alexander allegedly was not offended by this answer, but praised Dandamis' attitude and refrained from insisting that he come[21].

However, this was probably more than just flattery; Onesikritos evidently had a genuine admiration for his king, precisely because he combined political with intellectual powers. Such is the intention of Onesikritos when he quotes an Indian sage. Dandamis as saying that Alexander was the only philosopher at arms' i.e. the only conqueror who happened also to be a philosopher[22].

The ideas of gymnosophists as briefed by Dandamis to Onesikritos are as follows :

> "The best teaching is that which removes pleasure and pain from the soul; and that pain and toil differ, for the former is inimical to man and the latter friendly, since man trains the body for toil in order that his opinions may be strengthened whereby he may put a stop to dissensions and be ready to give good advice to all, both in public and in private........"

After understanding the commonalities between Indian and Greek philosophy, Dandamis accepted the Greeks as sound minded in general, but found them wrong in their preferences of formal custom to nature; for otherwise they would not be ashamed to go naked. Dandamis remarked, "the best house is that which requires the least repairs[23].

Dandamis tells Alexander :

> "I have just as much of the earth as you and every other person; even if you gain all rivers, you cannot drink more than I. Therefore I have no fears, acquired no wounds and destroy no cities. I have just as much earth and water as you; altogether I possess everything. Learn this wisdom from me. Wish for nothing, and everything is yours"[24].

The king agrees so to the desirability of such a life. Unfortunately, he argues, his ties to his soldiers are too strong; for this reason he cannot renounce the world[25]. Thereby even Alexander, the world-conqueror, accepts the moral superiority of asceticism. Alexander approves of the ascetics' life style. Only practical considerations prevent him from imitating it himself[26].

While, returning from India, Alexander reaching at Patala at the mouth of Indus ordered the building of a harbour and docks to secure a sea-connection with the West. He wanted a thorough survey of the coastline and a report on the conditions of life there, presumably as a preliminary to opening up the route between India and Mesopotamia. Nearchos was commissioned for the venture of finding a way to the mouth of Euphrates.

The account of voyage as furnished by Nearchos[27] gives a vivid description of the places and races encountered the distances covered in stadia, the navigational facilities available in the route. Climatic changes and few hints on maritime trade. The names of places along the whole route between the Indus to the head of the Persian gulf, the references to local shipping and ocean pilots with accurate informations about the coastal region in Nearchos' account, bear testimony to the fact that the route was already in use.

The brief expedition of Alexander had some interesting consequences in the context of Indo-Greek relations. One of these was the establishment of the sceptic school of thought in the Hellenistic world, which is considered to be the outcome of Jain influence on its founder Pyrrhon, who was in India with Alexander. We came to know from Diogenes Laertios that in company of his master Anaxarchos, Pyrrhon had travelled everywhere including India, where he had met the Indian gymnosophists and Persia, where he came into contact with Magis. He had accompanied Alexander in his Indian expedition. This led him to adopt a philosophy taking the form of agnosticism and suspension of judgements.

Pyrrhon had propounded a logical device known in philosophy as the tetralemma i.e. to say about a phenomenon that it either is, or is not, or is and is not, or neither is nor is not. The principle of Syadvada in Jainism stresses choice among seven predicates. In Greece except Scepticism this type of judgement is apparently unknown. Furthermore, Sceptic's nihilistic attitude towards knowledge also supports the theory of Jain influence[28].

On Indian soil, the campaign resulted in the establishment of several Greek settlements. During the course of his campaigns, Alexander is said to have founded several Alexandrias at various places. He is said to have established Alexandria-Buclephala on the East bank of the river Hydaspes (Jhelum) and Alexandria Nicaea on the West bank of the Hydaspes. The other Alexandria cities which we have in India were on the upper Acesines (Chenab)[29], the one at the confluence of the Chenab and the Indus and another in the country of Sogdians. At the end of his Indian campaigns he also built a harbour and dockyards in the city of Pattala on the mouth of the Indus[30]. The cities and towns thus established by Alexander must have contributed significantly in inter exchange of Indian and Greek cultural elements.

Probably, the most significant effect of the Macedonian campaign was the example, it provided to Indian chiefs. Before Alexander's invasion on India, the Indian ideal of *Chakravartin*, i.e., the universal king lived in the realm of mythology only. But in Alexander for the first time the Indian rulers could see the concept of *Chakravartin* in reality. The founder of Mauryan empire, who was just a lad at this time might have been motivated by Alexander's example.

In 305 B.C. Seleukos Niketor, established as ruler of Syria, Mesopotamia and Persia over the reminder of Alexander's inheritance, attempted to get back the lost provinces of Alexander's Indian conquests. Chandragupta Maurya opposed Seleukos with such a formidable army that the latter had to recognise not only the sovereignty of Chandragupta over Punjab but also to cede additional territories of Gandhara, parts of Arachosia and Gedrosia in exchange of 500 war elephants from the Indian chief, Seleukos' daughter was also probably married to Chandragupta Maurya. Seleukos also sent an ambassador Megasthenes to Chandragupta's court, where he had lived for several years. Megasthenes' work *Ta Indika* which survives in numerous fragments, is considered to be the most valuable work on Indian affairs. Described by Patrokles as one not in haste (epidromaden). Megasthenes' long stay in the sub-continent enabled him to describe the whole of Indian life from royalty to remotest tribe. His rich informations consist of India's geography, rivers, mountains, fertility, animals, plants, Pataliputra, the customs of the Indians, the division of the society, public adminstration, the Indian philosophers and many other subjects. It was probably written to show that India was even a better land than Hekataios' Egypt that it was an ideal Platonic state where philosophers reigned and that all civilizations sprung from India not Egypt[32].

According to Megasthenes Janpadas like Polis had their humble beginnings Indian which gradually developing into an association of the aggregate of families began to form the ruling tribes. Megasthenes evidence draws our attention towards the form of state developed by the Mauryas[33].

Platon's similarities with Upanisadic philosophy, which has drawn the attention of many scholars was already noticed by Megasthenes during his Indian sojourn. It may be noted that not only does Platon represent the Upanisadic doctrine of reincarnation but also the Upanisadic style of tale and dialogues for propounding his thought. Furthermore, Platon's concepts of three elements of soul, three-fold social order and city soul analogy may be well corroborated with ancient Indian ideals. It will also be interesting to study the evolution of the concept like justice in Platon's *Republic* and Dharma in the Shantiparva of *Mahabharat* in reorganising social and political institutions in ancient India and ancient Greece. In fact originating from the concept of rta in India and dike in Greece both of them imbibed the peculiar empirical and moral characteristics.

Seleukos' successer Antiochos I (280-261 B.C.) had also deputed his ambassador Daimachos in the court of Amitrochatis identified with Chandragupta Maurya's son Bindusara. Amitrochatis' which in the Indian language of the time meant (Slayer of foes) which was an appellation of the King

Bindusara[34].

Daimachos is also said to have written a book on India but very few fragments, which are on geographical features of India have survived from his work. Another book on India of same time was written by Patrokles, who had served as military commander both under Seleukos and Antiochos I. But unfortunately like Daimachos, his survived fragments are also very few in number.

Hegasandos refers that Amitrochatis the king of India wrote to Antiochos to purchase and send him grape syrup, figs and a sophist. And Antiochos wrote back' "figs to be sure and grape syrup we will despatch to you, but it is against the law in Greece to sell a sophist[35].

Bactria (Afganistan) under Greek rule was a flourishing country of many towns and cities; its capital, Baktra (Modern Balkh) was a great entrepot for trade between Babylon and India. In the 3rd century B.C. Chandragupta's grandson Ashoka sent Buddhist missionaries to Bactria, where he erected rock inscriptions composed to Greek by someone who was obviously familiar with the vocabulary of Hellenistic philosophy[36]. A thousand year later (7th Cen. A.D.) the Chinese pilgrim HsuanTsang counted one hundred Buddhist monasteries and three thousand monks in the city of Baktra alone[37]. The XIIIth Major Rock Edict of Ashoka refers to Buddhist missionaries sent to the region of Greeks. They were Antiohos II Theos, King of Syria and West Asia (261-247 B.C.) Ptolemaios Philadelphos, King of Egypt (285-247 B.C.), Magas, King of Cyrene (285-258 B.C.) Antigonos II Gonatos, King of Macedonea (277-239 B.C.) and Alexander II, King of Epirus (Circa 272-240 B.C.).[38]

According to Polybios (born circa 200 B.C.) Antiochos III (223-187 B.C.) who had campaigned against the Bactrian Ethydemes had renewed his alliance with an Indian king called Sophagasenos. Beside a huge tribute Antiochos also received some elephants from the Indian king. The Sanskrit version of Sophagosenos is Subhagasena, was probably the ruler of one of the splinter kingdoms of North-West India, into which the Mauryan Empire had broken up[39].

Ptolemaios Philadelphos II (285-246 B.C.) ruling in Egypt had sent an ambassador Dionysios to the Mauryan court. Whether he presented his credentials to Bindusara or Ashoka remains uncertain. Like Megasthenes, Patrokles and Daimachos, Dionysios also wrote a work on India but it is completely lost.

According to the *Mahavamsa,* at the foundation of the great tope by the King Duthagamini in the year 157 B.C. the senior priest of Yona from the vicinity of Alasadda (Alexandria) the capital of the Yona country attended it, accompanied the thirty thousand priests. The number is of course, an exggeration. Strabo states on the authority of Nicolaus of Damascus that an Indian embassy including a thinker who burnt himself to death at Athens in 200 B.C. was sent to Augustus by the Indian king Poros[40].

During all this period, India and the West had extensive trade relations. When Alexander chase in Egypt the site for a city which was destined to prepetuate his name, the preparation for the blending of Eastern and Western cultures started. For a thousand years Alexandria continued to be a centre of intellectual and commercial activity because it was the meeting place of Jews, Syrians, and Greeks. *Milindapanho* mentions it as one of the places to which the Indians regularly resorted.[41]

The leading Greek geographer Eratosthenes (275-200 B.C.) was an ardent admirer of the Indians. Among the civilized barbarians, he cited Indians at the top, followed by the Romans, Arianes (Persians) and Cartheginians. Eratosthenes wrote a work Geography, in the third book of this work, which gives a description of the world with maps, we have references to India. His transworthy and scientifically well founded information on India was much utilized by geographers and historians after him.

The description of Greek writer Iambulos (end of 3rd C. or beginning of 2nd C.B.C.) speaks highly about the friendly attitude of some Magadhan king towards the Greeks. Diodoros mentions that once when Iambulos was ship wrecked, he was brought by the natives into the presence of the king at Polibothra (Pataliputra), a city which was distant a journey of many days from the sea. And since the king was friendly to the Greeks and devoted to learning, he considered Iamboulos worth of cordial welcome; and at length, upon receiving a permission of safe conduct he passed over first of all into Persia and latter arrived safe in Greece[42].

In Indian literature, the text like *Yuga Purana*, Patanjali's *Mahabhasya*[43] and Kalidasa's *Malavikagnimitra* (Act V) corraborate the advancement of Greek conquests. Finally through coins we come across the name of more than 40 kings of the Indo-Greek kingdom of Bactria and North-West India. The Greek expedition from Bactria had led to the establishment of Greek rule in North-West India and Punjab. Towards east they had also probably reached as far as Pataliputra and in the south had conquered Saurashtra and Gujarat.

The amalgamation of Indian and Greek cultural elements was best reflected during the rule of Indo-Greek kings. Contrary to Hellenistic countries elsewhere where the Greek rulers had maintained their Hellenistic identity, encourage large scale immigration of Greeks and Greek way of life was popularized including the language which had become the lingua-franca; the Greek kings in India become to assimilated to their milieu. Whereas, in Egypt and West Asia the Greek kings had followed a policy of Greek acculturation, in India rather they themselves were accultured as has been rightly pointed out by Narain that in South Asia, "they came, they saw, but India conquered[44]. Here they adopted Indian religion and customs and used the language of the local people. The best known personal example of this cultural fusion is certainly Menandros, identified with king Milinda of the Buddhist text Milindapanho (Questions of Milinda), who was a devout adherent of the Buddhist faith. Menandros appears in folk tales as the hero of certain stories which originally were told about Buddha or the emperor

Ashoka. The great conqueror Alexander has not even the faintest allusion in any Indian text. India has always honoured a poet or a philosopher, never a conqueror. Alexander was a conquerer only, while Menandros was a philosopher King.

The two Indo-Greeks kings Agathocles (171-160 B.C.) and Pantaleon (171-160 B.C.) issued bilingual coins with inscriptions in Kharosthi and Brahmi as well as in both Greek and Prakrit. We have the example of Heliodoros, who according to Basenagar pillar incription came as the ambassador of the Indo-Greek king Antialcidas of Taxila, to the court of Vidisa King Bhagabhadra, was converted to the cult of Krishna-Vasudeva and commemorated his visit by erecting a Gruda-column to the sacred-shrine of Vishnu in Vidisa[45].

Several references to Greek as *Yavanas* in Indian epic and Puranic literature bear testimony to the fact that the*Puranas* as well as the composition of some parts of the *Mahabharata* and the *Ramayana* took place after the settlement of Bactrian Greeks on India soil. The *Puranas* refer to some eight Yavana kings[46].

According to Philostratos (A.D. 170-246), an Indian village where all the inhabitants spoke Greek was visited by Apollonios of Tyana. An Indian king Phraotes (Gondophernes?) conversed with Apollonios in Greek and informed him that he had read Euripides' Herakledai[47].

In epic and Puranic text of India there are several striking parallels of Greek myths and legends. Correlations occur, for instance between the legends of Santanu Ganga and Peleus-Thetis; Urvasi and Pururavas and Eros-Psyche, Ruru-Pramadvara and Alcestis-Admetus, Kamsa-Krishna and Kronas-Zeus, Sikhandin's and Iphis' changes of sex; the mantic sharp sight of Nala's companion Rituparna and Calcha's contestant Mopsus. Archery feat in Svoyamvara of Draupadi and in Penelope's marriage; *Maya* Sita and *Eidolon* Helen. Death of Krsna and Duryodhana, and Achilles' death and so on[48]. In most of these cases the formats of the tales are essentially the same. These resemblances are so remarkable that the theory of Greek influence on these legends appear to be highly probable after the settlement of Bactrian Greeks on India soil.

The archaeological evidences too corroborate the view that the Greek legends had become a part of cultural expression in certain regions of India by the early centuries of Christian era. The coins of Indianised Greeks and the Kushanas depict Greek deities. The Trojan horse motif emerges in a stone relief discovered in the vicinity of Peshawar. All these evidences lead us in acknowledging the fact without any hesitation that some Greek themes certainly found their way into Sanskrit literature.

The use of the word *Yavanika* for curtain in Sanskrit dramas and similarities between dramatic concepts of Bharata and Aristoteles had led long ago the German scholars like Weber and Windish to believe in the Greek origin of Indian dramas. Various classical references draw our attention towards the actual performance of Greek dramas on Indian soil. In Sanskrit dramas we come across *Yavana* girls appearing on stage as a part of king's entourage. The word *Yavanika* is in no way connected with the *Yavanas*. It is in fact the corrupt form of the word *Javanika* which has been twice used by Bharata in the sense of stage curtain and not *Yavanika*, the Greek dramas had no stage curtain.

It is note worthy that due to historical contacts in ancient times we have evidence of some Greek loan words in Sanskrit and some Sanskrit loan words in Greek[49].

The Indians greatly admired the Greek expertise and scholarship in the scientific treatises. The Mahabharata refers to them as Sarvjna yavanas (Greeks possessing knowledge in all spheres)[50]. *The Brhat Samhita* mentions that although the Greeks are Mlechnos (barbarians), they deserve to be worshipped like the rishis (sages) on account of their perfect knowledge in astronomy[51]. The introduction of solar Zodiac signs or the twelve rashis, and seven grahas (planets) as well as the concept of the planets corresponding to the seven week days are considered to be the Greek contribution to Hindu astrology. The Romaka and Paulisa school of ancient Indian astronomy have been recognized by the scholars as of

Hellenistic origin.

The well-known ancient city of Taksasila was the main city of Peshawar Valley known as Gandhara. The excavation conducted at Taksasila reveal that the town Sirkap was built here according to a typically Greek layout. Here was developed mainly under the Kushanas the Gandhara school of sculpture in which the Buddhist images were represented in Greek style. Situated at the confluence of East and West the region was although exposed to Persian, Greek, Shaka and Kushana art activities, it was the Hellenistic art, the elements of which predominate in Gandhara images. The discovery of fully developed Hellenistic town at Ai-Khanoum in North-East Afghanistan further supports the Hellenistic origin of Gandhara images.

Ai-Khanoum is a complete Greek town with an acropolis, temple, mousoleum, gymnasium, stadium, theatre, together with several sculpture pieces in stone, stucco, clay and bronze—all clearly Hellenistic in concept style and technique. Their presence offers almost certain proof that the language, culture and educational system of the city were Greek, and that its citizens made strong efforts to preserve intact the integrity of their Greek civilization in its overwhelming oriental surroundings[52].

In the history of Indian coins, the coinage system introduced by the Indo-Greeks mark a significant change. They are the earliest dynastic issues and thus they represent a major departure from the earlier Punch-marked and uninscribed cast coins issued mainly by corporate bodies of traders. The fusion of two cultural streams, Greece and India, is reflected clearly in the legends, symbols and fabric of these coins. In fact they provide a proto-typal model for all the subsequent dynastic issues of India. The Indianisation of the Greeks, their art forms and conceptions, was so complete that Indo-Greek coinage belongs more to Indian numismatic history than to either Greek or West Asian.

What is generally called as the Indo-Roman contacts was

infact the interaction with the Hellenized Egypt under the Romans. It was an era of new discoveries enterprises and frequent voyages, for the world under the firm rule of Rome was ripe and ready for the fresh developments in the intercourse of civilization. The discovery of the full use of monsoon by the Greek sailor Hippalos had accelerated trade and commerce with India. The voyage to India had become shorter, as the Greek ships instead of following the coast were pushed by the monsoon directly to the Eastern shores of the Indian subcontinent and later to Ceylon and the gulf of Bengal. The Greek text Periplous of the Erythraean Sea by some unknown sailor described several parts of India and Ceylon. As a matter of fact trade to and from India increased so much during the Roman period that according to an account of Strabo Alexandrian merchants sent about 120 ships annually to India. Loukianos said that in two Olympiads a man could sail from the pillars of Herakles to India and back again three times with leisure to explore tribes by the way[53].

The Periplous of the Erythrean sea had found the Indians settled along with the Arabs and Greeks in an island situated on the coast of Africa. Dion-Chrysostomas' speech refers to the Indian inhabitants of Alexandria in Egypt. The Indian emphasis were frequently sent to Roman emperors. We have references to at least eight Indian missions sent to the courts of the Roman emperors Augustus (63 B.C. - 14 A.D.). Trajan (98-114 A.D.), Hadrian (117-38 AD), Antoninus Pius (138 - 61 A.D.), Elagabalus (218 - 22 A.D.), Aurelian (270-75 A.D.), Constantinos (306-37 AD) and Julian (361-63 A.D.)[54].

The numerous references to *Yavanas* in the early Tamil and the Sanskrit literature, cave inscriptions of Western India, and the discovery of a large number of Roman gold coins from South India bear testimony to the fact of the increased interaction between India and the Graeco Roman World. The various Roman artefacts like the potteries, clay-bullae, seals and discs, sculptural representations, terracotta figurines, metallic objects, beads, etc. occur in Pondichery, Tamilnadu,

Maharashtra, Andhra Pradesh, Karnataka, Gujrat, Rajasthan, Madhya Pradesh and the coastal belt of Orissa and West Bengal. The amphitheatre excavated at Nagarjunakonda in Andhra Pradesh was built at this time under the influence of the Greaco-Romans.[55] From Buddhist dedicatory inscriptions of Deccan at Nasik, Junar and Karla we get the names of atleast nine donors who all themselves Yavana (or Yonaka). They had become followers of Buddhism and had Indian names[56].

While the Greaco-Roman world had a fancy for Indian spices, precious stones and the various luxury items, the Indians had developed a liking for the Roman wine, pottery, glass wares metal utensils, statuettes etc. It is to be noted that though while innumerable items belonging to Graeco Roman world have been discovered from the Indian soil, we have very few Indian things on the western side. We know only about an ivory statuette of a Yaksini found at Pompoli and a bronze statuette of an Indian girl found in Oman in South Arabia.

Besides traders, the increased facilities of the voyages had also motivated many early Christian fathers to visit India for the propagation of Christianity. On the basis of the accounts of the early missionaries the begining of Christianity in Malabar may be safely taken back to the first two centuries A.D. (A.D. 260-340). From the existence of an early Christian Church in Malabar coast and Srilanka, which was governed from Persia, it may be assumed that some Bartholomew was probably responsible for founding the Malabar Church in 2nd C.A.D.

The Church Fathers belonging to the period of Roman domination furnish very reliable informations on India, particularly connected with religion and philosophical thought. The doctrines of the Brahmanas were expounded more authentically not in the text of classical literary tradition but in the writings of the Christian authors like Bardessanes of Edessa, and Clemens of Alexandria. Bardessanes speaks about the image worship of Siva Ardhanarisvara housed in a rock cut temple, which could be somewhere in the region of Maharastra, where the Yavana traders were settled and had made dedications to such temples.

That philosophers of India possess some special wisdom was developing as a wide-spread views in the Graeco-Roman world. Pythagoras, Demokritos of Abdera, Platon, Appolonios of Tyana, Lykurgos and Demitrios of Sounion were reported to have learnt wisdom from Indian Brahmins[57]. Even the Egyptians, Persians and Jews were mentioned to have derived their knowledge of philosophy from the Indians. Loukianos asserted that the philosophy had first visited India, from there it marched to Ethiopia, afterwards to Egypt and then to other nations.

Those engaged in philosophy in India, i.e. the Brahmins, were greatly admired by the Graeco-Roman authors. Apollonios' observation of the Brahmana philosophers as quoted by philostratos is as follows :

> "It is then not unreasonable on any part I think to have devoted myself to a philosophy so highly elaborated and that I am right in considering them to be wise and blessed. I beheld men dwelling upon the earth, and yet not upon it. I beheld them possessed of nothing and yet possessed of all things." (Leob)[58].

The contacts between India and the Greek world continued to remain throughout their ancient history. It is, therefore, possible, both to identify the nature of the links and to see their dynamics from epoch to epoch. The results of the cross fertilization between the two cultures in the domain of religion and mythology, art and architecture, fable and folklore, science and philosophy, coins and metallargy language and literature have attracted the attention of scholars, but they require a deeper investigation.

REFERENCES

1. Rawlinson, H.G., *Intercourse Between India and the western World*, pp. 1-15.
2. Gopal Lallanji, "Samkhya and Greek Philosophy" in *Graeco- Indica - India's*

Cultural Contacts with the Greek World. p. 244.

3. Rawlinson, H.G., *op. cit.,* p. 158.
4. Zannas, E. Lascarides, "The Hellenization of the East, "*Proceedings of the Fifth World Sanskrit Conference,* p. 942.
5. The presence of Indians in Alexandria is testified to by Ptolemy, Dion Cassius and St. Chrysostom. Rawlinson, H.G., *op. cit.,* p. 137.
6. Ojha, K.C., *The History of Foreign Rule in Ancient India*, Allahabad, 1968, pp. 14-17.
7. Sedlar, J. W., *India and the Greek World, op. cit.,* p.10.
8. *Herodotus*, VII. 65-66 (Loeb) III, 379-81; Sedlar, *op. cit.,* p.10.
9. Arora, U.P., "Ancient India and Ancient Greece" in *Life Thought and Culture in India* (600 B.C. to A.D. 300) Ed. G.C. Pande in *History of Science Philosophy and Culture in Indian Civilization*, Vol. 1, Part 2, New Delhi, 2001, p. 1045.
10. Panini, 4, 1, 49.
11. Aristoxenos in C., Mueller, *Fragmenta Historicorum Graecorum* (in 5 Vols.), Vol. II, Paris, 1841, Fragment 31, P. 81; Fernando Tola and Carmen Dragonetti, India and Greece before Alexander, *ABORI*, Poona, 1986, Vol. 67 (1-4) pp 159-194.
12. Chattopadhyaya, D.P., "Uddalaka Aruni : The Pioneer of Science" *Indian Historical Review,* Indian Council of Historical Research, Vol. XIII, No. 1-2 (July 1986-Jan 1987), New Delhi, pp. 37-57.
13. Philostratos, Travells of Apollonios of Tyana (Loeb), VII, 7; Sedlar, J. W., *India and the Greek World*, Totowa, 1980, p. 31-32.
14. Colebrooke, H. L., *Miscellanious Essays*, Vol.1, London 1873, 1. 436ff; Richard Garbe, *Philosophy of Ancient India,* Chicago, 1897, 39 ff; Rawlinson, H.G., "India in European Literature and Thought", in G.T. Garratt (Ed.), *The Legacy of India,* Oxford, 1937, P.5; Radhakrishnan, S., *Eastern Religion and Western Thought,* Oxford, 1939, pp. 142-43.
15. Sedlar, J. W., *op. cit.,* p. 101.
16. Arora, U.P., "The Folklore in Ancient Indian and Greek Literature", in *Essays on Indology, Polity and Administration- in Honour of Padmabusan Shri R.K. Trivedi*, S.D. Trivedi (Ed.) Delhi, 1989, pp. 341-349.
17. Arora, U.P., *Greeks on India*, Indian Society for Greeks and Roman Studies Publication, Bareilly, 1996, p. 107.
18. Sedlar, J. W., *op. cit.,* p. 68.
19. *Ibid*, p. 69; T.S. Brown, *Onesicritus*, Berkeley 1949, p. 25.
20. Strabo, *Geography*, XV 64-65 (Loeb) VII, III-13.
21. Sedlar, *op. cit.,* p. 69.
22. Velissaropoulos, Dimitraos, C., "The Ancient Greek Knowledge of Indian Philosophy" in *Graeco-Indica, op. cit,* Arora, U.P., (Ed.) p. 262.
23. Arora, U. P., "Ancient India and Ancient Greece" in *Life Thought & Culture*

in India (from 600 BC to AD 300), *op. cit.*, p.1048.
24. Sedlar, *op. cit.*, p. 72.
25. *Ibid,* p. 72.
26. *Ibid,* p. 73
27. Arora, U.P., "Ancient India and Ancient Greece" *op. cit.*, p. 1050.
28. Sedlar, J.W., *op. cit.*, p. 75.
29. Tarn, W. W., *Alexander, the Great,* Vol II, Cambridge, 1950, p. 237.
30. Arrian, *Anabasis*, VI, 15, 2, (Loeb).
31. Velissaropoulos, Dimitraos C., "The Ancient Greek Knowledge of Indian Philosophy" in *Graeco-Indica, op. cit.*, p. 267.
32. Arora, U.P., "The Reliability of Megasthenes' Indika", in *Contact Between Cultures,* Vol. 2, South Asia, Selected papers from 33rd International Congress of Asian and North African Studies, Toronto, Edited by K.I. Koppedrayer, New York and Queenston, 1992, pp. 1-5.
33. Arora, U.P., "Form of State Power in Mauryan India—Megasthenes 'Evidence' in *Facets of Indian History, Culture and Archaeology*, S.P. Gupta and K.S. Ramchandran (ed.), New Delhi, 1991, pp. 164-172.
34. Bevan, E., *House of Seloucus*, Vol. 1, London, 1966, pp. 297-298; Smith, V., *Early History of India,* Oxford, 1924, pp. 129-130.
35. Arora, U.P., " Ancient India and Ancient Greece" *op. cit.*, p. 1053.
36. Sedlar, J.W., *op-cit.*, p. 62.
37. Thomas Watters, *On yuan Chwang's Travels in India,* London, 1904-05, i. p.108.
38. Thirteenth Rock Edict, Quoted in Radhakrishnan, *op, cit.*, p.156.
39. Smith, V.A., *op.cit.*, p. 237, n.I; H.C. Roychuadhari, *Political History of Ancient India,* Calcutta, 1950, p. 3504.
40. Radhakrishnan, S., *op. cit.*, p.157.
41. *Ibid.* p.157
42. Arora, U.P., "Ancient India and Ancient Greece" *op. cit.*, p.1055.
43. *Mahabhasya,* Ed.F. Kielhorn (in 3 Vols.) Bombay, 1892-1909, Vol. II, pp 118-19.
44. Arora, U.P., " Ancient India and Ancient Greece" *op. cit.*, p. 1056.
45. Marshall, *Journal of the Royal Asiatic Society*, 1909. pp 1053 ff; Chanda, *Memoirs of Arch. Survey of India*, No. 18.
46. Arora, U.P., *Motifs in Indian Mythology*; *Their Greeks and Other Parallels*, Delhi, 1981, 177ff.
47. Philostratos, *Apoll Tya*. III, 12, (Loeb).
48. Arora, U.P. *Motifs in Indian Mythology*, *op. cit.*, p. 130-132, 97-98, 90-92,124-125.
49. Chandra, Lokesh, "*The Sublime and the Infinite in India and Greece-connection and Parallels*," S. Doshi (ed.) Marg. Pub., Bombay, 1985, pp.13-14; U.P. Arora, "Ancient India and Ancient Greece", *op. cit.*, p.1059.

50. *Mahabharata*, III, 445, 36. (Crit. edn.)
51. *Brhat Samhita,* II, 15, (Kern's ed.)
52. Bernard, Paul, "Ai Khanum on the Oxus: a Hellenistic City in Central Asia", *Proceedings of the British Academy*, 53, 1967, pp 71-95; Wheeler, Mortimer, *Flames over Persepolis,* New York, 1968, pp. 78-87.
53. Arora, U.P., " Ancient India and ancient Greece" *op. cit.,* p. 1061.
54. *Ibid.*, 1061.
55. Gupta, Sunil, "List of Explored and Excavated Early Historic Sites in India Yielding Material Evidence of Indo-Roman Trade", *Yavanika*, Journal of the Indian Society for Greek and Roman studies, No. 3, 1993, pp. 75-91.
56. Shastri, Ajay Mitra ,"Yavanas in Western Indian Cave Inscription", *Yavanika,* No. 3., 1993, pp. 58-66.
57. Gregorios, Paul, "The Monastic Tradition," S.D. Doshi (ed.)*op. cit.,* Marg Pub., pp. 33-34.
58. Philast. *op. cit.*, VI.11.

PYTHAGOREANISM AND INDIAN ASCETICISM

Pythagoras, a late sixth century BCE contemporary of Xenophanes, was like him, an Ionian (from Samos), who latter settled in southern Italy. There at Croton, he established a community bound not only by a shared philosophy based on reason, but also by religious beliefs. From the earliest formation of this community any advances that were made in Pythagorean doctrine were attributed to Pythagoras himself, so it is very hard to discern earliest form of Pythagoreanism amid reports about its later accretions.

The two defining factors of Pythagoreanism are its mysticism and its concern with mathematics. Many of the beliefs which governed the ethical and moral behaviour of Pythagoreans, such as their belief in the transmigration of souls after death (they thought souls could pass into other bodies, including the bodies of animals, which led to the exclusion of meat from there diet), were based on mysticism rather than reason and are not easy to reconcile into a unified whole with their philosophical theories[1].

The religion of Pythagoras was based on the Orphic teaching with its austere asceticism, its voluntary poverty and community of goods, its belief in rebirth and respect for animal life[2]. Pythagoras looked upon Orpheus as the chief of his patrons[3]. With regard to Pythagoras, indeed, we are certain of only two things of his cardinal tenents, viz. the immortality of the soul, and the transmigration of souls. It can be said that, the founder of the school, Pythagoras was himself an ascetic because we have find unmistakable traces of the ascetic mode of life among the oldest Pythagoreans. Even Herodotus speaks of the prohibition of burying the dead in woollen clothes as being not only on Orphic, but also a Pythagorean, ordinance[4].

The interdict against the use of beans seems likewise to belong to the early school. It cannot be doubted that the early Pythagoreans were distinguished by their *simple life*. A peculiar feature in their asceticism, from the 4th cent B.C. at least, seems to have been silence[5], originally resorted to, no doubt, as a means of avoiding sacreligious or ill-omened language in their religious practices. It should also be noted that anticipations of sexual asceticism, or continence, are apparently found in connexion with the primitive school.

Meagre as these notices are, they are sufficient to show us that purity in the ceremonial religious sense was the ideal of the 'Italic' philosophers no less than of the Orphic cults. Moreover, when we compare with them the teaching of Pythagoras regarding the immortality and the transmigration of the soul, and that of Philolaus regarding the human body as a house of detention wherein the soul expiates its guilt, it would appear that early Pythagorean asceticism sprang from the same fundamental causes, and had the same objects in view, as that of Orphism, the influence of which upon the former is unmistakable.

So we may say that Pythagoras enjoined an ascetic way of living[6]. Abstention from meat was a principal requirement. In some instances Pythagoreans lived like monks in communities with common property[7]. The most famous of these Neo-Pythagoreans, however, was the wandering religious reformer Apollonios of Tyana (first Cen. A.D.). According to Philostratos, his biographer, Apollonios led a strictly ascetic life, giving away most of his property, refusing to marry, observing a vow of silence for five years, avoiding meat, wine and sex, and subsisting by begging[8]. Allegedly this was the same rule of life Pythagoras himself had established for his semi-monastic brotherhood in the 6th century B.C. Clearly the Hellenistic age viewed Pythagoras as a religious thinker. Thus the Neo-Platonist Iamblichos once remarked that all of Pythagoras regulations were aimed at promoting a relationship with God[9].

We may put Pythagoras' birth round about 570 B.C. or a few years earlier. The length of his life was variously estimated in antiquity, and most probably he died at about seventy-five or eighty[10]. His father Mnesarchus of Samos is described as gem-engraver, and it would be in accordance with regular Greek custom for Pythagoras to be trained in his fathers craft.

But to escape life under the tyranny of Polycrates, Pythagoras left Samos and migrated to Croton, the leading Achaean colony in South Italy. Croton was still suffering the demoralizing effects of her defeat by the Locrians at the river Sagra, and historians of the Greek West observe a marked improvement after arrival of Pythagoras[11]. He appears to have attained without delay a position of authority and influence in the city and founded his school there. From now on the name of Pythagoras is linked indissolubly, not with the Ionian or Eastern, but with the Italian or Western schools of thought of which he is the fountain-head[12]. What we may say, from our knowledge of the Pythagorean philosophy, is that his motive in acquiring power (like that of his near contemporary Confucious) was not personal ambition but a zeal for reforming society according to his own moral ideas. There is no reason to doubt the general statement which we find in Diogenes (VIII, 3) that he gave the Italians a constitution and with his followers governed the state so well that it deserved the name of aristocracy ('government of the best') in its literal sense. One may suspect that the aristocracy of which Pythagoras was a leader was not simply of the old land-owning type, but had strong connexions with trade[13].

The ascendancy of Pythagoras and his followers was uninterrupted for some twenty years, during which Croton extended her influence over the neighbouring cities and in many of them the leading positions were occupied by members of the Pythagorean brotherhood. At the end of this period a Crotonian named Cylon stirred the people to revolt[14]. In the Cylonian conspiracy a number of leading Pythagoreans were rounded up and killed, and it seems to have been the signal for outbursts of anti-Pythagorean activity in other cities also, which made it difficult for Pythagoras, banished from Croton, to find a resting place. According to the most credible accounts, he finally reached Metapontum, where he died. About his death there are naturally a number of more or less romantic stories, but the most probable seems to be that of Dicaearchus, that he was forced to take refuge in a temple of the Muses, where he starved to death.

The rebellion of Cylon, which must have taken place about the turn of the sixth and fifth centuries, seems to have caused only a very temporary check to Pythagorean activities, and their influence was even extended over the next forty or fifty years. But it was a troublous period of growing unrest, which led to a second major anti-Pythagorean outbreak in the middle of the fifth century. In this the house at Croton that had belonged to Milo was said to have been burned down, and according to Polybius[15] the revolutionary movement spread through the whole of Magna Graecia. The meeting - houses of Pythagoreans were destroyed, the leading men of each city perished, and the whole region was in turmoil. This catastrophe, which is dated by Minar to 454 B.C.[16] brought about the first emigration of Pythagoreans to the mainland of Greece and led to the establishment of Pythagorean centres at Phlius and Thebes. Even now, the Pythagoreans who stayed behind seem to have regained a certain amount of political influence in Italy, and to have continued their life as a society, chiefly at Rhegium. Later still, however, when in the words of Aristoxenus 'political conditions got worse', all are said to have left Italy except Archytas of Tarentum[17].

After this we may say that the life of Pythagorean societies was by no means peaceful or uninterrupted , and that from the second half of the fifth century they existed in small separate bands scattered widely over South Italy and Greece. The effect of this on the continuity of their Philosophical tradition was naturally serious. According to the description of Porphyry and

Iamblichus, the prominent Pythagoreans who lost their lives in the troubles carried their knowledge with them to the grave, for it had been kept secret, only those parts being divulged which would have conveyed little meaning to outsiders. Pythagoras had left no writings of his own, and only a few dim sparks of philosophy were kept alight by men like Lysis and Archippus of Tarentum who escaped, and who were abroad at the time of the troubles. These exiles were so cast down by events that they lived in isolation, shunning the company of their fellow-men. They collected in note form whatever had been written down by an older generation, supplemented by their own memories. Each one left these commentaries, when and where he happened to die, in thrust to son, daughter or wife, with instructions that they be kept within the household. The trust was faithfully kept, and the notebooks handed down for several generations, but our sources agree that as an active sect the Pythagorean society practically died out during the fourth century B.C. They preserved their original ways, and their science, although the sect was dwindling, until, not ignobly, they died out. Thus was their epitaph written by Aristoxenus[18], speaking of those who were his contemporaries and acquaintances.

It emerges from this troubled history, first that the Pythagorean school continued to exist through the classical period of Greek thought in the sixth to the fourth centuries B.C. and secondly, that from the middle of the fifth century it existed in the form of separate, scattered communities in various parts of the Greek world. It is only natural that these communities should develop on different lines, and that we should hear, as we do from Aristotle, that 'some Pythagoreans' held certain doctrines and some held others, although all acknowledged allegiance to the same founder.

Pythagoras has been regarded by some scholars as no more than the founder of a religious sect, others have emphasized almost exclusively the rational and scientific side of his thought. Both these portrayals are too one-sided and extreme to be plausible. In fact in the sixth century B.C. such a combination was not only possible but natural. The religious doctrines of immortality and transmigration are assigned to Pythagoras on incontrovertible positive evidence. His character as one of the most original thinkers in history, a founder of Mathematical science and philosophical cosmology, although not directly attested by such early and impregnable sources must be assumed as the only reasonable explanation of the unique impression made by his name on subsequent thought. It was both as religious teacher and as scientific genius that he was from his own life-time and for many centuries afterwards venerated by his followers, violently attacked by others, but ignored by none. Now, we may say safely is that for Pythagoras religious and moral motives were dominant, so that his philosophical inquiries were destined from the start to support a particular conception of the best life and fulfil certain spiritual aspirations.

Philosophy for Pythagoras and his followers had to be first and foremost and basis for a way of life, more than that, for a way of eternal salvation. When the study of man and the cosmos is undertaken as a means of help and guidance in right living, the resulting system of nature must be one that will afford such help. To the Pythagoreans the most important part of philosophy was that which taught of man, of the nature of the human soul and its relations with other forms of life and with the whole.

We may assert about Pythagoras that from at least the middle of the fifth century the Pythagoreans were known to practise certain superstitious taboos (on burial in wool[19] Herodotus; compare Heraclides on eating flesh and beans: here at any rate there is not contamination from Academic doctrine, and the prohibitions are of course much older). Silence and secrecy were prominent features of their behaviour. They formed a society of their own, practising what was to their contemporaries a distinctive and extraordinary way of life. Philolaus, a leading fifth century Pythagorean, preached the wickedness of suicide, basing it on a secret *logos* of which the purport was that men are not their own masters but belong to the Gods[20].

As to the more scientific side of their teaching we have learned from Plato that they were the acknowledged experts in astronomy, harmonics and the science of number. They regarded all these studies as closely allied, because in their view the key to the understanding both of the movements of the stars and of the notes in the musical scale lay in the establishment of a numerical relation. We may allow ourselves to note that the actual union of astronomy and harmonics in the remarkable theory of the 'harmony of the spheres', adopted by Plato, is described and attested as Pythagorean in the same century by Aristotle[21]. This is the view that physical objects moving as rapidly as the heavenly bodies must necessarily produce a sound; that the intervals between the several planets and the sphere of the fixed starts correspond mathematically to the intervals between the notes of the octave, and that therefore, the sound which they produce has a definite musical character.

Pythagoreanism contains a strong element of the magical, a primitive feature which sometimes seems hard to reconcile with the intellectual depth which is no less certainly attested. Their retention of primitive material is well illustrated in their collection of sayings called *Acusmata* or *Symbola*. Some are straightforward moral precepts, but others had to be latter explained as having a hidden, oracular meaning in accord with Pythagorean moral or political ideals. In fact the majority are easily recognizable as primitive taboos. The list of them, which we have in Diogenes, Porphyry, Iamblichus, Hippolytus may be said with confidence to go back to a collection made by Aristotle in the work which he wrote on the Pythagoreans, and which is explicitly quoted as the authority for some. Out of many attributed to Pythagoras, the magical origin of which is obvious, the following will serve as examples :

To abstain from beans.

Not to pick up what has fallen from the table.

Not to stir the fire with knife.

To rub out the mark of a pat in the ashes.

Not to sit on a bushel-measure.

Not to wear a narrow ring.

Not to have swallows in the house.

To spit on one's nail-parings and hair-trimmings.

Not to make water or stand on one's nail-parings or hair-trimmings.

To roll up one's bedclothes on rising and smooth cut the imprint of the body.

To touch the earth when it thunders[22].

The moral interpretations attached to these picturesque sayings in our sources show plainly enough that they had nothing to do with them in the beginning. To stir the fire with a knife was taken to mean rousing a man's passions with sharp words, to sit on the bushel was to be content with what one has or to rest on one's laurels, to roll up the bedding meant to be always ready fo travel, that is, ready to leave this life for the next, swallows stood for chatterers, and so forth[23].

The Pythagorean order was a religious fraternity. Admission to the fraternity was gained by initiation, i.e. by purification followed by the revelation of truth. Purification consisted not only in the observance of rules of abstinence from certain kinds of food and dress but also in the purification of the soul by theoria, or the contemplation of the divine reality. Plato in the *Phaedo* states as the Pythagorean doctrine the view that men are strangers to the world and the body is the tomb of the soul, and yet we must not escape from it by suicide. For Pythagoras, pure contemplation is the end of man, the completion of human nature. To the question what are we born for he replied, 'To gaze upon the heavens'[24]. When by the contemplative process the soul is perfected, that is, purified from the taint of its subjection to the body, there would be no need of further rebirths. Pythagoras is believed to have reached this threshold of divinity[25]. Aristoxenus says of Pythagoras and his followers: 'Every distinction they lay down as to what should be done or not done aims at communion with the divine. This is their starting point; their whole life is ordered with a view to following God and it is the governing principle of their philosophy[26].

Professor Burnet says : 'if we can trust Herakleides, it was Pythagoras who first distinguished the "three lives", the Theoretic, the Practical, and the Apolaustic, which Aristotle made use of in the Ethics[27]. According to Burnet,[28] "the doctrine is to this effect we are strangers in this world and the body is the tomb of the soul, and yet we must not seek to escape by self-murder; for we are the chatteles of God who is our herdsman, and without his command we have no right to just as there are three sorts of people who come to the olympic games. The lowest class is made up of those who come to buy and sell and next above them are those who come to compete. Best of all, however, are those who come to look on. The greatest purification of all is science and it is the man who devotes himself to that, the true philosopher, who has most effectually released himself from the "wheel of birth".

Pythagoras held, as the early Upanishad thinkers did, that all souls are similar in class and the apparent distinctions between human and other kinds of beings are not ultimate. Iamblichus informs us that Pythagoras held that the islands of the blest were the sun and the moon. In the Upanisads the moon is mentioned as the dwelling-place of spirits[29].

The earliest reference to Pythagoras is in a few verses quoted by Xenophanes in which we are told that Pythagoras once heard a dog howling and appealed to its master not to beat it, as he recognized the voice of a departed friend[30]. Another anecdote which has become famous through Ennius and Horace tells us that Pythagoras was gifted with the power of remembering his former births, and he claimed to have been Euphorbus among others. Pythagoras believed not only in rebirth but in purification of the soul. The cycle of births is regarded as a means for the growth of man's higher nature. The theoretic is for him the highest form of life. He was also known as an important scientific man. According to Aristotle, Pythagoras first buried himself with mathematics and numbers.

The only mention of Pythagoras in Plato is in the*Republic* where he tells us that Pythagoras won the affection of his followers by teaching them a way of life which was still called Pythagorean[31].

A peculiar feature in the asceticism of the Pythagoreans from the fourth century at least seems to have been silence. Porphyry writes of Pythagoras as follows : 'What he said to his disciples no man can tell for certain, since they preserved such as exceptional silence'. However, the following facts in particular became universally known : first that he held the soul to be immortal, next that it migrates into other kinds of animal, further that past events repeat themselves in a cycle process and nothing is new in an absolute sense, and finally that one must regard all living things as kindered. These are the beliefs which Pythagoras is said to have been the first to introduce into Greece[32].

According to Porphyry, 'his teaching took two forms, and of his followers some were called *mathematici* and some *acusmatici*. The *mathematici* were those who had mastered the deepest and most fully worked-out parts of his wisdom, and the *acusmatici* those who had only hear summarized, precepts from the writings, without full explanation[33]. Nevertheless, the thesis that there were two kinds of Pythagoreans[34], the one chiefly interested in the pursuit of mathematical philosophy and the other in preserving the religious foundations of the school, is both inherently probable and supported by a certain amount of positive evidence, among which we may certainly reckon the contradictory reports that have just been quoted concerning the views of Pythagoras on religious abstention from certain foods[35].

Being a mathematician, Pythagoras expressed his cosmogony in mathematical terms. The primal Monad takes the place of the world egg. The world is a mixture of light and darkness, the formless and the form. The mathematical and mystical sides were side by side in Pythagoras and, according to tradition, a split[36] occurred within the school between the

Mathematikoi or the rationalists, whose interest was in the theory of numbers, and the *Akusmatikoi*, who followed up the religious side of the movement. We have in Pythagoras a rare combination of high intellectual power and profound spiritual insight[37].

The great musician of legend impressed Pythagoras, who was led by his experiments in music to the understanding of numerical ratios and hence to the foundation of mathematical science. For Pythagoras the universe is not only an order or observance of due proportions but a '*harmonia*' or being in tune. The human soul must also strive to imitate the orderliness of the universe[38].

The doctrine that all life was *homogenes* not only united men in the ties of kinship with animals, but, most important of all, it taught them that their best nature was identical with something higher. It gave them an aim in life, namely to cultivate the soul, shake off the taint of the body, and rejoin the universal soul of which their individual souls were in essence parts. So long as the soul was condemned to remain in the wheel of transmigration—so long, that is to say, as it had to enter a new body of man or animal after the death of the one which it had previously tenanted—so long was it still impure. By living the best and highest type of human life it might ultimately shake of the body altogether, escape from the wheel of rebirth[39], and attain the final bliss of losing itself in the universal, eternal and divine soul to which by its own nature it belonged[40].

We have seen above that Pythagoras himself taught tansmigration, and may also be safely credited with the complex of ideas with which transmigration is bound up: the doctrine that the human soul is immortal, that is owes its immortality to its essential kinship with the divine, universal soul, and that it may hope to return to its divine source when purified. The first form of the Pythagorean view mentioned by Aristotle sounds the more primitive and the second a refinement on it in a spiritual direction, though 'what moved them' was no doubt still thought of in what we should call material terms as the air (which indeed it is), identified with *pneuma* or the breath soul[41].

Two different notions of soul, then, existed in contemporary belief, the *psyche* which 'vanished like smoke' at death, and which medical writers rationalized into a *harmonia* of the physical opposites that made up the body; and the more mysterious *daimon* in man, immortal, suffering transmigration through many bodies, but in its pure essence divine. This too could be called *psyche*, as it was by Plato. Both survived side by side in the general current of religious thought, and both also survived in the curious combination of mathematical philosophy and religious mysticism which made up Pythagoreanism.[42]

About the relation of the soul with God Pythagoras statement is as follows : "Let your desire and exertion in this world be directed towards the union with *the first cause*, which is the cause of your existence, that you may endure for ever. You will be saved from destruction and from being wiped out; you will go to the world of the true sense, of the true joy, of the true glory, in everlasting joy and pleasures". Further, Pythagoras says: "How can you hope for the state of detachment as long as you are clad in bodies? And how will you obtain liberation as long as you are incarcerated in them?"[43]

Limit (*peras*) and the unlimited (*apeiron*) were set by the Pythagoreans at the very beginning of things as the two contrasting principles by which the world evolved; and of them they saw *peras* as good and *apeiron* as evil. To quote a simple statement of this, Aristotle says in the *Ethics* : 'Evil belongs to the unlimited, as the Pythagoreans surmised, and good to the *limited*'[44]. Now the world is living and divine, and so good. It can only be any or all of these because it is limited, and displays an *order* in the relations of its component parts. Full and efficient life depends on organization. We see this in individual creatures, which we call organic to indicate that they have all their parts arranged and subordinated as instruments (*organa*) towards the end of keeping the whole being alive and enabling it to perform its funtions. So with the world there may be minor irregularities, but the major cosmic events are marked by their regular order.

Dawn and sunset, summer, winter and the intermediate seasons follow one another in unvarying succession. For the Greeks the perfect example of this eternal regularity was provided by the wheeling stars, which exhibited an everlasting and perfectly circular motion. One can see the reason for the paramount position assigned by the Pythagoreans to astronomy among the sciences.

In short, the world is in the full sense a *kosmos*, and we may allow ourselves to note a statement about Pythagoras which, whether literally true or not, is a significant pointer to doctrines which were regarded as characteristically his: he was traditionally supposed to have been the first to apply the name *Kosmos* to the world, in recognition of the order which it displayed.

It would appear then that the ultimate principles are the two contraries limit and the unlimited. With these are equated numerical oddness and evenness respectively, and they thus form the principles of the number-series which in turn is to provide the elements of all existing things. Of the treatment of the unit there are two accounts known to Aristotle: some Pythagoreans derived it from a combination of limit-odd with unlimited-even, whereas others constructed two columns of contraries in which the unit appeared alongside limit, goodness, etc. These columns contain all their principles, and therefore include the principles of numbers, which all exemplify oddness and evenness. It is not to be doubted that for all Pythagoreans alike the unit stood for what is limited in opposition to the infinite or undefined (*apeiron*). The only difference between the two schools of thought is that whereas one of them identified it with the active principle of limit itself, the other saw it as the first product of that principle imposing itself on the undifferentiated mass of the *apeiron* and so initiating the introduction of order and limit which was necessary to produce a *kosmos* within it.

The followers of Pythagoras and Empedocles, and most of the Italian philosophers, say that there is a certain community uniting us not only with each other and with the Gods but even with the brute creation. There is in fact one breath pervading the whole cosmos like soul, and uniting us with them.' Nothing could be more natural than that the world should grow from seed like any other living creature. The formation of a cosmos was seen as the imposition of Limit on the Unlimited but equally as the impregnation of female matter by the form-giving sperm of the male. One may compare the inclusion of male with limit and female with unlimited in the table of opposites.

The doctrine of metempsychosis unquestionably provides more specific analogies (with India), causing scholars to speculate that the idea as it occurred in Greece was ultimately derived from India. Metempsychosis was undeniably a prominent concept in Indian thought: all the major Indian religions took it for granted. In Greece the Orphics, Pherekydes, Pythagoras and Empedokles apparently all believed in it[45].

The notion that spirits or souls of dead persons may inhabit or "possess" animals or plants is widespread among both ancient and modern peoples in many parts of the world. Known as metempsychosis or transmigration of souls, it is found in developed form in the ancient world only in India and Greece. Metempsychosis appears in rudimentry form in the Upanishads[46] and subsequently became incorporated into the ethical teaching of all the major Indian thought-systems down to the present day. Though vastly more important in Indian than in Greek religion, it was nontheless known in Greece as early as the 6th cenury B.C., and played a significant role in Orphism and Pythagoreanism. Plato in the early 4th century B.C. could already refer to it as "an ancient tradition"[47].

But in both India and Greece, metempsychosis in its characteristic and fullest development was a decisively ethical doctrine. The present status of every living being whether human or animal, man or woman, high or low-caste, happy or miserable-was believed to be the direct result of the quality of its behaviour in previous earthly existences. Certain Greek mystery-cults apparently held that the soul becomes purified only through a series of successive rebirths. In India, metempsychosis was taught as an ethical doctrine by Buddhist and Jains, Vishnuites and Shivaites, adherents of the Samkhya and Vedanta philosophies, and by the practioners of yoga. Formulated as the law of *Karma* (i.e. 'act' or 'deed'), ethical metempsychosis served to sanction traditional mores, inasmuch as proper behaviour was defined according to custom. Strange from the western viewpoint is the fact that *karma* was believed to operate as a kind of natural law, not requiring the intervention of any personalized form of deity[48].

Pythagoras is linked by Greek writers with Egypt, and with India besides-apparently because he too taught metempsychosis. According to a tradition already current in classical times, Pythagoras had lived for a while in Egypt, where he presumably consulted the priests concerning their ancient sacred lore. Our earliest evidence for this notion is a remark by Isokrates (4th Cen. B.C.), who is probably recounting accepted belief. However, Herodotas too may have had Pythagoras in mind when he referred to "certain Greek writers" who, he claimed, had learned metempsychosis in Egypt, but whose names he mysteriously refused to divulge[49]. Quite possibly this alleged connection of Pythagoras with Egypt represents an attempt to legitimize his ideas by linking them with hoary tradition. In any event, a Greek philosopher's visit to Egypt even as early as the 6th Century B.C. is in no way incredible Graeco-Egyptian trade relations certainly existed at that time, and long before. Indeed, the Egyptians' reputation as originators of the arts of civilization may well have encouraged educated Greeks to seek them out.

But Pythagoras' alleged connection with India is far more dubious. The extent statement that he visited that country—all made by authors removed from Pythagoras' own lifetime by an interval of five to seven centuries—are unsupported by any credible evidence. In the late-Hellenistic age informed Greeks were aware that the Indian Brahmins believed in metempsychosis; thus the conclusion was not far to seek that Pythagoras had acquired his ideas in India. The intellectual fashion of the day undoubtedly played a role here: it was common in the Hellenistic period to attribute Greek ideas to remote and exotic sources. The assertion that Pythagoras in the 6th century B.C. visited India—a country of which barely the name was known in those days in Greece-is unlikely in the extreme. We are probably safe in attributing this curious notion to the Hellenistic (but certainly not classical) Greek view that the philosophers of India possessed some special wisdom[50].

One more possible reflection of the idea of *Karma* and metempsychosis occurs in the *New Testament's* book of James. The Greek expression rendered in King James' translation as "the course of nature", actually means "the wheel of birth". As the Indophile Schopenhauer pointed out more than a century ago, this has a typically Buddhist flavour. Inasmuch as Orphics and Pythagoreans also used this phrase, the immediate source of the Biblical expression was presumably Greek, not India. Nonetheless the words evoke the idea of metempsychosis; and the verse as a whole would be perfectly at home in a Buddhist document[51].

The similarities between the Indian and Greek versions of the idea extended not merely to soul-wandering in itself, but also to its connection with a system of ethics. Hindus, Jains and Buddhists all assumed that the*karma* produced by a person is good or evil deeds extended through a series of earthly existences and determined that persons' status as animal or human being, high or low-class, in each of his lives. Likewise the Greek Orphics and Pythagoreans believed in a causal link between each person's current social status and his good or evil acts in previous existences. Prior to the Hellenistic age and the period of Buddhist expansion, the idea of ethical metempsychosis apparently found expression nowhere except in India and Greece.

This circumstance has naturally suggested the possibility that the idea of ethical metempsychosis originated in India and spread thence to Greece. The fairly exceptional occurrence of this idea in Greece, combined with the Greek's own conviction that it was a foreign concept, clearly suggests that metempsychosis was not native to Greece[52].

In the 6th century B.C. (when the Persian empire came into existence) is probably too late to be of significance for the origins of Greek metempsychosis. Almost certainly the doctrine was earlier present in Greece. According to Diogenes Laertios, Pythagoras (6th cen. B.C.) was the first person in Greece to teach metempsychosis as a metaphysical idea. Apparently this means that as a matter of religious belief, accepted by faith or tradition, it was already old—a virtual impossibility if it had come from India. The Orphics too, who believed in ethical metempsychosis, were probably active in Greece prior to the 6th century B.C. The Greek belief that Orpheos lived even before Homer indicates at least that he was considered ancient. Pythagoras perhaps learned of ethical metempsychosis from Orphic practitioners, giving to their religious idea a philosophical justification[53].

But it is difficult to draw any general conclusions from such scattered and apparently unconnected evidence. Perhaps the communities which produced the gold plates did have some relationship to Egypt. It is not impossible that Orphic practitioners did likewise. On the other hand, the similarities are not precise enough to exclude the possibility of coincidence. Egypt offers no satisfactory solution to the question of the origins of Greek metempsychosis. Firstly, there is no evidence for Egypt other than Herodotos' statement and the reputed visit of Pythagoras to that country. Both of these probably represent a logical, but not historical association between two known forms of soul-wandering. Furthermore, the theory of Egyptian origin presupposes a significant religious effect at considerable remove. Egypt, if not so distant as India, was nonetheless remote terrain to the Greeks of the 7th or 6th centuries B.C.; and religious ideas are obviously less likely to be adopted by foreigners than such visible items as artmotifs or architectural styles. Most significantly, the Egyptian concept of soul-wondering differed considerably from that of the

Orphics and Pythagoreans[54].

Whether the Pythagoreans forbade meat-eating absolutely is not clear from ancient sources. Many authors have given their views over this issue, some of them, are as follows : Porphyry says that 'Pythagoras exhibited such purity and such abhorrence of killing and killers that he not only abstained from animal food but would have nothing to do with cooks or hunters'. According to Strabo, Onesicritus states that Pythagoras 'commanded men to abstain from animal food'[55]. Aristotle in his work on the Pythagoreans said that Pythagoras counselled abstention from white cocks because they are sacred to the lunar God or to the month, and are suppliants-sacred to the lunar God because they announce the hours. Moreover, white is of the nature of good, black of evil. Also to abstain from any fish that are sacred, since it is not right that the same creatures should be assigned to Gods and to men'[56]. Porphyry states in the list of the *Symbola* of Pythagoras : 'Of sacrificed animals he bade them not to eat the loin, testicles and privy parts, marrow, feed or head'. Porphyry adds as the reason Pythagoras's symbolic interpretation of these parts. They signified for the animal respectively the foundation, genesis, growth, beginning and end. Together these are the leading parts of the body. He added that they must abstain from beans 'as they would from human flesh'[57].

This abstention from meat must be viewed in light of the fact that animal sacrifice constituted the central act of Greek city-state religion[58]. Through this ritual the citizen reaffirmed his membership in the body politic; and ordinarily meat-eating was inseparable from the sacrifice. We know that the Pythagoreans sacrificed cereals, raw plants and perfumes (incense, myrrh) instead of meat. In so doing, and in eliminating meat from their diet, they may have sought to reduce the religious distance between themselves and the Gods, thereby negating Prometheos' original dichotomy between those who eat meat and those who (being immortal) need not do so. Some ancient authorities claim that Pythagoras himself abstained from meat-eating though others say that he did not forbid the tasting of sacrificial meat[59].

According to Guthrie[60] Iamblichus tells us that according to the Pythagorean *acusmata* only animals which it is proper to sacrifice may be eaten, because only into these does the soul of a man not enter. This sounds more like the genuine Pythagorean reason than the incompatible explanation attributed to Aristotle that it was not right for men and Gods to share the same creatures. According to Plato, the Pythagoreans explained their abstention from meat on the ground that animals and human beings have the same type of souls, and that it is impious to act unjustly toward one's own kindered[61]. Pythagoras' near contemporary, Empedokles, took approximately the same line; he abhorred animal sacrifice on the ground that one might thereby slay a close relative[62].

It has been observed among Pythagoras' followers that two schools of thought existed on the subject of meat-eating. Conceivably this division followed the lines of rationalist versus traditionalist[63]. According to Aristoxenos, the Pythagoreans permitted the eating of goat meat and pork and forbade only mutton and ox-meat. These exclusions had a certain rational : not only that the God Dionysos was supposed to assume an ox's form on occasion[64], but that the sheep and the plow-ox are humankind's close companions and essential to civilized life. By contrast, the pig roots out planted seeds; the goat eats vines and destroys grapes, Greek myths made plain these distinctions in declaring the pig to be the enemy of Demeter, Goddess of agriculture, and the goat the enemy of Dionysos, God of vegetation and wine.

This might also reflect a division between "ascetic" and "political" Pythagoreans that the existence of two opposed attitudes towards meat-eating within the same Pythagorean order—i.e. total abstention; or prohibition only of mutton and ox-meat. Clearly, men who totally rejected the central ritual of Greek religious life were unlikely to be effective politically. Perhaps for this reason the "politicals" compromised on the matter of meat-eating, refusing to touch only those animals already recognized by Greek myth as harmful to civilized life. Within the same brotherhood, however, other members may have renounced civic participation in order to follow more consistently their ascetic proclivities. Some such explanation could account for the contradiction in the ancient sources as to whether the Pythagoreans were or were not complete vegetarians[65].

Now we would see about these rules in India. Like the Pythagoreans, the Indians of this period sometimes observed a distinction between meat eating in general and the tasting of meat in the context of a sacrifice to the Gods. Although now-a-days the doctrine of *ahimsa* (non-injury to living beings), which includes the total prohibition of meat-eating is almost universally observed in India, it certainly does not antedate the Christian era. The laws of Manu (Second century B.C.), specify that Brahmins may offer beans and birds in sacrifice, and that these things may be tasted. Even if done everyday, meat eating is no sin when associated with a sacrifice. On the other hand, to eat meat at any other time is forbidden[66].

The injunction against eating beans is the another curious dietary regulation, which appears both in India and in Greece at an early date. Some of the oldest extent ritual texts of India, dating perhaps from the 10th century B.C., forbid bean-eating for the period during which the sacrificer prepares for the sacrifice. Beans were felt to be unclean, unholy, unworthy of the sacred ceremony[67]. In classical Greece the same prohibition is linked to the name of Pythagoras, from whom the philosopher Empedokles (early 5th cen. B.C.) perhaps learned it[68]. One of Empedokles' poems includes the lines :

"O wretches, utter wretches, from beans withhold your hands."[69]

Most people assumed the word to refer to the vegetable, as it commonly does. But those who have studied the poem of Empedokles with the greatest care and insight say that in this context it signifies testicles, which after the enigmatic and symbolic style of Pythagoras are called beans because they bring about pregnancy and are the source of human generative power. Thus Empedocles in this line is trying to dissuae men not from eating beans but from sexual indulgence[70].

Classical and Hellenistic authors cite a wide variety of reasons for the prohibition of beans, all of which assume some connection between that vegetable and the forces of nature. For example, beans were thought to be full of life-force, or to arise from the same primal matter as human beings, or if buried in the earth or in dung to assume human shape, or being flatulent, to possess animal properties[71]. Plato tells us to go to bed in such a condition of body that there be nothing to induce wandering or disturbance of the mind. This is commonly thought to be the reason why the Pythagoreans are forbidden to eat beans, which have a flatulent tendency inimical to the pursuit of mental tranquillity[73]. Because beans have a stalk without nodes, they were believed to serve as a ladder of communication by which human souls could pass between the earth and Hades. Tales were told of a bean turning into the head of a child, or into blood; or when bitten, giving off the odour of human semen or of blood shed through murder.

The Pythagoreans actually claimed that bean-eating was equivalent to cannibalism of one's own parents. Thus the bean evidently represented rottenness and decay, sexuality and death—all qualities which distinguished human beings from gods[73]. Avoidance of beans was apparently also linked to the belief in metempsychosis, inasmuch as the same people who held that doctrine also forbade bean-eating—namely the Orphics. Pythagoreans and Empedokles. The Orphics actually used beans as offerings to the dead[74]. Plinuis reports (first cen. A.D.) that certain of the Pythagoreans held that the souls of the dead live in beans, though this again may represent a rationalization of the ancient taboo.

It will be seen that none of these testimonies antedates the fourth century B.C., by which time the prohibition of flesh had already become a matter of doubt and controversy. They fall into three classes. First those that affirm the prohibition of animal food without qualification, like Eudoxus and the less decisive voices of Onesicritus and the comic poets. Secondly, those (among them Aristotle) who describe the prohibition as selective, certain species or parts of animals being forbidden on religious or superstitious grounds. Abstention from some of the creatures mentioned as a common enough superstition outside the Pythagorean brotherhood and indeed outside the Hellenic sphere. Examples are collected by Boehm. Cocks for instance were forbidden to epileptics, who were supposed to be daemonically possessed and Caesar notes that the British held it impious to eat them. The religious reasons adduced by the Pythagoreans are expressly linked by some of our authorities with their belief in transmigration. Sacrifice was limited to certain animals, and these might be eaten because of a belief that the soul of a man never enters them. Perhaps the same, or perhaps a different, school of Pythagoreans held that even of sacrificial animals certain parts were to be avoided, including those, like testicles and marrow, which were particularly associated with the vital force.

We may conclude that abstinence from flesh, on the religious ground that to eat it is a form of cannibalism, was a tenet of Pythagoreanism from the beginning. A sacramental tasting, on special occasion, of the flesh of the forbidden animal is not an exception; rather it brings the system into line with universal primitive practice. Later, when rationalists and the devotees tended to take separate roads, it was denied by some who still laid claim to membership of the school. In support of this conclusion we may add that the belief and practice are independently known to have been current in the thought of the early fifth century, especially in the West. Empedocles of Acragas reasoned explicitly that because of the transmigration of souls a man who eats flesh may unwittingly devour his own son or his own father in altered shape; and a similar abstention was enjoined in the Orphic writings.

One very credible possibility of Indian influence upon

Hellenistic religion appears in the person of Apollonios of Tyana, famous Pythogorean philosopher, ascetic and religious reformer of the first century A.D. Apollonios combined Greek and Oriental elements in his religion. Nearly everything that is known of him derives from one single source - the biography of him written by the sophist Philostratos ca. 217 A.D.

According to Philostratos, Apollonios admired the Brahmin's life style: he believed that the Pythagorean rule of life had been taught by the Brahmins to the sages of Egypt, from whom Pythagoras learned it. Possibly he also thought that Pythagoras, his spiritual mentor, had visited India : an obscure reference by Philostratos to the effect that Apollonios "verified" Pythagoras' statement about a certain Indian river might be interpreted in his fashion. But if Apollonios felt that he followed in Pythagoras' footsteps to India, Philostratos makes no mention of the fact. On the contrary, his *Life of Apollonios* may itself have been one source for the commonly-held Hellenistic opinion Pythagoras had travelled to India.

As related by Philostratos, Apallonios lived his life according to the accepted Pythagorean pattern. As a young man he studied philosophy at a town near Tarsos called Aigai. In his sixteenth year he resolved to imitate the life-style anciently attributed to Pythagoras himself. In this way he denied to eat meat or drink wine, ate only dried fruits and vegetables, walked without shoes, clothed himself in linen (thereby declining to wear animal skins) and let his hair grow long. He lived in the temple of Asklepios. Indifferent to worldly possessions, Apollonios renounced most of the inheritance left by his father; and following Pythagorean custom, took a vow of silence which he faithfully kept for five years[75].

All traditions about Apollonios agree that his travels were wide-ranging. His object was the attainment of wisdom : indeed he said to the Brahmin: "I consider that your lore is profounder and much more divine than our own." He asked the Brahmins to teach him, which they gladly accepted to do; and he participated in their religious rites. Like the Indians he believed in metempsychosis, which was an article of faith among the Pythagoreans: he claimed to have been a ship's pilot in his most recent earthly life. Apparently, it was Apollonios' intention to disseminate Indian wisdom in the Hellenistic world[76]. How much of Apollonios' life-style was the legacy of Pythagoreanism rather than direct Indian example is difficult to say. But, if Philostratos is correct, Apollonios himself believed that the Pythagorean way of life had come from India to Greece by way of Egypt[77].

Two of the principal Neo-Platonist philosophers, Porphyrios and Iamblichos treat Apallonios as an authority on Pythagoreanism.[78] But it is impossible to ascertain how much of the *Life of Apollonios* reflects the actual historical personality of its subject, and how much is merely the idealized re-creation of a prototypal Pythagorean wise man. Philostratos gives Apollonios the characteristics of a model Pythagorean practitioner : strict asceticism, including the five years of silence and prohibition with respect to food and clothing; a cryptic and symbolic mode of expression, supposedly characteristic of the Pythagoreans, journeys to the Egyptian wise men, Persian Magi and Indian Brahmins; the doctrine of soul-wandering and a refusal to pray to the Gods for worldly blessings[79]. Apollonios' extent letters confirm his Pythagorean tendencies. Nonetheless it is probably fair to say that Philostratos' biography reflects the ideal of a spiritualized Pythagoreanism as it existed in the 3rd century. The alternative view of Apollonios—namely, that he was a mere magician—is not inconsistent with the Pythagorean tradition. Pythagoras himself (6th cen. B.C.) had been philosopher, mystic, shaman and purveyor of superstitious all at once: reputedly possessing special insight into nature, but also a close relationship with Gods and demons. In Philostratos' time the notion of "Pythagorean" was probably itself abbivalent, denoting low level magic as well as a higher spirituality. Furthermore, the Pythagoreans cultivated secret knowledge; thus to the uninitiated their rule of life was necessarily suspect.

Thus, of all the known Western visitors to India Apollonios could have been the most likely medium for effectively communicating the finer points of any system of Indian philosophy in their original form[80].

The Greek philosophy although it incorporated religious beliefs remained secular and open to all, while the sacred teachings of the Indians were transmitted from teacher to disciple and presupposed a certain initiation. However, similarities and differentiations are there indicating that no conclusions can be drawn in closed horizons. The Pythagorean and the Orphic societies, for instance, preserved their teachings through an oral transmission and the study of their confidential doctrines was possible only to initiates who could fulfil certain preconditions. A similar approach was followed by Buddha and Mahavira, who dismissed birth and sex distinctions. Initiation into the monastic orders was based solely on ideological and ethical grounds. More liberal in approach were the meterialists who taught openly to all people without any distinction whatever[81].

The Pythagorean and the Samkhya philosophers were mainly concerned with questions related to the nature of the world and implied scientific methodologies to explain the form and the constitution of the world. General parallels between the two systems might be drawn on the dualistic concept of reality (limit-unlimited and purusa-prakrti) and on soteriological considerations, but there is nothing equal in the Indian system to the Pythagorean life which incorporated into one whole religious rituals, sharing property, participation in social affairs, and the study of mathematics and music. The attempt of certain scholars to compare the Pythagorean theory of numbers with the dualistic philosophy of Kapila, because the Sanskrit word "Samkhya" (from Sankhya) has the meaning of number, is however unconvincing. The Samkhya philosophy apart from the enumeraion of the twenty-four categories of Prakrti is not known to have dealt with the doctrine of numbers at all. The Pythagorean theory that the essence of number is the essence of material things is a unique contribution in the history of human thought.

So, there was a problem concerning the influence of Samkhya on Greek philosophy. With Colebrooks the problem acquired a deeper scholarly seriousness. He attempted a minute analysis of the problem by comparing the principles of Samkhya with those of Pythagoras[82] and came to the conclusion that Pythagoras was indebted to Indian instructors[83]. Barthelemy Saint Hilaire also supported the probability of Pythagoras's theory of metempsychosis being of Indian origin[84]. The ideas of redemption and bondage as the liberation of soul from matter and the confinement of soul by matter, of metempsychosis and of the beginningless and endless existence of the soul as propunded by Plato were traced by him to Pythagoras and, through the latter, ultimately to India[85].

Leopold Von Schroeder made a very exhaustive study to show the Indian origin of all the doctrines ascribed to Pythgoras. According to him Pythagoras acquired his knowledge in India itself from what he identified as an older form of Samkhya philosophy[86].

Pythagoras' conception of the soul as harmony reminds us of the Buddhist denial of the existence of permanent spiritual substance. A musical illustration occurs also in the *Brhadaranyaka Upanisad*, but the notes here constitute the phenomena of the universe while the soul (atman), the musical instrument (drum, conch, lute). In the *Chandogya Upanisad*, the soul is the unhearable (asrutam) while the phenomena, the hearable (srutam).

Herodotus suggests that Pythagoras got the doctrine of rebirth from the Egyptians, but 'the Egyptians did not believe in transmigration at all and Herodotus was deceived by the priests or the symbolism of the monuments. Even if the theory by a development from the primitive belief in the kinship of men and beasts, it is difficult to account for the other parts of the system, taboos on certain kinds of food, the rule of silence which the members of his fraternity were required to observe, the ascetic emphasis and insistence on release assured to those who are initiated. Iamblichus, the biographer of Pythagoras, tells us that he travelled widely, studying the teachings of Egyptians, Assyrians and Brahmins[87].

Rawlinson writes[88] : "It is more likely that Pythagoras was influenced by India than by Egypt. Almost all the theories, religious, philosophical and mathematical taught by the Pythagoreans, were known in India in the sixth century B.C., and the Pythagoreans, like the Jains and the Buddhists, refrained from the destruction of life and eating meat and regarded certain vegetables such as beans as taboo'. Professor Winternitz[89] is of the same opinion : 'As regards Pythagoras, it seems to me very probable that he became acquainted with Indian doctrines in Persia'. Gomperz writes : 'It is not too much to assume that the curious Greek, who was a contemporary of Buddha, and it may be of Zoroaster too, would have acquired a more or less exact knowledge of the East in that age of intellectual fermentation, through the medium of Persia[90].

The Pythagorean school was influenced by Orphic culture. Likewise it believed in the immortality of soul, in the doctrine of rebirth, and in the purification of soul through ascetic practices like self-control. Pythagoras, like the Upanisadic philosophers, believed that all souls are identical by nature[91]. The apparent distinctions between human beings and other beings are not ultimate. A man, through theoria, "the contemplation of the divine," can realize his true nature and be free from the wheel of transmigration. It is said that Pythagoras had travelled widely. He was greatly influenced by India in his religious, philosophical and mathematical teachings. Even in the formation of his famous theorem of the quadrature of the hypotenuse he was inlfuenced by India where it was already known in the older Vedic times, long before Pythagoras[92]. Like the Jains and the Buddhists he refrained from violence and eating meat and regarded certain vegetables as taboos[93].

Whether or not we accept the hypothesis of direct influence from India through Persia on the Greeks, a student of Orphic and Pythagorean thought canot fail to see that the similarities between it and the Indian religion are so close as to warrant our regarding them as expressions of the same view of life. We can use the one system to interpret the other[94]. Loukianos related that philosophy first visited to India, and from there marched to Ethiopia, afterwards to Egypt and then to other countries. The theory of recognizing Egypt as the origin of wisdom was discredited and philosophers like Pythagoras, Demokritos, Platon, were reported to have been influenced by the learned men of India[95].

RERFERENCES

1. Cartledge Paul, *Ancient Greece*, (Cambridge Illustrated History), Cambridge, 1998, p. 293.
2. Radhakrishnan, S., *Eastern Religions and Western Thought*, 1939, New Delhi, p.148.
3. *Ibid*, p. 140.
4. *ERE*, James Hastings, p. 81.
5. *ERE*, op, cit, P.81.; S. Radhakrishnan, *op. cit.*, p. 141.
6. Radhakrishnan, S., *op. cit.*, p. 140.
7. Lohse, *Askese und Monchtum*, p. 71.
8. Philostratus, *Life of Apollonius*, I.1-2, 8,11, 14 (Loeb) I, 3-5, 19-21, 29, 37-39.
9. Sedlar, J.W., *India and the Greek World*, Totowa, 1980, p. 244.
10. Minar, E.L., *Early Pathogorean Politics in Practice and Theory,* Baltimore, 1942, appendix.
11. Dunbabin, T.J., *The Western Greeks, Oxford*, 1948, pp. 354-360.
12. Guthrie, W.K.C., *A History of Greek Philosophy*, Cambridge, 1962, p. 175.
13. *Ibid.*, p. 178.
14. *Ibid.*, p. 78.
15. Minar, E.L., *op. cit.*, p. 75.
16. *Ibid.*, p. 77.
17. Guthrie, W.K.C., *op. cit.*, p.180.
18. Guthrie, W.K.C., *op. cit.*, p. 180.
19. ERE "*ASCETICISM*", p. 81, James Hastings Vol. I.
20. W.K.C. Guthrie, *op. cit.*, p.167.
21. *Ibid.*, p.167.
22. *Ibid.*, p.183.
23. *Ibid.*, p. 184.
24. Aristotle, Jaeger, E.T. 1934, p. 75.

25. Radhakrishnan, S., *op. cit.,* p. 141.
26. Cornford, F. M., "Mysticism and Science in Pythogorean Tradition"; *Classical Quarterly,* 1922, p.142.
27. Radhakrishnan, S., *op. cit.,* p. 141.
28. Burnet, *Early Greek Philosophy,* 1930, p. 98.
29. Deussen, *Philosophy of the Upanisads,* E.T. 1906, pp. 326ff.
30. Radhakrishnan, S., *op. cit.,* p. 140.
31. *Ibid.,* p.141.
32. Guthrie, W.K.C., *op. cit.,* p.186.
33. Guthrie, W.K.C., *op. cit.,* p.192.
34. Minar, *op.cit.,* p. 31-3.
35. Guthrie, W.K.C., *op.cit.,* p. 193.
36. *Ibid.,* p. 140.
37. S. Radhakrishnan, *op. cit.,* p. 142.
38. *Ibid,* p. 140.
39. Sedlar, J.W., *op. cit.,* p.121.
40. Guthrie, *op. cit.,* p. 203.
41. *Ibid.,* p. 307.
42. Guthrie,W.K.C., *op. cit.,* p. 319.
43. Alberuni, *Alberuni's India,* Chp. VII, p. 85.
44. Guthrie, W.K.C., *op. cit.,* p. 320.
45. Sedlar, J.W., *op. cit.,* p. 269.
46. *Chandogya* III. 14.1.; *Svetasvatara* V.7., *Upan.,* pp. 391, 740.
47. Sedlar, *op. cit.,* p. 22.
48. *Ibid.,* p. 23.
49. Isocrates, "Busiris, " Ch.28 cited by Guthrie, *Greek Philosaphy,* p.163.
50. Sedlar, *op. cit.,* p. 32.
51. *Ibid.,* p.122.
52. *Ibid.,* p. 269
53. *Ibid.,* p. 270
54. *Ibid.,* p. 272
55. Guthrie, W.K.C., *op. cit.,* p.187.
56. *Ibid.,* p. 188.
57. *Ibid.,* p. 188.
58. Sedlar, *op. cit.,* p. 38.
59. *Ibid.,* p. 38; Guhtrie, *op. cit.,* p.187.
60. Guthrie, W.K.C., *op. cit.,* p. 188.
61. Sedlar, *op. cit.,* p. 38.
62. *Ibid.,* p. 38.
63. *Ibid.,* p. 39.
64. Keith, " Pythogoras and Transmigration "*JRAS,* 1909, p. 588.
65. Sedlar, *op. cit.,* p. 39.

66. Laws of Manu, Ch.V. vv. 7, 22, 26, 30, 31., in Buhler, pp.170, 172-74.
67. Schroeder, *Pythogoras und die inder*, Leipzig, 1884 pp. 35, 36.
68. Sedlar, *op-cit.*, p. 40.
69. Guthrie, W.K.C., *op. cit.*, p. 189.
70. Guthrie, W.K.C., *op. cit.*, p. 189.
71. *Ibid.*, p. 184.
72. *Ibid.*, p. 189.
73. Sedlar, *op. cit.*, p. 40.
74. Keith, *JRAS*, *op. cit.*, p. 588
75. Sedlar, *op-cit.*, p. 191
76. Sedlar, *op-cit.*, p.192
77. *Ibid.*, p. 193.
78. *Ibid.*, p. 197
79. *Ibid.*, p.195
80. Gopal, Lallanji, " Samkhya and Greek Philosophy", in *Graeco-indica*, Ed. U.P. Arora, Delhi ,1991. p. 247.
81. Vassiliades, Demetrios Th. , "India and Greece : Early Philosophical Understanding", in *Indian Historical Review*, Vol. XXXII, No.1 (Jan. 2005), ICHR, New Delhi, 2005, p. 268.
82. *Miscellaneous Essays*, Second Edition, I, pp. 441f.
83. *Ibid.*, pp. 436f;p Wilson *Quarterly Oriental Magazine*, IV. II, 12.
84. Gopal, Lalanji, *op. cit.*, p. 242.
85. *Ibid.*, p. 242
86. Vassiliades, Demetrios Th.,"India and Greece : Early Philosophical Understanding", in *Indian Historical Review*, Vol. XXXII, No. 1 (Jan 2005), ICHR, New Delhi, 2005, p. 278.
87. Radhakrishnan, S., *op. cit.*, p.142.
88. Rawlinson, H.G., *Legacy of India*, 1937, p. 5.
89. Winternitz, *Visvabharati Quarterly*, Feb. 1937, p. 8.
90. Gomperz, *Greek Thinkers*, vol. I, p.127.
91. Tripathi, C.L., "Influence of Indian Philosophy", In *Neoplatonism and Indian Thought*, Ed. R. Baine Harris, Delhi, 1992, p. 280.
92. Rawlinson, H.G., *op. cit.*, p. 5.
93. Tripathi, C.L., "Influence of Indian Philosophy", *op. cit.*, p. 281.
94. Radhakrishnan S., *op. cit.*, p.143.
95. Arora, U.P., *Greeks on India-Skylax to Aristoteles*, ISGARS, 1996, p.172.

GNOSTICISM AND INDIAN THOUGHT

Gnosticism was a deliberate attempt to fuse Greek (Platonic) and Hindu elements. It is a name for the whole system of syncretistic religious thought, which covers many sects with widely differing tenets which prevailed in the Eastern provinces of the Roman Empire during and prior to the early days of Christianity. It existed long before the Christian era, though Christianity tended to look upon it as heresy. Many of the chief features of Gnasticism are those common to the *Upanisads* and the mystic traditions of Greece[1].

Many of the Gnostic sects believed in pre-existence and rebirth of human souls. They had also a magical theory of the spirit world. The disembodied soul travels by the dark or bright paths and is saved from the perils on the way by the magic word. 'The essential part' of these Gnostic conceptions 'was already in existence and fully developed before Christianity'[2]. What it did was to introduce into Christianity not the pure spirit of Greek philosophy but conceptions of Eastern religions which by the first century had taken their place everywhere in the Roman Empire. Its conceptions of dualistic theology, ascetic ethics, ecstatic experience of the real, and redemption from the trammels of flesh are derived from the Eastern cults. Kennedy states that .... Gnosticism is not pure Hellenism as some say; it is rather pure orientalism in a Hellenic mask[3].

All things have their law of being in themselves; suffering is the concomitant of existence, rebirth is the result of former acts and metempsychosis governs men with inflexible justice and with iron necessity. The office of Jesus is the office of Buddha; the elect alone are saved and the mass of mankind content to be born again[4].

The Gnostic view of creation is opposed to the Christian view as set forth in the first article of the Apostles' Creed : 'I believe in God, the Father Almighty, the Maker of heaven and earth.' For the Gnostics creation is not the act of the supreme God but of an inferior demiurge. The God of religion and the God of creation are distinguished. Again, the doctrine of the resurrection of the body is opposed to the Gnostic view, which separates spirit and body[5].

'That the seeds of the Gnosis were originally of Indian growth carried so far westward by the influence of that Buddhistic movement which had previously overspread all the East, from Tibet to Ceylon, was the great truth faintly discerned by Matter but which became evident to me upon acquiring ever a slight acquaintance with the chief doctrines of Indian theosophy'[6].

Rawlinson states that Gnosticism, a far more serious and noble creed, together with its later offshoots, shows traces of both Hindu and Zorathustrian influence. Its doctrine of the plurality of Heavens is essentially Indian : its "three qualities" resemble the "three gunas" of the Samkhya system[7].

Now we would discuss the elements and doctrines of Gnosticism:

In contrast to those religions which have a known founder and a continuous tradition, the great Gnostic thought-systems of the 2nd century A.D. appear to us full-blown. "Gnosis" in the wider sense of the word may well pre-date the Christian era, though "Gnosticism" as a group of well developed theologies probably does not. Gnostic concepts and terminology as known to us from the 2nd century system, can be found in both Jewish and Christian contexts in the first century A.D. This suggests the possibility of Gnostic influences upon Christianity in the latter's formative period. Ultimately the Gnostic sects either disappeared or became absorbed into other faiths; and the victorious Christian Church aided in the destruction of Gnosis' sacred scriptures.

The "basic myth"[8] of Gnostic elucidated the divine plan of the universe and humankinds situation within it. In so doing, it also provided the framework for a doctrine of salvation. Fundamental to Gnostic belief was a pre-historic divine drama which resulted in the creation of the earth and of human beings. However, the Eastern (i.e. Iranian) and Western (i.e. Syrian and Egyptian) forms of Gnosis explained this somewhat differently. The Eastern variant undoubtedly influenced by Zoroastrian antecedents, assumed a radical cosmological dualism. The beneficient God (called Light, Spirit or Father of Greatness) is an independent entity co-eternal and co-equal (or nearly so) with the evil deity (Darkness, Matter or Satan). At some point in the pre-cosmic era, fragments of the divine light became imprisoned in Matter. So Darkness was supposed to have created the world for the express purpose of imprisoning the sparks of divine light which constitute human souls. Thereby the stage was set for a process of redemption.

By contrast, the Western Gnostic theologies assumed a single first principle of the cosmos through which the world was created by a process of emanation. According to this variant of the myth, God gave off a portion of himself order to create his second-in-rank. This derivative deity or angel in turn produced another, and so on. Therefore, each intermediary power in the universe is lesser in dignity than its predecessor, and correspondingly removed from God. Among these lower emanations are the evil Demiurge (Satan) who created this world, as well as his wicked cohorts. By virtue of their distance from God, these inferior deities are also ignorant of him. Moreover, they attempt to prevent human souls from gaining knowledge of him. But because God has refrained from direct participation in the work of world-creation, he bears no responsibility for any of these evils.

Although in a cosmological semse, Eastern Gnosticism was dualist, Western Gnosticism monist, both taught a redical dualism on the plane of human existence. This earth was declared to be the product of a divine tragedy. Creation of the wicked Demiurge, it is dominated by satanic powers. Humankind too is evil, both in its physical and its psychic nature (the latter being defined to include both mind and will). Only the divine light-spark within each person, the so-called pneuma or soul, belongs to the realm of God. But the soul's long association with matter (i.e. with earthly goods and pleasures) has caused into "forget" its true nature. Gnostic metaphor describes it as "drunk", "benumbed", "asleep". Ignorant of its celestial origin and essential purity, it is nonetheless consumed with inexpressible longing for its heavenly home[9].

Gnostic thought thus reversed the typically Greek attitude toward the universe. For the Greeks, the very orderliness of the natural world—i.e. the regular paths of the stars and planets; the periodic recurrence of the seasons and of plant and animal life—made it the object of admiration. In Greek the word*Kosmos* means both "world" and "order". The heavenly bodies who were believed to be living , intelligent beings either possessed souls or were moved by Gods. The proof of this was the infallible regularity of their motions. Thus compared to the grandeur and perfection of the universe as a whole, the evil suffered by individuals was considered a minor matter. But in Gnosticism this sense of harmony between man and world was turned upside down. To the Gnostic believer the cosmic order is tyranny; the physical and moral law is an intolerable burden; and the influence of the heavenly bodies on human destiny signifies enslavement. The cosmos is a diabolical machine, in which humankind suffers and suffocates[10].

J .W. Sedlar states that redemption for the Gnostic believer signified liberation of the soul from the bonds of evil matter. The instrument of redemption was Gnosis. This word in Greek means "Knowledge", though in the technical vocabulary of the Gnostics it had little in common with reason or logic. Rather it denoted a knowledge not attainable in a natural manner—knowledge of mysteries and secret doctrine. In order to be redeemed, the entrapped soul must "know" or "remember" its heavenly origin. Such knowledge cannot be gained either by intellectual processes or by meditation, asceticism, good works or ritual observance. Moreover, it is not open to everyone, but only to a select few. Gnosis is the gift of the redeemer, who has descended from the realm of light in order to issue a "call" to remembrance. The saving knowledge which he brings is the instrument of liberation. Once freed of the shackles of ignorance, the soul will rise upward through the innumerable planetary spheres or heavens which surround the earth until it finally returns to its native realm of light. In the culmination of the world-process, all souls will return to God[11].

This typically Gnostic world-view exhibits a number of similarities with Indian religion. It shares certain features with the *Upanisads,* others with the *Bhagavad Gita*, still others with the *Samkhya* philosophy and with Buddhism. No single Indian system can be considered its complete counterpart. Rather it has analogies with many.

However, one Indian thought system does analyze the nature of the human being in a way reminiscent of the Gnostic contrast between psyche and pneuma. This is Samkhya one of the six major Indian philosophical systems, which also serve as the theological underpinning for the practical discipline of Yoga. The earliest systematic formulation of Samkhya as now known occurs in the *Samkhya Karika*, a work dating from perhaps the 5th century A.D. But elements of the system can already be found in a few passages from the middle and later *Upanisads* and in the Bhagavad Gita and Moksadharma[12].

According to Samkhya, this world is composed of a multiplicity of souls (*purus*) bond to matter (*prakriti*). Prakriti contains in itself not only inanimate matter, but also mental and emotional life. On the other hand, Purusha is pure consciousness, it does not participate in life, but is only a spectator of it. Though associated with prakriti, it is essentially isolated and uncontaminated by it. Samkhya recognizes no supreme being. It knows no all-encompassing single Purusha or otherwordly One to serve as transcendental component of the individual soul. Salvation in the Samkhya system occurs when a person, by means of intelligence (buddhi), comprehends that his true nature is consciousness (i.e. purusha), which is essentially independent of prakriti.

Purusha is not identical in nature with the *Upanisadic* atman, though both words may be translated as "soul" or "self". Although some passages of the *Upanisads* treat atman as the pure, abstract subject of consciousness, atman is also the life giving power, the essence of the total person. In the case of purusha, its most essential feature is alienation from life—i.e., isolation and non-involvement. In this it closely resembles the Gnostic pneuma. Both pneuma and purusha are associated (in Gnostic terminology : "entrapped") with bodies which by nature are their complete antitheses. Gnosticism explained this alienation as the result of a complete cosmic pre-history: the mythological drama which brought the world into being. Samkhya's creation-story is less elaborate. The original proximity of prakriti and purusha brought about an imbalance among the three *gunas* (i.e. the components of matter), thus producing the manifold earthly phenomena. The process is a kind of mechanical interaction, which is in no way the consequence of (a deity's) conscious decision. According to Sedlar, the purpose of creation was to provide the purushas, which are subjects of consciousness, with objects to perceive, i.e. with "enjoyments" and secondly to make possible the purushas' liberation from their bondage to matter[13].

Like Gnosticism, Samkhya is a system of individual salvation. Moreover, it provides theoretical justification for Yoga, the characteristically Indian method of physical and mental discipline by which the practitioner may eventually attain the ultimate mystic state. Indeed, Indian texts often refer to Samkhya and Yoga as the two halves of one single system. By contrast, Gnosticism never became associated with a sophisticated ascetic discipline.

But Samkhya and Gnosticism resemble each other in that both emphasize "knowledge" as the true path to salvation. Gnostics spoke of the "awakening" of the pneuma, while

Samkhya regards knowledge as arising in the material half of existence, the *buddhi* (intelligence) which is the first and highest evolute of prakriti. Classical Samkhya, moreover gave a partially rationalist interpretation to "knowledge" : it analyzed the three forms of knowledge as perception, inference and authority[14]. Even so, the ultimate knowledge—knowledge of the purity of purusha and the falsity of its association with prakriti—could hardly have been originally a logical determination. More probably, the categories enumerated by the Samkhya—Karika are the rationalist explanations of what was originally a mystic intuition, an "awakening" similar in nature to Gnosis.

The point of departure for classical Samkhya, as for Buddhism and less explicitly for Gnosticism, is the interpretation of earthly life as an inevitable condition of suffering and torment[15]. Thus, the object of religion is to procure release from suffering, which in turn requires spiritual alienation from the affairs of this world. Suffering is the direct result of involvement in wordly concerns—an involvement metaphysically explained in Samkhya as the association of purusha and prakriti, in Gnosticism as the "drunkeness" or "numbness" produced in the pneuma through its contacts with material life. Salvation is defined in negative term as "isolation" (*Kaivalya*) or release from bondage. Samkhya differs fundamentally from Gnosticism in that is lacks the figure of a divine redeemer who transmits to humankind the knowledge of the path to salvation. Furthermore, the multiple purushas of Samkhya possess no transcendental counterpart, because the system recognizes no supreme being. However, on this point its difference from Gnosticism is essentially one of degree. The Gnostic high God is so vastly removed from all relation to the world that he is, ineffect, absent. The resultant human feeling of world-alienation, so pronounced in Gnosticism, is if anything even more extreme in Samkhya. Not only is each purusha unrelated to any other, it is also without relation to God. It has no heavenly "home" to which it may ultimately hope to return.

But in the final analysis—despite the differing traditions

from which they arose-Samkhya and Gnosticism present remarkably similar responses to the human condition. In both systems the innermost nature of the human being is considered totally alien to every ordinary aspect of life. The soul is a foreigner on this earth, ill-at ease in the universe it inhabits. The highest object of human ambition consists in discovering "true" being—a being as far removed as it is possible to be from all human affairs[16].

In the beginning the scholars were inclined to find out the similarities between the Greek philosophy and the Samkhya system found were listed previously. Sir William Jones[17] as represented the statements made by the earlier scholars. According to him Kapila corresponds with Pythagoras and Patanjali with Zeno. Many other contemporary writers have also made the similar statements regarding the importance of Oriental influence specially of Samkhya on Greek philosophy but such statement had not been supported by any comparative study[18].

Garbe endeavoured to make the analysis about the exact nature of the views expressed by the philosophers in Greece and their effects in India. He has also tried to determine the specific Samkhya views as different from those principles which are the common features of different schools of Indian philosophy. Grabe was the first philosopher who has streached the need for finding out the probability of influence from India reaching Greek philosophers. He also kept in mind the consideration at the time of studying a question of the exchange of ideas between the distant countries[20].

Grabe's opinions about the correlation between Samkhya and Greek philosophy led to a lively discussion between him[21], Keith[22] and Oldenberg.

Keith in his *History of Samkhya Philosophy* admits the probability of Samkhya elements in Gnosticism but does not determine such parallels to be of definite help in finding the date of a real Samkhya.

J.W. Sedlar[23] has made the use of earlier studies to make

reasonable prppositions about the relation between Samkhya and Greek philosophy. According to him there is a close relation in the doctrine of metempsychosis in Greek philosophy with the common philosophical heritage of India of which*Upanisads,* Buddhism and Samkhya alike partake. He analyses with keen understanding the relevant features of Gnosticism[24]. According to him, there is a great likelihood for Gnostic system to have been influenced by Samkhya, he adds that no single Indian system can be considered as its complete counterpart, rather it has analogies with many, namely, *Upanisads, Bhagavad-Gita*, Samkhya and Buddhism.

The only author to add new information about the Brahmanas is St. Hippolytos, Bishop of Rome, who belonged to the first half of the third century. He possibly received it from south India, which was open through sea-route, though the overland route was violently snapped on account of political disturbances. His *logos* is Light, God or Brahman and tallies with *atman* in the *Upanisads.* His account resembles the teaching in the *Maitry Upanisad.* He speaks of Kenodoxia (vain opinion of *abhimana*), which may be identified with ahankara in Samkhya[25].

We may say, in the case of Gnosticism it has been admitted that, before its appearance as a co-herent system in the second century A.D., its direct antecedents cannot be identified, though we may find isolated motifs and the use of the term *gnosis* in a wider sense.There being no clear indication of the existence of Gnosticism in the first century A.D., the probability of Indian example causing the efflorescence of Gnosticism is strengthened[26]. The case of Egypt or any country other than Indian providing the stimulus for these features has not been seriously advocated[27]. It is admitted on all hands that the ideas under study are characteristic mostly of Indian systems, situations and thinking pattern.

The earliest available Samkhya text is the *Samkhya-Karika* of Isvarakrsna. Even the earliest date suggested for this text would create a chronological impasse for the Samkhya influence to permeate to Greek philosophy. The latest in the group of Greek tradition to show Samkhya influence are the Gnostics and the Neo-Platonists. Gnosticism, as a full blown system, belongs to the second century A.D., but is not seen before the beginning of the Christian era[28]. As against this, Isvarakrsna is generally placed in the early fourth century A.D.[29] though some people suggest as early a date as the first century[30]. Thus, the Samkhya elements in Greek thought could not have been derived from the *Samkhya-Karika.*

The Samkhya philosophy is correctly reputed to be the oldest in India. Though the claims for tracing its elements in the early Vedic literature may be disputed, it is admitted that it has a long career before Isvarakrsna standardized it. Likewise, Samkhya influence on origins of Buddhism may be debated, but its contemporaneity with early Buddhism is admitted. Efforts have been made to demonstrate that, notwithstanding some retouching and interpolations, the *Samkhya-Pravacana-sutra* or *Samkhya-sadadhyay* and *Tattvasamasasutra* are among the earliest Samkhya text which possibly were written by Kapila himself or by Pancasikha[31]. Early versions of Samkhya philosophy are known to occur in the middle *Upanisads, Mahabharata, Gita,* Asvaghosa's *Buddhacarita* and *Carakasamhita.*[32] The treatment of the history of Samkhya requires considerable reformulation on account of the clear proof that the *Devaladhrmasutra* contained a detailed and authentic account of Samkhya principles. Quotations from Pancasikha are also known to occur in later works. That these accounts of Samkhya preceded the *Samkhya-Karika* by many centuries is too well-known to require arguing.

Many ideas and expressions occurring in Gnostic writings are known to be the characteristic features of Samkhya. Such parallelisms are not confined to the text of *Samkhya-Karika.* Even in the case of *Samkhyakarika* the possibility cannot be ruled out that the parallels were preserved traditionally and were adapted by Isvarakrsna from earlier sources. A closer scrutiny of the Samkhya system found in texts which can be dated before the *Samkhyakarika* shows a closer similarity in a still larger number of cases. The Gnostic tenet of personal existence of intellect, will etc. is to be connected with the Samkhya doctrine of independent existence of *Buddhi, Manas,* and *Citta*[33]. Of these we may make a special mention of the *Devaladharmasutra*, the *Upanisadic* texts, the *Moksadharmaparva* section in the *Shantiparva* of the *Mahabharata* and the *Gita*. The dates of these texts are not settled. It is generally agreed that they are based on much old material which may be placed in the fifth-fourth centuries, though their present and final form was fixed as late as the second-third centuries of the Christian eras. Hence, we will not be far from realities of the case, if we take these texts generally to belong to the period roughly from the second century B.C. to the first century of the Christian era. Chronologically this suits the suggestion that the novel features in the Gnostic philosophy were the results of Samkhya influence.

The view of Gnosticism about coming of the soul on this earth has been defined in the "Purush" and "Prakriti" of Samkhya. Here purush is pure consciousness and after assimilating with "Prakriti" and matter has forgotten its divine origin. "Purusha" is tied in fatters of earthly allurements from where it can be free through yoga, meditation and intelligence of knowledge.

In the light of the above study we see that there were vivid similarities in the philosophy involved between the ancient India and Greece. There were great similarities between Samkhya one of the six orthodox philosophies of India and the Gnosticism of Greece. "Purusha" in Samkhya in India and Pneuma in Gnosticism of Greece are the similar terms. Both are of the opinion that the soul comes to the earth from almighty and getting influenced by the worldly allurements it forgets that it is the part of the divine and at the end it becomes one with Him. The soul can go back to the divine through the medium of intelligence and knowledge after being detached from this world and yoga is the other medium of it.

There are many resemblances between Gnosticism and the ideas of the *Upanisads* mainly the Brahman *atman* doctrine. The Gnostic light-spark (or pneuma) and the *Upanisadic* atman are both defined as the inmost-self of the human being. They are similarly treated as identical in substance with the supreme Power of the universe, i.e. with the Gnostic God or the Upanishadic Brahman. Each light-spark constitutes a portion of the heavenly Light; each atman is in essence identical with Brahman, the world-self. With this all, in both Gnosticism and the *Upanisads*, knowledge of this identity is similar to salvation.

There are also some differences between the thought-worlds of these two systems. In the *Upanisads* Brahman is the universe, namely its essence, self or inmost ruler. The Gnostic spirit or Light, though sometimes personified as the Father of Greatness, is almost equally impersonal; but it is the total antithesis of the world. It is the quintesential outsider, vis-a-vis the physical universe. It is an alien, a total opposite. For the Gnostics this earth is wicked and demonic, human beings participate in its activities only because they are sensul and ignorant. The higher self of the person, the pneuma or light-spark, is alient to this world to the level that it realizes its true identity with God.

"Knowledge" is also different in both the *Upanisads* and Gnosticism. Gnostic knowledge is the gift of a redeemer whose home is in a supernatural realm, and without whom no one can be liberated from bondage to this world. Knowledge in *Upanisads* is communicated by sages and "seers" who are only human beings, although persons especially advanced in matters spiritual. By the study and long meditation the saving knowledge of the *Upanisads* is self-attainable. The seeker's own efforts, unaided by divine intervention, can bring him to union with Brahman. So in a whole the *Upanisads* represent an infinitely more optimistic view of the human condition than Gnosticism does, and a vastly more positive assessment of the world. This is so despite the concern of the *Upanisadic* seers to give less importance to the phenomenal world by contrast with Brahman. The sages say that this present world is not the ultimate. The wise person will not become blinded by phenomena, by multiplicity. But whatever its deficiencies, the world remains Brahman. The *Upanisads* describe it as neither good nor evil, but merely transitory. They do not suggest the believer to deny the world, but rather to seek its essence, the permanent core which hides behind apparently manifold things.

An element which is largely missing in the *Upanisads* : a divine Redeemer, the God Krisna, has been introduced in the *Bhagavad Gita* into Indian religion. The God Krisna sheds his disguise and stood forth openly as the God who reveals the path to salvation. Krishna, to be sure, remains heir to the *Upanisadic* tradition, he describes himself as identical to both *atman* and Brahman[34]. He indeed resembles the Gnostic saviours because he is appearing as the incarnate form of the supreme power. But the parallel holds slight significance. No God in India approaches the exalted status of the GnosticFather of Greatness, or of the Judeo-Christian God. Gods in India are many : in this they resemble the angels and demons of Western religions, rather than the Gnostic or Judeo-Christian high God. They neither create, nor do they rule the world, although they perform miraculous acts and give aid to their devotees[35]. Nonetheless Krisna is his relationship to human kind functions similarly to the Gnostic redeemers. His essential message is one of faith. While the *Gita* pays its respects to the "way of knowledge", i.e. the path of self-salvation, it prefers to emphasize the individuals need for faith and dependence upon God. Krishna says to the devout : dedicate all your actions to me; believe in me and then your works will not produce Karma (sin). You will thus be liberated from rebirth and will join me hereafter in Paradise.

But both *Gita* and *Upanisads* differ from Gnosticism in regarding the soul i.e. the inner nature of the human being—as a single entity. Gnosticism, while defining the human light-spark (pneuma) as identical with the cosmic Light, nonetheless makes a firm distinction between pneuma and psyche—both words being sometimes translated as "soul". Psyche is the life-giving power within a person which includes the mind and the emotions. Pneuma (literally : "breath") is the purely divine element whose sole relation to the person's empirical existence is to produce in him a vague and infocused longing. Gnostic theology explains this longing as the homesickness of the pneuma for its place of origin, its heavenly home. But the *Upanisads* and the *Gita*, theologically less sophisticated than the Gnostic systems, do not divide the "self" into divine and human components. Atman in the Indian texts is the life-giving element within the person (psyche), but the divine element (pneuma) also. The entire universe, like the arche of old Greek philosophy, is considered a living, vital entity. Neither the *Upanisads* nor the *Gita* distinguishes between that portion of the inward self which belongs to this earth (mind or psyche) and that which does not (pneuma). Rather, both belong. For the *Upanisads* the problem of knowledge is to recognize the essence or true nature of the whole (i.e. Brahman) as distinct from its separate manifestations. Moreover, the "self" is the bearer of Karma. Karma, the "deeds" which determine the individual's status in future lives, is par excellence a mode of relation to this earth.

For Buddhists there exists no atman, purush, pneuma or psyche; therefore no alienation is possible between self and world. There every person consists only *dharmas* which are a bundle of energy-points or existence factors. Each dharmas life is just for a moment; each like a spark passing on its flame, ignites the next and disappears in an instant's time. All living beings are subject of this Buddhist theory of Dependent Origination. These dharmas are classified into five groups, or *Skandhas* : form, feeling, perception, will and consciousness. Buddhists dismiss as mere illusion the common sense idea that certain things in this world are permanent.

The Four Noble Truths are the core of Buddhist doctrine : the four Noble Truths state categorically that life in this world denotes suffering and that the cause of suffering is desire for and attachment to the things of this world. The Noble Eight fold path is the means to extinguish suffering and gives directions for the gradual elimination of desire and attachment. The Buddhist argument against attachment, however, is founded only secondarily upon a sense of revulsion from this wicked world. Unlike the Gnostics, who thought the creation of the world by Satan and its domination of everything earthly. Buddhists experience no such feeling of moral offense at the world. The fundamental Buddhist objection to earthly things is either that they are transient or that they are illusory.

It is right to say that Mara, the Buddhist Devil, is in some respects analogous to the figure whom the Gnostics call Satan, Belial, or even Yahweh, the "God of this world". Mara appears often in Buddhist legend as the tempter of Gautama or of other holy men; he rules the realm of sensual pleasures. But this world (which is eternal) has not created by him, nor is he its supreme Lord. Like other Indian deities, Mara is a subordinate being who is neither omniscent, omnipotent nor omnipresent[36]. In some cases Mara is for less important than the Gnostic Satan, who is Darkness embodied. Buddhism would scarcely suffer by the loss of him, whereas the existence of a powerful Devil is central to the entire Gnostic theology.

The closest conceptual analogy between Buddhist and Gnostic thought may lies in the similarity between the Buddhist Nirvana (Englightenment) and the Gnostic supreme Spirit (Light). Both are negative in character, though certainly not exclusively so; however, they are principally described in terms of what they are not. So in Nirvana there is no arising or passing away, no multiplicity, no movement, no suffering. Nirvana can be explained as extinction of the three principal evils of the world: hate, envy and delusion. *Nirvana* is total peace, complete rest. It is a counter-reality, the complete opposite of the everyday world of becoming *(samsara)*. It is a mystery. With this empirical world Nirvana bears no relationship. It is "alien" "wholly other" —just as the God of Gnosticism.

With the development of Mahayana Buddhism the concept of Nirvana began to change. In Mahayana texts Nirvana is increasingly described as a definite ontological category. In metaphysical terms, it is the ultimate Reality which is both transcendent and immanent; Buddhists call it the Buddha-nature, Emptiness, the Void, or Suchness (Tathata). Nirvana eludes every definition and unifies all contradictions. Like the pneuma in Gnosticism, Nirvana also constitutes the inmost nature of the human personality. Thus, the Gnostic redeemer "calls believers to become aware of the pneuma within them" Ch'an (Zen) Buddhism teaches that each person must find the Buddha-nature in himself; Buddhists of the Vijnanavadin-school seek the "reservoir of consciousness" (the world principle) beyond the superficial consciousness of the person.

In the more clear speculations of both Buddhism and Gnosticism, the ultimate nature of being is equated with knowledge. (Indeed, the Buddhist term *jnana*, "knowledge", derives from the same linguistic root as the Greek gnosis). According to Mahayana Buddhism, the universe as it essentially is (i.e. Suchness, the Void etc.) is knowledge, which means Nirvana, or Enlightment. Similarly, Gnostic theology teaches that the supreme spirit exists in a state of pure knowledge. The same is true of the pneumatic souls, the fallen light-fragments, once they have awakened from their sleep. Gnostics and Buddhists conceive of Wisdom (Gnosis*sophia*, Buddhist *prajna*) in analogous fashion: both are feminine and called "mothers" and "nurses"; both are equated with the law of the universe[37].

But according to both Buddhism and Gnosticism, knowledge represents more than the metaphysical Absolute. It is also the salvation bringing principle. Here some differences can be made. On one level, Gnostic knowledge denotes doctrine : the story of the creation of the world, the existence of the light spark or pneuma within the person, and the formulas or magic passwords by which the liberated pneuma, on its journey to God may outwit the devilish guardians of the outer-worldly spheres. This kind of knowledge corresponds to the Buddhist Noble Truths related with the universality of suffering and the path to salvation-teachings which may be intellectually understood, which presuppose a duality between the knower and the known. But the ultimate, salvation - bringing knowledge cannot be acquired through ordinary cognitive processes. Thus, the system of the Egyptian Gnostic Valentinos and his followers describes "perfect salvation" as "the cognition of the ineffable greatness"[38]. Knowledge is equivalent to the ultimate Reality, or salvation. Thus, an intuitive knowledge of the essential, innermost nature of the universe constitues the highest mystic state—a salvation which cannot be differentiate from final truth.

Ignorance is the thing which has covered or veiled the knowledge. In Mahayana Buddhism, knowledge denotes the removal of ignorance[39] ; in Gnosticism it means the awakening of the soul from sleep or drunkenness. In Buddhism the world existence is possible due to ignorance. In at least one form of Gnosticism, i.e. Valentinianism[40], ignorance is the real *cause* of the world (although in Gnosis generally it is the *result* of the divine fall into the lower world). The Valentinians claimed that the supreme Being originally existed in a state of pure knowledge.

Those creations lower down on the scale of existence were ignorant of their forefather. Thus ignorance means a deficiency or perversion of knowledge. The final product of the emanation process is our present world : "the solidified external expression" of the state of ignorance. Conversely, as each person on this earth wins the illumination of knowledge, the effect is of cosmic significance. It contributes to the eventual disappearance of a world created and maintained through ignorance[41].

Like in many forms of Mahayana, in Gnosticism generally, the saving knowledge was allegedly transmitted by a redeemer and accepted by the believer through faith . On the other hand a more optimistic view of human capabilities has been taken by Hinayana Buddhism. It regarded faith as merely an attitude of trust *(shraddha)* in the Buddha and it felt no need for a redeemer. In early Buddhist texts Gautama appears only as a teacher or "path-finder", not a saviour. He shows the way to salvation, but does not claim to lead people there himself.

Within Hinayana, that knowledge which brings liberation from this world can only be gained through a persons' own efforts, i.e. study, a moderate asceticism and meditation.

In Mahayana, there is a different view which placed increasing emphasis on the notion of salvation through faith. Indeed, they stated that salvation through one's own efforts was totally impossible. The new sects generally took as their patron some who was qualified by his spiritual merits to do so or had already entered Nirvana (i.e. a Buddha). Thus Buddhas and Bodhisattvas emerged in the Mahayana sect. Amida, Manjusri, Avalokita and other became objects of extreme devotion, and assumed a redeemer's role as manager of the saving message. The requirement of wide and intensive spiritual preparation for Enlightenment now disappeared. Only a simple, if sincere act of faith in the redeemer was necessary.

The best beloved of these redeemer-Buddhas was Amida (Amitabha) whose distinguishing characteristic was his all-embracing compassion. Sects devoted to Amida-worship gained tremendous popularity in the Buddhist world, especially in Japan. The older ideals of asceticism and long meditation had made Buddhism accessible mainly to monks; salvation-through-faith made it a layman's religion. The compassionate Buddhas and Bodhisatvas allegedly permitted such short-cuts only as a necessary but regrettable concession to the weakness of humankind in this late, degenerate age when salvation through personal effort is no longer possible.

It is common that the development of salvation by-faith doctrines went hand in hand with the elevation of the redeemers to supernatural status. In early (Hinyana) Buddhism Gautama was no divinity, but a more human being, though one far advanced in spiritual knowledge. But the Mahayana regarded its Buddhas and Bodhisattvas as divine beings residing in supernatural realms. When they comes on this earth they assume human figure : but their bodies are phantoms. The Gnostic saviour was likewise purely divine : his human appearance was illusory. But while the Gnostic saviour was generally regarded as a unique personality in Buddhism he was multipled many times over. The Buddhas and Bodhisattvas are many in numbers.

Gnostic theory told of multiple emanations from God, innumerable ages, heavens and planetary realms, while the Mahayana boasted an enormous pantheon of Buddhas and Bodhisattavas. Essentially all these emanations were secondary deities, some of which played key roles in their respective systems. Thus the God Hermes (Thoth) is supposed to have founded the Egyptian Gnostic sect of Hermetics. Two key Gnostic treatises, the *Poimandres* and *Pistis Sophia*, are stated respectively to the "Mind of the Absolute" and to the "Risen Christ". In the same way, all the Mahayana scriptures allegedly were written by Buddhas and Bodhisattvas. Both Gnosticism and Mahayana Buddhism borrowed lavishly from legends originally associated with older deities and reinterpreted them in light of their own distinctive theology[42].

Finally, the belief in metempsychosis is common to Gnosticism and all the major Indian religions. The Gnostic light fragment (pneuma, soul) which fails to free itself from the "sleep" of bondage to this earth will be unable to rise to its origin or heavenly home. It has to live many earthly lives. In this respect both the Gnostic and Indian thoughts differ utterly from the Christian one which assumes a single life for each soul. But Gnostic soul-wandering and Indian metempsychosis are nonetheless not similar. In Indian thought, a person's acts in this life determine the character of his future births. Gnosticism could not make this connection between present deeds and future births. Although performance of the sacraments and an ascetic life-style may help in the soul's liberation, the Gnostics in general showed little interest in the soul's future lives on earth. The Indian follower, unless far advanced in spiritual knowledge, is unlikely to aspire to immediate liberation, rather he hopes for a higher status in the next life and a gradual ascent to salvation through many lives. More passimistic, the Gnostic feels that no possible earthly life is worth striving for. On the other hand, he demonstrates a quite un-Indian optimism in believing that the soul is capable of attaining final liberation immediately after this current life.

So, these are the countless similarities which gives an idea that there was a possibility of Indian influence upon Gnosticism. In chronological order all the major Indian systems were ancient. The *Upanisads* and the *Bhagavad Gita*, Buddhism, Jainism and probably Samkhya all arose in India long before Gnosticism took form in the Hellenistic world. Unfortunately, there is little direct evidence for Indian influence upon any of the Gnostic sects. We can trace the Indian Gnostic connection mainly upon the general similarities between the two, and on this possibility that Indian religious ideas might had accompanied Indian merchants, ambassadors and holy men into the Hellenistic world.

REFERENCES

1. Radhakrishnan, S., *Eastern Religion Western Thought*, p.198.
2. Professor W. Bousset,"Gnosticism",*Encyclopaedia Britannica,* IIth ed.
3. Kennedy, "Buddhist Gnosticism",*JRAS,* 1902, p. 383.
4. Kennedy, "Buddhist Gnosticims",*JRAS*, 1902, pp. 411-12.
5. Radhakrishnan, S., *op. cit.,* p. 206.
6. King, C.W., *The Gnostics and Their Remains Ancient and Mediaeval,* 2nd ed. 1887. p. XIV.
7. Rawlinson, H.G., *Intercourse Between India and the Western World,* New Delhi, 1992, p.177.
8. Wilson, R. Mcl., *The Gnostic Problem,* London, 1958, pp. 32-33.
9. Sedlar, J.W., *India and the Greek World,* p.126.
10. Wilson, R.Mcl. *op. cit.*, pp. 39-197.
11. Sedlar, J.W., *op. city.*, p.127; Kazanas, N., "Advaita and Gnosticism" in *Indian Historical Review*, volume XXXII, No. 1, (Jan. 2005), ICHR, New Delhi, 2005, p. 221.
12. Wilson, R.Mcl., *op. cit.,* p. 223.
13. Josephus, Flaviius, "*The Jewish War,*" 11.119, in Josephus (Loeb) 11, 369; Kazanas, N., "Advaita and Gnosticism" in *Indian Historical Review,* Volume XXXII, No,. 1, (Jan. 2005), ICHR, New Delhi, 2005, p. 225.
14. Larson, Gerald James, *Samkhya Karika* XXI, in *Classical Samkhya; An Interpretation of Its History and Meaning*, Delhi, 1969, pp.258-99.
15. *Ibid*, I, p. 257; Kazanas, N., "Advaita and Gnosticism" in *Indian Historical*

Review, Volume XXXII, No. 1, (Jan 2005), ICHR, New Delhi, 2005, p. 209.

16. J. W. Sedlar, *op. cit.*, p. 131; Kazanas, N., "Advaita and Gnosticism" *op. cit.*, p.208.
17. Jones, W., *Works* (Quarto edition), 1799, 1, pp 360-61 quoted in Gopal Lallanji " Samkhya and Greek Philosophy" in *Graeco-Indica: India's Cultural Contacts with the Greek World,* edited by U.P. Arora, Delhi.1991.
18. Garbe, R., *The Philosophy of Ancient India*, pp. 56-57, quoted in Gopal, Lallanji, *op. cit.* p. 242.
19. *Samkhya Philosophie,* p.p. 113-37 quoted in Lallanji Gopal, *op. cit.,* p. 252.
20. *The Philosophy of Ancient India,* quoted in Lalanji Gopal, *op. cit.,* p. 252.
21. *Samkhya Philosophie*, quoted in Lallanji Gopal, *op. cit.,* p. 252.
22. Keith, A.B. " Pythagoras and Transmigration." *JRAS,* 1909, p. 252.
23. Sedlar, J.W., *op. cit.,* p. 22, 24, 124-25, 129, 131.
24. *Ibid.*, p. 126-27, 284-85.
25. Fillozat , J. "Ancient India and Graeco Roman World", *Proceedings of the Fifth World Sanskrit Conference,* p. 836-37.
26. Sedlar, J.W., *op. cit.,* p. 124-25, 285.
27. Rawlinson, H.G. *op. cit.,* p.158.
28. Sedlar, J.W., *op.cit.*, p.158.
29. Keith, A.B., *A History of the Samkhya Philosophy,* p.79; J. Takakusu, *JRAS,* 1905, p. 33.
30. Velvalkar in *Bhadarkar Commemoration Volume,* p. 178; Shastri, U.V., *Samkhyadarshan ka Itihasa*, p. 537.
31. Shastri, U.V., *op. cit.,* pp. 93-343.
32. Larson, G.J., *Classical Samkhya,* pp. 99-139.
33. *Mahabharata,* XII. 275.16.
34. Wilson, *Gnostic Problem,* p. 40; Kazanas, N., "Advaita and Gnosticism", *op. cit.,* p. 205.
35. Quispel, " Gnostische Anthropos" pp. 204.
36. Mathew Black, *The Scrolls and Christian Origins,* New York, 1961, p.166.
37. Josephus, 'Jewish War', II. 133-42 (Loeb), II, 373-77.
38. *Ibid.*, II, 151-52 (Loeb) II, 381.
39. Pliny, *Natural History*, V, XV, 73(Leob) II., 277.
40. Radhakrishnan, S., *op. cit.,* p. 205.
41. Dupont Sommer. A. *The Essene Writings from Qumran*, Oxford, 1961, p. 359-60, 371.
42. *Ibid*, p. 114; Kazanas, N., "Advaita and Gnosticism", *op. cit.,* p. 200.

NEOPLATONISM AND INDIAN THOUGHT

In the Neoplatonism of Plotinos, (A.D. 205-70) we have the fruits of the religious syncritism which arose from the conquests of Alexander, the Great and the undertakings of the Roman Empire. It revived the mystic tradition of the Greek cults and its resemblances not only to Alexandrian Judaism but to Vedanta philosophy are well-known, Ritter introduces his account of Neoplatonic philosophy with his general title "Diffusion of Oriental modes of thought among the Greeks"[1].

The following are the chief points of the system. The original essence is pure being and absolute causality. It is also the good in so far as everything finite is to find its aim in it a being without magnitude, without life, without thought. One should not even call it existence. It is something above existence and above goodness, and at the same time an operative force without any substratum. As operative force it is continually begetting something else, without being itself changed or moved or diminished. The first principle is perfect self-sufficiency[2].

Plotinos (205-70 A.D.) the founder of Neo-Platonism explained the universe in a manner complex, abstruse and logical, though comprehensible only to an educated minority of Greeks. His system has certain affinities with the Indian religions; and Plotinos himself made a serious effort to visit India to learn from the Brahmins. Thus, the possibility exists that Neo-platonism owes something to Indian influences.

Plotinos himself spent much of his life at Alexandria, where he was presumably in contact with the important intellectual currents of his time. Originally from Lykopolis (Asyut) on the Nile he was probably a Hellenized Egyptian[3], which suggests that his philosophy may bear some traces of native Egyptian thought patterns. As a young man he went to Alexandria to study philosophy, but was dissatisfied with all his teachers there until he discovered Ammonios Sakkas, whose student he remained for eleven years[4].Various attempts have been made to interpret the designation of "Sakkas" is most probably the variant of "Shakya"—the name of the Buddha's tribe in India, or might mean (Indian) monk in general. To suggest that Ammonios was either an Indian or a Greek of Buddhist sympathies seems presumptuous; yet linguistic arguments indicate that "Sakkas" is more likely to mean "Shakya" than anything else. We know there were Buddhist at Alexanderia during his lifetime; so it is not impossible. According to Porphyrios, Plotinos as a mature thinker propounded the system he had learned from Ammonios[5]. Thus, we do not even know to what extent Plotinos was original......

Unquestionably he demonstrated more than just a passing interest in Indian wisdom. Wishing to seek knowledge at first hand from the Magi of Persia and the Brahmins of India, he attached himself to the army with which the Roman emperor Gordianus III was about to march into Asia. Nonetheless, in embarking upon so dangerous an adventure at the mature age of 39, Plotinos must have had some definite notion of the content of Indian (and Persian) philosophy. Presumably he had acquired this at Alexandria, the most cosmopolitan city of the age. Perhaps too he was influenced by the prevalent Hellenistic view that the divine revelation had first appeared in the East, or that Brahmins, Magi, Egyptians or Hebrews had furnished the sources for Greek philosophy. For an Alexandrian thinker of the 3rd century to attempt to visit India merely establishes him as a product of his times.

Plotinos philosophical ideas are recorded in 54 treatises, now arranged into six sets of nine; or *Enneads*. All were written in his late middle age. When he was 50, Plotinos went to Rome, where he held philosophical lectures open to the public, the *Enneads* are apparently their result[6]. They are not systematic expositions of doctrine; each one already presupposes knowledge of the entire system[7].

The central concepts of Plotinos' philosophy are : (1) the infinity of the knowable world, and (2) the unity of the human soul with the essential, underlying nature of the universe. Both are exceptional in Greek philosophy. The Greeks viewed the cosmos as a limited and defined structure (thus a sphere was considered the perfect form). However, certain notions suggestive of Plotinos' ideas about the soul do occur in the thought of some of his predecessors[8].

However, Plotinos' philosophy belongs to the dominant Greek tradition both in its rationalistic ordering of principles and in the importance it attaches to intelligence (*Nous*) as the spiritual principal prevading the universe. For Plotinos the world is a fixed intellectual order, a hierarchy extending downward from the Supreme Being—the One—through the Intelligence, the World-Soul, and finally the world of the senses. As such it connects the lowest forms of physical life with the highest forms of spirituality. Souls are the organizing forces in physical bodies and also their governors; thus every natural force is a soul[9]. He considered individual souls as parts of the World Soul, but not in the same sense in which physical particles constitute separate portions of a larger corporeal whole. Plotinos' World-Soul is pure spirit. Its power arises from its ability to contemplate and penetrate the higher orders of being, firstly the Intelligence and finally the One.

It is difficult to understand the relation of souls to bodies, in the system of Plotinos. His master Plato taught two different theories on this subject. Plotinos is similarly contradictory. On the one hand, he supposes that souls leap downward into bodies through their audacity and desire for independence, attracted by their own images. Association with the body produces the soul's impurity and vices. On the other hand, he regards the production of living bodies as a natural function of the soul owing to her desire to be fruitful, to adorn what is below her, and to develop her power[10]. Association of body and soul is therefore good and necessary. Some commentators have suggested that both the views of Plotinos were close to reality. As a religious thinker, he was conscious of the soul's need to abstract itself from material attachments in order to attain moral purity and ultimately to experience the mystic union with God. But as a metaphysician he regarded the existing structure of the universe as valid and necessary[11].

Directly above the World-Soul in Plotinos' scheme of things is the intelligence, including all things in the universe as well as the fixed, eternal relations among them. The intelligence is the cosmic order, the essence of everything, the totality of all cosmic realities, and the collectivity of the Platonic ideas. It is both one and many. Moreover, intelligence is a spiritual as well as a rational principle. Through contemplation the soul may attain a mystic vision of the various portions of the cosmic system, seen in their essential nature. In this way the individual soul can make intelligence prevail in itself. Thereby it ascends to the Supreme Inelligence which is its own higher principle.

Beyond the Intelligence lies the One, the ultimate source of all beings and the principle of cosmic unity. All things proceed from the One, which overflows to produce multiplicity. But whereas the supreme intelligence is unified by the system and order which binds the individual intelligences, the One is in no way multiple. It is the equivalent of Plato's supreme Idea, the Idea of the Good. Only by direct intuition can it be known, not through any intellectual or rational processes. The soul ascends to the One by way of the Intelligence, having prepared itself by a virtuous life and acts of purification. As it rises, it loses the characteristics which formerly bound it to the body. All normal conciousness disappears, because consiousness demands multiple objects. In this culminating mystic experience an immoveable calmness reigns. Their is neither knower or known; the soul is alone with God[12]. He felt that priests and temples, ceremonies and prayers were all superfluous. The soul could ascend by its own efforts, and the mystic vision would arrive as a consequence.

Plotinos undermines, with his distinct vision of the One, a principle that had apparently been fundamental to Greek thought that the limited and finite is the perfect, while the unlimited and infinite is the imperfect. In contrast, Plotinos claims infinity, unlimitedness and formlessness to be the One's nature, and then calls the ultimate ground. Plotinos here unveils a new awareness in western thinking, that of a positive infinity, no longer viewing indeterminateness as an imperfection. And because of this absolute transcendence of the One the most appropriate analysis of the One is a negative analysis[13].

It is Plotinos's refusal to give ultimate status to form, individually and intelligence that radically sets him apart from the Greek tradition in which he operated. For the purpose of transition, let us again locate Plotinos's attitude toward intelligence. There seem to be two aspects of intelligence. First, there is the articulated system of definite notions, the intelligible order, the fixed model of the sensible order. This is the Greek and generally the western emphasis. Secondly we find thought directed toward itself, where subject-object distinctions disappear, and where finally intelligence is transcended and the self is merged with the universal principle. This seems foreign to Greek and most of western thought. The first considers rational knowledge of the universe, the second considers a mystical union of beings in the One. The relation of the individual to the universal had always been a Greek problem. But Plotinos moved to show that the universal is present in its entirely in all things without losing its universality. He no longer sought rational knowledge of the universal, but a mystical union where individual consciousness disappears. This is a withdrawal from particular forms, and all ethical and intellectual aspects of the soul, where the self is lost in contemplation. And it is generally this emphasis on contemplation as the ultimate reality that most conclusively connects Plotinos with the thought of India.

The *Upanisads* are fundamental to the philosophy of India. Each different form of Indian thought has always had to reconcile itself with them. With the coming of the *Upnisads*, Vedic hymns and rites were replaced by a search for the one reality behind all flux. This was also a movement from the "objective" to the "subjective". The key to the one is found within the depths of the human self. The *Upanisads* often criticize ritualistic religion : liberation is an internal, not external experience. The goal of the liberated self is not the bliss of a heaven or rebirth in a better world, but freedom from the objective, *Karma* and union with the Absolute, which is not in any "state".[14]

Absolute being is not an existing quality or object of thought. It transcends all attempts to grasp it, as it is the source of all manifestations. It can only be described negatively, as the formless, nameless, etc. In relation to concrete beings, it is non-being, but in itself it is the fullness of Being. In the *Maitri U.* (VI.3) we find that Brahman has two aspects, the formless and the formed. Though Brahman can take form, in the world, the formless is the fundamental reality, the "cause" of the formed effect. And in the *Brhad-araṇyaka U.* we hear the statement at IV.5.15 that Brahman is *neti neti*, not this not that.

As in Plotinian thought, this absolute transcendence of Brahman demands that it be beyond intellect. Mind and sense, which operate through subject-object distinctions, are misleading, are *avidya* or "ignorance", if blind to the intuitive level of vidya or "wisdom" which characterizes "knowledge" of Brahman. If the Real is seen as an object of knowledge, it cannot be known. True knowledge or *vidya* is an integral creative activity of spirit knowing nothing external to it. Truth is not an expression or reflection of reality, it is reality itself. The*Mundaka U.* (I.1.4) distinguishes between two kinds of knowledge, higher and lower, *para vidya* and *apara vidya*. This distinction seems to correspond to the Plotinian distinction between "knowledge" or vision of unity and knowledge of multiplicity. *Para vidya* is a knowledge of imperishable Being; *apara vidya* is a knowledge of perishable beings. The latter is not false; one can seek Brahman in a particularized manner, yet if it is sought merely as particular and not grounded in *para vidya*, the result is still bondage and ignorance. It seems that *apara vidya* culminates in intellect and *para vidya* manifests as vision, an experience. Again this corresponds to the difference between Nous and the vision of the One. One can understand the *Vedas* and the teachings on Brahman, but this understanding will always be insufficient without the actual *experience* of one's ground, the vision, the clarity of illumination. One can know God only by becoming godlike, not by thinking about God (thus the importance in Indian religion of yoga, or non-theoretical techniques to further expanded *experience*).

The *Kena U.* states that :

> To whomsoever it is not known, to him it is known : to whomsoever it is known, he does not know. It is not understood by those who understand it; it is understood by those who do not understand it (*Kena U.* II. 3).

In the *Svetaśvatara U.* (I.1) we find that Brahman is the cause of all things. So Brahman as cause is Brahman as *Iśvara*, or Lord, the principle of creation. Isvara is the creator working through the power of *māya*. Brahman in relation to the world is Isvara; but Brahman's absolute nature transcends Isvara. This corresponds to Plotinos's notion that the One in relation to the universe is Nous, the divine Ideas as source of the universe.

Therefore, as the *Māndukya U.* tells us (2), Brahman has four quarters, this can be analysed as four levels of being : (1) A transcendence prior to any concrete reality, Absolute Brahman; (2) A causal foundation of all differentiation, Iśvara or cause—Brahman; Iśvara is looked on as prajna, a supreme intelligence which holds all things in an undifferentiated condition, a divine wisdom which sees things as a primordial whole, unlike human reason which sees things in parts and relations; (3) An interior essence of the world, a World-Soul, effect—Brahman, called Brahma or Hirañya-garbha. This World-Soul emanates from Iśvara, the creator (*Śvetaśvatara U.* III.4; VI.8; *Mundaka U.*I.19); (4) A manifest world of multiplicity, called *virāj*. These are four coexistent sides of one reality. The Absolute is not a sum of these, or an elimination of any. It is an ineffable unity in the midst of which conceptual distinctions are possible, but only to serve *our* understanding. Brahman has strict distinctions only phenomenally.

Now, if we look back over these four aspects of reality and compare them with the Plotinian realms; (1) One, the absolute, undifferentiated, formless source; (2) Nous, the divine ideas, principle of creation; (3) World-Soul, the agent of creation; (4) the sense world-we find a remarkable similarity of structure.

So the levels of being as described in the *Upanisads* can be expressed through the following equations :

1. A = *Viśva* = waking state = external objects = *Viraj* = world;
2. U = *taijasa* - dream state = internal objects = *Hiraṅyagarbha* - World-Soul.
3. M = *Prajna* - dreamless state = mass of cognition, wisdom = *Iśvara* = creator;
4. Silence = *tūriya* = transcendental state = source of all = *Brahman* = place.

And these levels can easily be seen to correspond to Plotinos's stages of reality:

1. Sense world and the individual soul immersed in its externality;
2. World-soul creating the world from within itself;
3. Nous, the creative principle, unity of divine Ideas;
4. One, undifferentiated source of all.

The *Upanisads* thus teach the intimate unity of the self of man and Brahman. The wise see God abiding in their self (*Śvetāśvatara U.* VI.12). The knower of Brahman becomes merged with Brahman. The individual self sees its true reality as the source of all (*Kāivalya U.* 20-23). It is the task of the individual Self to become the Universal Self, and this is not attainable through the *Vedas*, intellectual knowledge, discipline or brain power (*Subala U.* IX.15), but only through a union[15].

This union is the transformation of the soul, the absorption in the divine, seeing one's self in all beings and all beings in one's self (*Isa U.*6). One who realizes this is released from sorrow, as all sorrow results from duality. The self loses itself, casting off all name and form it enters into the unmanifest (*Mundaka U.* III.2.8). Such is a release from the cycle of birth and death. The wheel of time and change, the achieving of the state *Kaivalya*, aloneness (*Kaivalya U.*25). All of this of course corresponds to Plotinos's flight of the alone to the Alone.

In its initial condition, sometimes the soul is depicted as wandering about, thinking itself different from Brahman, looking on multiplicity as its sole reality (*Śvetaśvatara U.* 1.6). This is quite similar to Plotinos's image of the soul wandering through the sense world. Union with Brahman cures the soul of this *avidya*, or individuality seen in itself independent of its ground, and brings about *vidya*, or awareness of Brahman. This *avidya-vidya* scheme is somewhat comparable to the Plotinion fall-return imagery. Sorrow is seen as the helplessness, resulting from being lost in the objective world; salvation involves getting beyond object-thinking to the realm of pure Being (*Svetasavatara U.* IV. 7).

We have been able to see deep similarities of thought between Plotinos and the *Upanisads*. We find the soul initially trapped in a fallen awareness, attending to multiplicity and change as the only reality. The task of soul is to purify and deepen its awareness to reveal the absolute, formless source behind these manifestations. And this awareness is not external but internal, found at the depths of the soul. The soul is this Absolute at its depths, hence its individuality is transcended, individuality as an ultimate principle is transcended. The world is an emanation (immanence) of a formless ground (transcendence) form is not the ultimate reality, it must ultimately deny itself, transcend itself, and return to its ground. This is the process of reality, that of emanation and return, reflected in the thought of Plotinos and the *Upanisads* in a noticeably similar fourfold organization.[16]

Now we would discuss the fundamental doctrines of Neoplatonism which are similar to Indian doctrines.

The One : In Neoplatonism, the One is another name for God. It is the Absolute spirit. It is pure being and the absolute causality. It is also the "Good". Everything finite finds its aim in it and flowsback into it[17]. It has no attributes at all; it is a being which has no magnitude, which has no life, which has no thought. It excludes all knowledge; Plotinos says, "imagine a well (pegi) without origin; it gives itself to all rivers; but it is not diminished by that; it remains quietly in itself[18]. It gives us an idea of the absolute described in the peace chant of the Hindu purnam, where plenitude proceeds from plenitude yet it remains plenitude undiminished and undisturbed[19].

***Emanation* (Creation)** : Plotinos says that since all things, even those without life, impart of themselves what they can, the most perfect cannot remain in itself but must pass over. Hence, the creation is not something different from the Absolute. It is the overflow of the Absolute. He compares the Absolue with an overflowing spirit which by its excess gives rise to that which comes after it[20], or a central source of light which illumines all things[21]. It can be compared with the Hindu concept of *Lila*. Both Plotinos and the *Upanisads* hold that God does not disperse Himself in individual or natural things. There is a continual process from first to last, but the cause remains itself as it was[22].

Nous : Nous is the first emanation of the original essence. It is a complete image of the original essence and archetype of all existing things. Mind knows its objects not like perception of external things, but as one with itself[23]. As this unity involves the duality of thinking and being thought, it is not the highest but the second in order of supermundane causes. It is being and thought at the same time. As image the Nous is equal to the original essence, as derived it is completely different from it. It is for Plotinos the highest sphere the human spirit can reach and at the same time pure thought itself. This doctrine of Nous may be compared with the personal (*Saguna*) *Brahman* of the *Upanisads.*

Soul : The soul is an immaterial substance like Nous, its image and product. It stands between the Nous and the world of phenomena. It is the principle of life and motion in things. It is of two kinds: the World Soul and the individual soul. The first can be compared with the doctrine of *Hiranyagarbha* of the *Upanisads* and the second with the *jivatman*. Like the *Upanisads*, Plotinos maintains that the soul can return to itself through the practice of virtues and ascetic purification.

When soul release from the body it dwells in God which is reality and true being. It is a world which cannot be seen with our physical eyes[24].

Hule: It has been described by Plotinos as "matter" and in many other ways. It is the same as evil, "privation" "a lie", a phantom.[25] It is indeterminate nothing and yet not nothing. It can be compared with the doctrine of *maya* which is appearance yet not a mere blank. It is something positive. In the words of Puech, it is magical and illusory. Being the product of matter this sensible world is also a mere illusion[26].

Rebirth : Plotinos, like the *Upanisads*, believes in the doctrine of rebirth. For him even animals have souls. So long as we do not attain the highest widom we are bound to successive rebirths, which are like one dream after another or sleep in different beds[27].

Law of Karma : Plotinos says law of *Karma* is a universal principle that each soul after death goes where it longs to be. Those who have exercised their human faculties are born as men; those who have lived a sensuous life are born as lower animals.[28] He also refers to the absorption of disembodied souls in the Universal soul, and this can be reached through an ascetic and contemplative life.

It is common in both Plotinos and Upanisads that through the analytic process of the dialectic, the mind reaches its cherished goal and after reaching it becomes quiescent and unified. It is supreme unity which is beyond even self-knowledge. Here the soul loses its identity and becomes "One". In the words of Plotinos :

> But in the vision that which sees is not reason but something greater than and prior to reason, something presupposed by reason as is the object of vision. He who then sees himself when he sees will see himself as a simple being, will be united to himself as such, will feel himself, become such. We ought not even to say that he will see, but he will be that which he sees, if indeed. It is possible any longer to distinguish between seer and seen, and not bodily to affirm that the two are one[29].

Like the *Upanisadic* philosophy Neoplatonism believes in the technique of entering into spiritual consciousness. Through Meditation we can free the soul from its subjection to the body and attain union with the Divine. In order to attain this union we must strip everything of the body until the vision is attained. We must abstract from the body, from the soul, from sense perceptions, appetites and emotions, and from even the intellect with its duality. Then the soul touches and gazes on the supreme light. In this account we may see a replica of the Indian theory of contemplation[30]. Porphyry tells that during the period of five years when he lived with Plotinos, Plotinos was four times in union with God. Likewise he laid more emphasis on *Jnana* (wisdom and contemplation) than on*karma* or ritual ceremonies and looked upon *Karma* as an enfeebled product of contemplation; and in the true spirit of mystic systems he rose above the political barriers of nations and states[31].

Porphyry and other Neoplatonic philosophers also followed the path carved by their great teacher-Plotinos.

Porphyry (AD. 230-300) popularized the teachings of Plotinos. For him the aim of philosophy is the salvation of the soul. The source of evil is not so much in the body as in the desires of the soul. Strict ascetisim is enjoined. Porphyry advocates abstinence from animal food in his *De Abstinentia*, which is a treatise against the eating of animal food. He gives an account of some Indian views on the authority of Bardesanes, who derived his information from an Indian embassy to the Imperial court early in the third century.

Iamblichus, who died in the reign of constantine, about A.D. 330, was considerably influenced by Pythagoras, Plato, and Plotinos, though he converted Neoplatonism into a theurgic spiritualism. He lived at the time of the collapse of the ancient world, when life tended to be oppressive and futile and the sense of man's unworthiness increased. Man could obtain unification with the central source not by his own efforts but by theurgic practices which must be performed correctly-Mystical exercises and even magical ceremonies as expounded by Iamblichus got into the Christian Church and practice.

Ascetic and contemplative virtue is rated higher than the practical. Proclus gave a somewhat devotional orientation to the Neoplantonism of Plotinos. Prayer for Plotinos was the turning of the mind to God; to Proclus it was humble supplication for divine aid. The self-sufficiency for which the attainment of bliss lay in man's unaided capacity gives place to a dependence on God. Proclus found a place for gods above the Nous and immediately below the One. He had superstitious respect for theurgy. He agrees with Iamblichus in thinking that individual things are united to the one by the mysterious operation of the occult "symbols" which reside in certain stones, herbs, and animals. While Plotinos and Porphyry believe more in human wisdom and spiritual vision, Iamblichus and Proclus are impressed by the blessings of divination and the purifying powers in initiation. Proclus accepts ecstatic experiences[32].

In the hands of Plotinos successors, Neo-platonism gradually lost much of its rationalist quality. Increasingly it emphasized ritual and ascetic practices, and assimilated itself to the ways of Oriental mystery-religions. While the fundamental impulse of assisting the soul's ascent remained, the means for doing so became increasingly magical in nature. The later Neo-Platonist school attached great importance to a book known as the *Chaldaean Oracles*. All the major Neo-

Platonist thinkers after Plotinos were devoted to this book. Prophyrios in the late 3rd century and Iamblichos in the 4th edited commentaries upon it. In the 5th century Proklos and Timaeus were the two most valuable books in the whole world[33].

While even Plotinos' system has important analogies with Gnosticism, the Neo-Platonism of his successors resembles it far more. Plotinos had assumed three principles of the intelligible world order—the One, the Intelligence and the World—Soul but subsequent Neo—Platonists added a multiplicity of other creations. They postulated a series of angels, demons and heroes forming an uninterrupted chain, beginning in heaven and progressively degenerating into the realm of nature. The soul they regarded as a spark of the original divine fire, which is defiled by contact with matter and thus becomes the slave of destiny. But through piety and incontations it can liberate itself.

The popular influence of the Neo-Platonist school after the 3rd century rested more upon its religious and occult practices than on the philosophy of Plotinos, its greatest representative. Plotinos' system was too difficult and intellectual and his life-style too self-contained, ever to appeal to masses of people. He felt, for instance, that organized religion was unnecessary. When on one occassion a disciple suggested that they attend temple services, Plotinos replied : "It is the business of those divinities to come and visit me and not mine to attend on them."[34] He practices only a modest asceticism because he felt that ordinary virtue cannot cause the soul to become assimilated to the divine[35]. But his student and close associate Porphyrios-whose great service to Western philosophy was the popularization of Plotinos' ideas - already abandoned this attitude. Porphyrios felt that ritual observances were important.

Porphyrios, in his book, describes abstinence from meat as a tenet of the Indian "*Brachmanai*" and "*Samanaioi*" : "to touch animal food, is considered by them as equivalent to extreme impurity and impiety". Porphyrios notes with approval that these

Indian holy men "are so disposed with respect to death, that they unwillingly endure the whole time of the present life...... and therefore they hasten to liberate their souls from the bodies (with which they are connected)"[36].

The Neo-platonist turn to cult practices and asceticism became even more prominent in Iamblichos, the best known of Porphyrios' disciples whereas in Porphyrios' writings philosophy still dominates over religion, Iamblichos made the "*Chaldaean Oracles*" into his principal guide to the purification of souls. He felt that even the mystic ecstasy could be produced by occult ceremonies and ritual acts.

Iamblichus[37] accepted Plotinos's teachings with little variation. He asserted that man could obtain unification with the central source (God) not by his own efforts but by theurgic practices which must be performed correctly.

Proclus teaches that beyond all bodies is the soul's essence; beyond the souls is the intellective principle; and beyond all intellectual substances is the One. The soul is incorporeal and independent of the body and therefore imperishable. He accepted the Neoplatonic trinity and explained the existence of the universe along Plotinian lines.

Like mystics proclus advocates world citizenship. His saying, "the philosopher ought not to observe the religious customs of one city or country but ought to be the common hierophant of the whole world", reminds us of the *Vasudhaiva Kutumbakam* of Indian philosophy. He had superstitious respect for theurgy. He agrees with Iamblichus that individual things are united to the "One" by the mysterious operation of the occult symbols which reside in certain stones, herbs and animals[38].

Apart from these doctrines there are some other ones which have striking resemblances with the doctrines of Indian philosophy. For instance, the three hypostases of Plotinos resemble three bodies of Buddha[39]. The Neoplatonic comparison of divine activity to the effortless and unpremeditated radiation of light by the sun reminds us of the description of *Brahman* in *Upanisads* and of Buddha in the

Buddhist texts[40]; and the doctrine of *Kenodoxia* (emptiness)[41] is a counterpart of the Upanisadic doctrine of *Avidya,* or "Ignorance". The Hypocratical treatise "On Winds" resembles the more ancient doctrine of *Prana* which forms a well known topic of the *Taittiriya Upanisad*[42]. The *Maitri Upanisad* stresses that we have to destroy our *abhimana* and get rid of the sheaths hiding the self[43]. A medical theory in Plato's *Timaeus* resembles Indian medical theories[44]. The duration of the Heracleitian "Great Year" (10-8) is a decimal fraction which is based on Indian calculation[45]. The doctrine of the infinity of *Brahman* and the world, and the doctrine of identity between God and soul and between knowledge and *Brahman* are well-known topics of the *Upanisads.*

We can trace some elements of Vedic origin in Philostratus's *Life of Appollonius of Tyana*. There are references to Avamedha, to Vedic rites, and to Yogic powers. There are certain striking resemblances in the matter of passage to Heaven. In the*Rgveda*, heaven is the home of the soul to which, after death, it returns purified; before reaching Heaven it has to cross a stream and pass by Yama's watchful dogs, "the spotted dogs of Sarama". Further, the cradle of Neoplatonism was not the quiet university town of Athens, but the great manufacturing city of Alexandria which was at that time not only a great intellectual centre but also the place where East and West rubbed their shoulders, where the wisdom of Asia was in high repute and where men of wisdom like Philostratus expressed the highest veneration for the learning of the Indians and even went to India to consult the Brahamanas.[46]

The scholars who try to find the hypostases of Plotinos in the "Trinity" of Plato and the simile of One and the sun in the *Republic* and other Platonic dialogues; the doctrine of *Kenodoxia* in Parmenides; the doctrine of infinity of*Brahman* and world in Melissus's "Being", in Anaxagoras "Nous", and in Heracleitus's "Soul"; and then emphatically assert that Neoplantonism is a legitimate development of Greek thought and Plato's own speculations—forget the fact that these philosophers were also influenced by Indian thought through Orphicism and Pythagoreanism.

In fact, the philosophy of Plato and even that of his independent disciple Aristotle was a kind of splendid digression from the main current of Greek speculation. Plato's growing sympathy with Orphic and Pythagorean teachings; the devoutness and solemnity of his later attitude towards religion; the ethical rigorism of his old age, with its strongly marked ascetic tendency, his interest in Oracles and demons and the momentary appearance of an "evil soul" in the*Timaeus* all point the way the wind was blowing. Iamblichus, the biographer of, Pythagoras and one of the greatest philosophers of Neoplatonism, clearly admitted that Plato, Aristotle and he himself were all Pythagoreans.

So we may say that some of the fundamental doctrines of Neoplatonism which have striking similarities with the doctrines of Indian philosophy were well-established in the *Upanisads* at least in the 6th century B.C. long before the rise of Neoplatonism.

In the words of Dr. Inge, "the Platonic or the mystical outlook on life for which religion is at once a philosophy and a discipline" was first felt in Asia especially in the *Upanisads* and Buddhism[47] and it influenced the entire Greek culture. In fact, Greek culture rose against an oriental background from which it was never isolated save in the minds of classical scholars"[48]. Tarn is also of the same view. According to him, "Egyptian, Persian and Indian cultural influences were absorbed into the Greek world from very early times"[49]. In the words of Prof. Mayer, we may conclude that though alien in origin, alien to the spirit of Hellenism, predominantly Indian in character and content, walking in the shadow without support from the state, the Orphic the Eleusinian, and the Pythagorean brotherhoods and the Platonic schools prepared the way for later Platonism and for certain elements in catholic the ology[50].

In the presence of these historical data we may conclude that Indian thought might have played a great part in the development of the doctrines of Neoplatonism, and that Neoplatonism might be the result of the religious syncretism which arose from the conquests of Alexander, the Great and the undertakings of the Roman Empire.[51] Modern ontologists also support the above conclusion and hold that all the resemblances between the similes used by Greek and Indian writers cannot be explained simply by reflection on earlier Greek ideas[52].

The elements of asceticism and unworldliness in Neoplatonism appealed strongly to the Fathers and Doctors of the Christian Church. Neoplatonism was an early influence on Christian thinkers. The philosophy was firmly joined with Christianity by St. Augustine, who was a Neoplatonist before his conversion. It was through Neoplatonism that Augustine conceived of spirit as being immaterial and viewed evil as an unreal substance (in contradistinction to Manichaean doctrine). The early Christian prelate St. Augustine, in his *Confessions*, acknowledged the contribution of Neoplatonism to Christianity and indicated the profound influence exerted by its doctrine on his own religious thinking. The Christian apologists *Clement of Alexendria* and Origen had vied with the incipient Neoplatonic tradition for control of the Platonic heritage. The writings of Pseudo-Dionysius and Boethius display Neoplatonic influences. In the Middle Ages, elements of Plotinos' thought can be found in St. Thomas Aquinas and John Scotus Erigena, particularly in the identification of the One with God and the Divine Mind with the angels. The system influenced medieval Jewish and Arab philosophy, and G.W.F. Hegal's metaphysics had Neoplatonic ingredients. Although a number of medieval theologians and philosophers, notably the German mystic Meister Eckhart, were deeply influenced by Neoplatonism, Roman Catholic dogmatists condemned its unorthodox tenets. In the 15th century, however, Neoplatonism became more generally accepted. The German Roman Catholic speculative philosopher, Nicholas of Cusa and other mystics sought to overcome the doubt arising from the limitations of human knowledge by espousing the theory of direct human intuition of God, a theory closely akin to the Neoplatonic doctrine that the soul in a state of ecstasy has the power to transcend all finite limitations. The humanists of the Italian Renaissance, in their reaction against the previously dominant rationalistic philosophy of Aristotle, turned to the idealistic meta-physics of Plato and thence to Neoplatonism. Notable in this connection was the Italian scholar Marsilio Ficino, who, under the patronage of the wealthy nobleman Cosimo de' Medici, translated and annotated the works of Plotinos, Porphyry and Iamblichus.

Neoplatonic metaphysics and aesthetics also influenced the German Romantics, the 17th century English metaphysical poets, William Blake and the Cambridge Platonists. Many mystical movements in the West including those of Meister Eckhardt and Jacob Boehme, owe something to the Neoplatonists. In England, the 17th century Cambridge Platonists exhibited marked affinities with Neoplatonic philosophers. A number of 19th and 20th century thinkers and writers have been influenced by Neoplatonism, among them were several of the most important British romantic poets including William Wordsworth, John Keats and Percy Bysshe Shelley.

REFERENCES

1. Radhakrishnan, S., *Eastern Religion and Western Thought*, p. 208.
2. *Ibid.,* p. 209.
3. Porphyry, "Life of Plotinos, " In Guthrie, Kenneth S., (ed.) Plotinos, *Complete Works,*London, 1918, p. 5.
4. *Ibid.,* pp. 7-8.
5. *Ibid.,* p. 8.
6. *Ibid.,* pp. 5, 8, 35-38.
7. *Ibid.,* p. 15
8. Sedlar, J.W., *India and the Greek World*, p.201.
9. Plotinus, *Enneads,* V. I.3; (Guthrie) pp. 177-78, 57.
10. Enneads, IV. 7.13, IV.8.5, pp. 83, 128-29.
11. Blumenthal, H.J., *Plotinios' Psychology: His Doctrines of the Embodied Soul,* The Hague, 1971, pp. 2-3.

12. Cumon, *Lux Perpetua,* Paris, 1949, pp. 347, 359.
13. Lawrence J. Hatab, "Platinus and the Upanisads", in *Neoplatonism and Indian Thought* ,ed. by R. Baine Harris, Delhi, 1992, p. 28.
14. *Ibid.,* p. 31.
15. *Ibid.,* p. 38.
16. *Ibid.,* p. 41.
17. *Taittiriya Upanisad* 3.1.1.
18. *Enneads* X. 5-7.
19. *Brhdaranyaka Upanishad* 5.1.1.
20. *Enneads,* V. 2.1.
21. *Kathopanisad,* 2.2.15.
22. *Enneads,* V.2.2.
23. *Enneads, V.5.1.*
24. *Enneads,* III. 4.24.
25. *Enneads,* II. 5.5.
26. Tripathi, C.L., " The Influence of Indian Philosophy on Neoplatonism", In *Neoplatonism and Indian Thought* , Harris, R. Baine (ed.). p. 275; Staal, J.F., *Advaita and Neoplatonism,* Madras, 1961, p.192.
27. Tripathi, C.L., *op. cit.*, p. 275.
28. Porphyry and Iamblichus do not agree with Plotinus. According to them, human souls are never born as beasts and birds.
29. Trans. Inge, W.R, quoted in his *Philosophy of Plotinos,* vol II, 1918, p.141.
30. Brehier, E., *La Philosophie de Plotin,* Paris, 1938, p. 10737 quoted in Staal, *Advaita and Neoplatanism,* p. 236.
31. Radhakrishnan, S., *op. cit.*, p. 214.
32. *Ibid.*, p. 218.
33. Cumont, *Lux perpetua*, *op. cit*., pp. 361-63.
34. Porphyry, " Life of plotinos" p. 18.
35. Whittaker, *Neo-Platonists*, Cambridge, 1918, p.113.
36. Porphyry, *On Abstinence*, IV. 17, p. 171.
37. D. *Circa*, 330. A.D.
38. Radhakrishnan, S., *Eastern Religion*, *op. cit.,* p. 218.
39. Staal, *Advaita and Neoplatonism*, p. 239.
40. Gompopa, *Jewel Ornament of Liberation* , trans. Guenther, Chap 21, pp. 271-4, quoted in Wallis, *Neoplatonism*, p.15, n. 2.
41. Tripathi, C.L., *op.cit.*, p. 278.
42. *Taittriya Upanishad,* 2.3.1.
43. Staal, *Advaita and Neoplatonism,* p. 245.
44. Tripathi, C.L., *op. cit.*, p. 278.
45. *Ibid.,* p. 278.
46. Inge, W.R., "Neoplatonism", in *Encyclopaedia of Religion and Ethics,* Vol. IX, ed. James Hastings, p. 308.

47. Inge, W.R., *The Platonic Tradition in English Religious Thought,* 1926, pp.7, 9.
48. Dodds, E.R., *Humanism and Technique in Greek Studies*, 1936, p. 11.
49. Tarn, W.W., *The Greeks in Bactria and India*, 1938, p. 67.
50. Mayer, *Political Thought*, 1939, p. 7.
51. Radhakrishnan, S., *op. cit.*, p. 208.
52. Wallis, *Neoplatonism,* p. 15.

MANICHAEISM AND INDIAN ASCETICISM

According to A.A. Bevan, Manichaeism, the religion of Mani or Manes, is one of those systems which are usualy classed together under the name of gnosticism. The Manichaean religion arose in Babylonia about the middle of the 3rd cent. A.D., and during many generations exercised great influence both in the East and in the West.[1] Manchaeism was long treated as a Christian heresy, but it is more clearly understood as an independant religion, drawing on the diverse resources of Christianity, Zoroastrianism, and Buddhism.[2]

In the persian Empire of the Sassanids, Manichaeism was born. Its founder, Mani, was born in A.D. 215 on Babylonian territory and promulgated a creed which was a blend of Zorastrian dogmas and Gnostic teaching. It held up an ascetic ideal of celibacy, poverty, and fasting.[3] It emphasized the Antagonism of the two principles of light and darkness. Dr. S. Radhakrishnan states that "Manichaeism spread among all the Christian subjects in Persia who spoke Aramaic. Mani gave a large place to the teachings of Jesus, which caused him to be accepted as a Christian heresiarch. His creed, however, forbade the worship of images, disapproved the killing of animals for sacrifice, and so provoked the wreath of the Roman emperors. It became Buddhist in China and Christian in Europe."[4]

Manichaeism spread out over most of the known world from Spain to China. But the religion disappread from the West in 10th century, and from China in the 14th century, and today it is not in existence. During the Roman Empire, Manichaeism got a strong position in North Africa—St. Augustine was a Manichaean for 9 years before his conversion to Christianity.

For about 80 years starting in 762, Manichaeism was the state religion of the Turkic people Uighurs.

As we know that this religion is named after the name of its founder Mani. So we will first of all discuss about the life of Mani, the founder of Manichaeism.

With regard to the history of the founder we are mainly dependent on Muhammadan writers. The accounts of the principal Muhammadan authorities may be briefly summarized thus.

> "Mani the son of F-t-q (Patik) was born in Babylonia about A.D. 216. His father was originally a heathen, and frequented an 'idol-temple' at or near Ctesiphon, the Persian capital, 'as other-people were want to do'. But shortly before the birth of Mani he abondoned his former religion, and joined the sect of the Mughtasila (those who practise ablutions). Mani at an early age became convinced that he had received divine revelations, and that he was chosen to preach a new faith. Before he was twenty-five year old he had privately gained a few disciples, but he began his public propaganda on the day when Shapur, the son of Ardashir, was crowned king, March 20 A.D. 242. He succeeded in securing the patronage of the king's brother Peroz, and through him obtained access to the king himself. In the course of his journeys he is said to have visited Central Asia, India, and China, but it does not appear that he ever penetrated into the Roman Empire. He composed numerous books and epistles in Aramaic, and at least one book in Persian, probably the work known as *Shapuraqun*, which according to Al-Biruni, was written for king Shapur. We learn from Ephraim Syrus that Mani illustrated his writings with coloured pictures; his fame as a painter survived for many centuries in the East. He is also said to have invented the peculiar alphabet which the Manichaeans afterwards employed. Mani was put to death by king Bahram, who reigned from about A.D. 274 to 277, his corpse, or,

> according to others, his skin stuffed with straw, was hung up, by order of the king, at the gate of Gunde-Shapur, an important city which lay a little to the East of the ancient Susa. In after times that gate was always known as the 'Mani-gate'. The execution of Mani was evidently due not so much to the personal caprice of the king as to the enmity of the Zoroastrian priesthood. At the same time the Persian government made a strenuous, but wholly fruitless, attempt to exterminate the adherents of the new religion." [5]

Mani contended that he was the greatest and last prophet or paraclete sent by the Father of light. His teaching was claimed to be superior to prophets who proceded him because, unlike Zoroaster, Buddha, and Jesus, Mani published an authoritative canon of at least seven major works. His system includes an elaborate mythical cosmogony and eschatalogy conceived in terms of two absolute principles, Light and Darkness, and an ascetic way of salvation. A unique feature of Manichaeism was paintings which illustrated his system of redemption. Mani claimed continuous revelations and inspiration from an angel, "the Twin", who as his heavenly alter ego prepared and protected him as a teacher and initiated him in the way of salvation. Miraculous healings were also attributed to Mani to authenticate his divine mission.[6]

According to an - Nadim's Fihrist, a 10th century Arabic work which informs that Patik, father of Mani, abondoned the imperial city (Ktesiphon) and moved to Maishan, where he joined a Baptist religious group. Situated in southern Babylonia around the Tigris-Euphrates mouths, the region of Maishan was noted for its mixture of nationalities and cults. Here Mani grew to adulthood : Parthian by heritage, in a Babylonian milieu and exposed to a variety of ethnic and religious influences. Undoubtedly this background played its part in suggesting to him the desirability of amalgamating diverse beliefs into a new and all-embracing world religion.[7]

Maishan, however, occupies a prominent place in the history

of Gnosis. The famous Gnostic poem known as "Hymn of the Soul" referes to it. This hymn describes the descent of the divine redeemer to earth from the realm of Light. His first stop upon reaching the earth and his last before returning to heaven is:

> ....Maishan the great
> The harbour of the merchants
> That sits upon the shore of the sea.[8]

So when Mani grew up in Maishan, presumably in contact with the multifarious influences in that cosmopolitan place, we may conclude that the extraordinary mixture of nationalities in Maishan must have contributed to Mani's vision of creating a religion acceptable to Christians, Persians and Indians all at once.

The Elchasites and the Mandaeism were the two faiths from where Mani had borrowed some principles of his new religion.This may be established beyond a doubt that the Elchasites were indeed the group to which Mani belonged as a boy. Thus Mani's early association with the Elchasites demonstrates that one of Christianity's offshoot forms contributed in a fundamental way to the future prophet's religious heritage. The Manichaean sacred books give clear indications of borrowing from Mandaeism. Mandaeism and Manichaeism use analogous technical terms and ritual gestures, e.g. the laying on hands and the kiss of peace. Mandaeism and Manichaeism are both forms of Gnosis. Perhaps it was through Mandaeism that Mani first encountered the characteristically Gnostic view of existence.

When Mani was twelve years old he experienced his first revelation As we have discussed earlier Mani's purveyor was an angel called the "Twin", who came from the supreme God known as "King of the Paradise of Light." The "Twin" motif is a common one in Gnosticism; it denotes the person's celestial self, or double. Mani identified this angle—Twin as the Paraclete. This it was revealed that Mani himself was the Paraclete. Mani asserts that the Paraclete.

> "............ revealed to me the secret mystery That was hidden from the worlds and the generations, The mystery of the Depth and the Height.
> He revealed to me the mystery of the Light and the Darkness,
> The mystery of the battle and the war And the great war........ which the Darkness stirred up.[9]

Mani claimed to have already been informed of his future mission, and to have received the doctrine he would later preach throughtout the Persian empire. Always he stressed the celestial provenance of his message :

> "The truth and the secrets of which I speak....... I have not received from men or from earthly creatures, and also not from the reading of texts............ The most holy Father............. in his grace drew me out of the common crowd, which does not know the truth. He revealed to me his secrets.[10]

The celestial "Twin" appeared once again when Mani was 24 years old and spoke to him : "The time has now come for your to step forth publicly." Decisive though it ultimately was for the founding of the Manichaean Church, this second revelation did not immediately lead Mani to depart from among the Elchasites . Evidently he viewed himself not as an apostate, but rather as a reformer who would purify Elchasite doctrine.

According to all extant accounts, Mani began his public mission in India. He travelled by ship, presumably via the usual route from the Persian Gulf to the Western Indus Valley. His presence in Baluchistan, and thus presumably also in Sind, is attested by one of the Manichaean documents unearthed at Turfan in Central Asia. Almost certainly Mani's experience of India was limited to this northwest region. Here Persian infuence had been felt at least since king Darius time. Here too the Buddhist Church was active. King Kanishka, one of the Indo-Scythian rulers who had succeeded the Parthians in this region, was famous as an active patron of Buddhism. Although it is possible that Mani had already learned something of Buddhism in Maishan, where a large variety of cults flourished. It is likely that the Buddhist feature of his religion derive principally from this visit to India.

One reasons for his Indian trip was probably political : untill Shapur came to the throne, he could not expect a favourable reception for his teachings within the persian empire. Perhaps too he was already inspired by the vision of uniting all the major religions of the world in to a grand and all-encompassing synthesis. Christianity he already had absorbed from his Elchasite back-ground; Zorastrianism was the offical religion of the Persian empire; but Buddhism he must have known mainly by nearsay until he visited India. Quite possibly he wished to observe Buddhists at first hand, on their own territory. However, it is probable that when he went to India the Gnostic framework of his thought was already established. Probably in India, too, he discovered the model for his Elect those filthy and ragged wanderers, with never-cut nails and wild hair, emaciated of body and pallid of countenance, oblivious to personal health or danger, and enduring the most fearful privations, but terribly in dread of sexuality and of doing harm to animals. Like Indian ascetics, the Manichaean Elect did not work, but spent their time praying and preaching, meditating and weeping over the world's sins.[11]

When Mani had spend about a year in India (241-42 A.D.) he received word of Ardashir's death, and returned at once to Persia. According to *Fihrist* one of Shapur's brothers arranged a meeting between Mani and the king, Shapur I, who in consequence accorded Mani complete freedom of preaching throughout his realm. Conceivably Shapur saw in this new creed the possibility of creating religious unity among the diverse territories of his vast empire. However, in 271 A.D., King Shapur died, and during the reign of his successor Bahram (272-75 A.D.) the Zoroastrian priesthood hostile to Mani gained ascendancy at the Persian court. Through their influence Mani was thrown into prison, where he either died naturally or was executed. But it was too late to extinguish his religion, which after thirty years of widespread preaching in the Persian empire had attracted numerous followers. At Mani's death, his Church was already well launched on its career of world conquest.[12]

According to W.A. Hoffecker, "After the death of Shapur, Mani was charged by Persian priests with perverting the traditional religion. The new king, Vahram I, imprisoned him, and a prolonged trial ensued. Mani was chained (known to his followers as his "crucifixion") and greatly weakend by fasting. He died twenty-six days after giving a final message to his Church. His followers memorialized Mani's death in their Bema festival celebrated yearly in March."[13]

Manichaeism, like other forms of Gnosticism, professes to be at the same time a religion and a philosophy, inasmuch as it not only sets up an ideal of holiness, but also undertakes to explain the constitution of the world. It attempts to arrive at philosophical truth by means of a method which, to us, appears wholly unphilosophical. Though the Manichaeans confidently appealed to human reason and were always ready to defend their conclusions by argument, they did not pretend that those conclusion had been reached by abstract logic or by any kind of scientific inductions. On the contrary, they claimed, no less than the primitive Christians, to be in possession of a direct revelation from God. Thus Mani himself says in a passage which Al-Biruni quotes from the *Shapuraqan*,[14] "Wisdom and deeds have always from time to time been brought to mankind by the messengers of God. So in one age they have been brought by the messenger called Buddha to India, in another by Zaradusht (Zoroaster) to Persia, in another by Jesus to the West. Thereupon this revelation has come down, this prophecy in this last age, through me, Mani, the messenger of the God of truth to Babylonia."

In short, the teachings of Manichaeism can be explained in this way that that was a most important example of Gnosticism. Central in the Manichaean teaching was dualism, that the world itself, and all creatures, was part of a battle between the good, represented by God, and the bad, the darkness, represented by a power driven by envy and lust.

These two powers were independent from each other, but in the world they were mixed. Most human beings were built from material from the bad power, but in everyone there was a divine light, which needed to be released from the dark material of the body. In Manichaeism creation is regarded as a cosmic catastrophe, this even applies to man. What had happened was that the Good forces had been forced to create the world, as a defence of the divine realms. The threat came from the bad powers that had discovered that there was a world of light, and this they could not resist. When the world and all creatures were created, the attacking darkness was mixed with some of the divine light.While the battle between light and darkness had been fought in cosmos untill creation, creation made the world of man the new battle ground. Everything that gives light in this world belongs to the divine realms, while everything that absorbs light, belongs to the darkness.

In this world, small pieces of light is constantly disentagled from the darkness, and the sun and the moon are two chariots bringing these pieces from the world and back to the divine world. The meaning of life is therefore the same as the meaning of the world, namely to participate on the divine side of this battle. Every man carries inside him a seed of light, and the only way to help free this seed from darkness is through by gnosis. Gnosis (knowledge) is the insight in this process of cosmic battle and insight in how to fight envy and lust. The gnosis can be discovered by man's intellectual capacities, but is at the same time something that is revealed, through messengers like Buddha, Jesus and Mani.

In the words of Sedlar, it has been said that in the Manichaean religion, the soul's journey was regarded as a physical transference from place to place, e.g. from the moon to the sun, then to the planets and the fixed stars.[15]

The starting point for Manichaeism, as for Gnosis generaly,

was the experience of the alienated soul, terror-struck at its own existence in this world. Manichaeans considered this earth as irretrievably wicked, overrun with demons, a place of wretchedness and torment in which the soul is a stranger. Happiness is possible only beyond the grave and beyond this world. The manichaean hymns vividly express this conception (here the soul speaks, for example):

- Who will willingly save me from the pit of destruction, and from the dark valley where all is harshness?
- Where all is anguish and the stab of death. Never to eternity is there safety there. It is all full of darkness and fume-filled fog.[16]

Who will take me up to that happy realm, so that joy shall be mine in union with all (its) inhabitants.[17]

As a logical consequence of this attitude, the Manichaean Elect were expected to have no interest in what Mani called "the four enterprises, on account of which men kill each other," namely (i) eating, (ii) sex, (iii) property, and (iv) war.[18]

By the different mythological ways, Manichaeism explained the origins of the world and the causes of the soul's alienation, as well as the possibility of salvation. Fantastic and absurd by any rationalist standard, these myths served to personify the powers of good and evil, justify the ethical demands of the faith, and give believers the hope of ultimate liberation from this world of suffering.

It can be said that the Manichaean system is based upon the idea of the essential and eternal contrast between good and evil, between light and darkness. At all events, it is clear that he represented evil, or darkness, as something capable of thought and volition : in other words, his dualism was of the imaginative, or poetical, not of the philosophical kind.[19] So, the essence of Manichaeism was the principle of absolute dualism : the primal conflict beween God represented by light and spirit, and Satan, represented by darkness and the material world. Human beings, created by God, were divine in spirit but they carried within them seeds of darkness, sown by Satan, because of their material bodies. Salvation, as taught by Mani, requires liberating the seed of light, the soul, from the material darkness in which it is trapped. This is achieved by strict celibacy and ascetic practices.[20]

Two distinct substances have existed from the beginning of time, in personified form the Father of Greatness and the Prince of Darkness. But despite this cosmological dualism, Manichaeism recognized no fundamental dichotomy between spirit and matter. Spiritual (ethical) principles assume concrete form as physical qualities (eg. Light, Darkness), while each pysical object posesses a moral rank according to the quantity of Light or darkness it contains. Whether the Manichaean universe is truly dualist might be disputed, since the evil element is carefully not called "God", and the superiority of the Good is indicated by its ultimate victory over Evil at the end of the world.[21] But Manichaean believers unquestionably felt an acute consciousness of the reality of sin, which they projected into an essential and eternal principle, Good and Evil they regarded as substances in their own right, existing together from eternity. Capable of intermixture but not of transformation.

The main features of Manichaeism were enunciated in an elaborate cosmogonical myth of two absolute and external principles which manifest themselves in their eras or "moments".

The first moment describes a radical dualism in a previous age. Light and darkness (good and evil) were both coeternal and independent. In the middle moment Darkness attacked and became mixed with light in a precosmic fall of primal man. This resulted in a second creation of the material world and man by the evil powers in which Light is trapped in nature and human bodies. Redemption of Light occurs by a cosmic mechanism in the heavens by which particles of Light(souls) are drawn up all fill the moon for fifteen days. In the last phases of the moon Light is transferred to the sun and finally to paradise. In the last days of second moment a great war is to be concluded with judgement and a global conflagration lasting

1,468 years. Light will be saved and everything material destroyed. In the third moment light and Darkness will be separated forever as in the primordial division. The following is an abstract of the account given in the *Fihrist* about the creation of the world and the war.

> "Originally, the light and the darkness bordered on one another, but were unmingled, the light-being limitless above and the darkness limitless below. The light is identical with God, who is called 'the king of the Paradises of Light', but the realm of light includes also an atmosphere and an earth which are co-eternal with the Godhead. Moreover there are various other beings called gods, who are subordinate to the king of the Paradise of Light. Out of the darkness arose Satan, the Primal Devil, who 'did not exist from all eternity, although the elements of which he is composed are eternal.' At first he wrought havoc in his own domain, and then invaded the kingdom of Light. 'When he saw the flashes of light, he conceived a hatred for them, shuddered, and rejoined his native elements. He made a second attack, and the king of the Paradises of Light, in order to repet him, produced a being called the Primal Man, who went forth armed with a fivefold panoply—the breeze, the wind, the light, the water, and the fire. Satan, on the other hand, arrayed himself in the smoke, the consuming flame, the darkness, the scorching blast, and the cloud. After a long struggle Satan prevailed over the Primal Man. The heavenly powers then interventted and rescued the Primal Man, but the elements which formed his panoply became mingled with the elements of darkness. Out of this confused mass the heavenly powers fashioned the actual world which we inhabit. Not only all animal and vegetable organisms, but even objects which we regard as wholly inanimate, such as metals, contain portions of divine light. Hence the distinction which we are accustomed to make between natural and spiritual phenomena does not exist in

> Manichaeism, since it represents all the processes of nature as part of a spiritual contest. The visible universe is, in fact, a vast and complicated machine devised by God for the purpose of enabling the elements of Light to effect their escape. When the light contained in the earth separates itself from the darkness, it ascends in the form of a pillar, called 'the pillar of glory', first to the moon, thence to the sun, and thence to the higher regions. This process continues untill at length the final separation is brought about by a conflagration, which will last 1468 years. Thereafter the light will be secured for ever against the assaults of the darkness."[22]

Sedlar states that the father of Greatness was unprepared for battle. This battle was taken place because of a result of the turmoil within the Dark realm, some of the demons (archons) inhabiting it were thrown up against the boundary of Light. They wished to posses the Light-realm for themselves. Ceasing their internecine strife, they gathered up their forces for war. On the other hand nonetheless the Father of Greatness chose not to defend his realm with the five Aeons (projections of himself) which already surrounded his throne. Instead he declared :

> Of my Aeons
> None will I send into battle
> For I created them for peace
> Rather I will go myself
> And carry on this war.[23]

The ultimate defeat of light and the resultant mixing of light-fragments with Darkness must thus be under-stood as a voluntary sacrifice—a sacrifice culminating in the final defeat of Darkness.

When the attack took place on the realm of the Father of greatness he called into existence an emanation called the Mother of life, who is turn produced Primal Man. As Primal

Man lay vanquished and stupefied in the realm of darkness, the Father of Greatness called the "living spirit" into being. The Living Spirit moved to the boundary of darkness and issued a "summons", to which Primal Man gave a "response". Upon hearing the response, the Living Spirit extended his hand to Primal Man and drew him upward to the world of Light. His sons, however, remained behind in the realm of Darkness.

There followed a kind of struggle in which Light attempted to liberate the remaining light- particles, while Darkness sought to retain them in captivity. According to the part of Light's battle-plan the Living Spirit flayed the archons, fashioned the sky from their skins, the mountains from their bones, and the earth from their excrement. He created the sun and the moon from those light fragments which were still undefiled and the stars from the slightly-defiled particles. A gigantic cosmic wheel was established to draw the liberated particles of light upward to the moon and the sun, the "ships of light". Henceforth during the first half of each month the rescued fragments rise upward in a pillar of light (the Milky Way) to the moon, which gradually becomes full. The waning of the moon in the latter half of the month means that the particles are passing on to the sun. From the sun they move onward to the paradise of Light. Mani's religious mission was supposed to have hastened, but not caused, this cosmic process of salvation.[24]

In this way we can say that the most singular part of the Manichaean system is that which relates to the origin and history of mankind. It is clear at least that the first human beings, whom Mani called Adam and Eve, were represented as the offspring of devils, the object of the devils in producing them being to imprison, and so to keep in their own possession, a portion of the elements of light. The heavenly powers, in order to frustrate the purpose of the devils, sent Jesus (who is here regarded as a celestial being) to instruct Adam on the subject of " the paradises and the Gods, Hell and the devils, the earth and the heaven, the sun and the moon, and in particular to warn him against sensuality. As to the history of

Adam and Eve many details are given, some of which have been borrowed from the OT, some perhaps from sources unknown to us, while some appear to be wholly fantastic.[25]

Sedlar gives the explanation of this creation of the world as this Manichaean pre-history not only provided an explanation of the earth's origin; it also justified the believer's sense of alienation from the world around him. Allegedly the Golden Age lay in a distant past before the earth was ever created. In non-mythological terms, the story of Darkness' attack upon Light presumably represented a projection of the Manichaean sense of sin, which was always a pronounced feature of the faith. The mingling of Light and Darkness, which the Manichaean probably experienced in human terms as the moral ambivalence of human nature, was poisonous to both. Thus this world's very existence is the products of Evil's aggressive act against the Good. Humanity is the offspring of two repulsive demons, who after a meal of monsters produce Adam and Eve. Life on this earth is a condition of degradation, expressed by such terms as "defilement", "soiling", "drunkenness", or "entombment". The highest motivation of the Manichaean believer is to abondon this wicked world and return to the original paradise of Light. The hymn says :

> "The enemy of my soul is the world, its riches and its deceit. All live hates godliness: what am I doing in the place of my enemies."[26]

The teachings of Mani as to the duties and ultimate destiny of individuals was in accordance with his theory of the universe as a whole. Since the visible world has as its aim the separation of the light from the darkness, practical religion must consist mainly in the furthering of this process. The divine element in man must be freed from its fetters in order that it may return to its heavenly source. The theory affirm only the existence of two opposite tendencies in man. And, just as the soul is not wholly good, so the body is not wholly evil; for according to the *Fihrist,* the Manichaeans held that after the death of the righteous man the 'powers' contained in his body, namely, the water, the fire, and the breeze, have to be extracted by 'the sun the moon and the shining gods,' and then 'the rest of his body which is altogether darkness is cast into hell'.[27]

Escape from this world consitutes salvation, and the means of salvation is knowledge. "Knowledge" in Manichaean terms means awareness of the divine pre-history of the universel and the present condition of the soul—which in Manichaeism is not identical with a light-particle, but is itself a mixture containing light. By means of knowledge (gnosis) the soul acquires an inward independence from the attractions of this world. Only the soul illumined by knowledge is capable of resisting Darkness, and not all souls can be saved. The illumined souls must be ready to receive the message of the redeemer (Jesus, Buddha etc.) who performs the same function for human beings that the Third Messenger (Mithra) earlier performed for the universe as a whole. They must also follow the precepts of the Manichaean faith.[28]

But although it was the duty of all Manicheans to take part in the liberation of the light from the darkness, their share in the great work naturally varied according to their several capacities. A Broad distinction was made between the ordinary Manicheans, who were known as 'Hearers' or ' the combatants', and the inner circle of teachers or ascetics, whom Western writers call 'the Elect'.

The "Elect" were persons already illumined, who were preparing for their soul's final liberation; "Hearers" were the laymen who helped them do it. Taken alone, the strict ascetic regimen which Manichaeism imposed upon its Elect would have made the maintenance of life impossible. Believing that all plant and animal life contained light-fragments, the Elect were forbidden to harm either. The Elect could neither sow nor harvest, mill or bake, engage in hunting, trade or of course war. These occupations represented injury to the light-substance. Manichaeans believed that the earth suffers when it is plowed; fruit complains when it is broken; food is injured by cooking;

water is defiled by bathing. These wicked deeds were obliged to recognize their own sinfulness in having frightened, hurt or killed living creatures. The Elect received their food from the Hearers while pronouncing an abjuration formula, thereby absolving themselves of all complicity in the crime. Meat eating—the worst of all culinary sins- was forbidden to them entirely, in as much as animals were the offspring of the archons and thus the image of their parents. Moreover, meat-eating allegedly excited sexual desire.

The main characteristic of the Elect was not that they had the exclusive right, or power, to perform certain acts but rather that they possessed a fuller knowledge of religion and abstained from certain things which were lawful to the rest of the community. This duty of abstention was called by the Manichaeans ' the three seals' on the mouth, hand and thoughts. The first—'seal' imposed restrictions with respect to food and speech, the second with respect to outward acts, the third with respect to thoughts and desires. Thus the Manichaean asceticism implied no thought of expiation; the idea that self inflicted suffering at ones for sin—an idea which has exercised so disastrous an influence in some sections of the Christian Church—was quite foreign to the religion of Mani.[29]

W.A. Haffecker states that the Elect were " sealed" with a threefold preservative: purity of mouth, abstaining from all ensouled things (meat) and strong drink; purity of life, renouncing earthly property and physical labour which might endanger Light diffused in nature; and purity of heart, for swearing sexual activity.[30]

The prohibitions which he issued are based upon the belief that certain acts, such as the destruction of life and the intercourse of the sexes, are essentially Satanic, and therefore retard the liberation of the light[31]. Contempt for the body was a natural consequence of Manichaean doctrine. Fasting constituted a primary obligation. The Elect were permitted to take only one meal daily, and that a spartan one; they seem to have been perpetually hungry. Sunday and Monday (the sunday and moon-day) were days of complete fasting; and for an entire month each year—just prior to the greatest festival of the year, the Throne Feast—they took no food between sun-up and sun-down. So extant sources depict the Manichaean Elect as lean and bony. Their approved diet consisted of raw fruits and vegetables, especially those which by their light colour demonstrated that they contained large quantities of light-substance. Melons and cucumbers were particularly favoured; bread with a little salt was allowed. Milk wine and all intoxicating beverages were forbidden. The permitted drinks were water and the unfermented juices of raw fruits.

The Elect were likewise required to abstain entirely from sexual intercourse, which they felt imitated the copulation of the demons by which whole human race came into existence. Manichaeans experienced evil most strongly in the form of concupiscence the desire for satisfaction of the flesh which finds its most characteristic expression in sexuality. Desire they personified as the demon Az, who thought desire and coitus to all the other demons, the witches, the angry devils, and the archons in Hell. Az also created the male and female forms of humanity. On Manichaean premises sexual desire is the worst of all possible defilements. And if sexuality is evil, procreation is still worse, because the creation of new human bodies hinders liberation of the enslaved particles of light.[32]

Thus, for instance, all Manichaeans were forbidden to kill animals, but it would seem that the Hearers were permitted to eat flesh. The Elect abstained from both flesh and wine; they were also forbidden to pluck fruit or vegetables, so that the food on which they subsisted had to be supplied by the Hearers.[33]

Women were considered forces of darkness, binding men to the flesh.[34] They rationalized on the ground that in Adam's body light substance was dominant, whereas dark elements prevailed in the body of Eve. On other hand women joined the ranks of the Elect and receive due praise in Manichean hymns, they were treated for the most part as clear inferiors.

Manichaeans thought that the body was the product of demons due to which the Elect refused to care for it in any way. They were content to dress in rags; their usual clothing was long robe of rough material. Some Manichaean texts inform that they might change garments only once a year. The Elect were for bidden to wash, to comb their hair, or to cut their fingernails. They wandered about with wild, dishevelled hair and long nails, clad in filthy and tattered robes and covered with dirt and dust. Furthermore the Elect paid no attention to bodily illnesses; the use of medicine was forbidden for them. Nordid they make any effort to escape physical danger, either from people or from wild animals.[35]

For the Manichean Elect wandering was an essential part of their religious obligation. They were allowed neither permanent residence nor personal belongings: property and a fixed domicile would mean attachment to this earth on which Darkness predominates. They travelled exclusively on foot; to ride on an animal would denote excessive concern for bodily comfort. Some Manichaean Monasteries did exist in Central Asia, perhaps under Buddhist influence, and Augustinus mentions the presence of one at Rome. But at least in principle these were permanent abodes merley temporary resting-places for travellers who would soon resume that wanderings.

The Elect avoided work in any form on the ground that work hinders development of the spiritual life. They were totally dependent upon the Hearers for sustenance. Correspondingly, almsgiving was a duty incumbent upon all Manichaean laymen[36]. The main occupation of the Elect was prayer, accompanied often by hymn singing, which they regarded as the most effective way to liberate the entrapped particles of light. In addition, he engaged in silent meditation, especially on the subject of death. Of the prayers, which were recited several times in the day, the following specimens are given by the author of the *Fihrist*:[37]

1. "Blessed is our Guide, the Paraclete, the Ambassador of

light, blessed are his guardian angels and adored are his shining hosts"

2. "Adored art thou, O shining one, Mani our guide, sources of brightness, branch of life, thou great tree which art wholly medicine."
3. "I adore and prostrate myself before all the Gods, all the shining angels, all the lights and all the hosts, who proceed from the great God."[38]

In this way Manichaean worship included fasting, daily prayers and sacramental meals which differed greatly from the lord's Supper. Hearers served the Elect "alms", fruit such as melons believed to contain great amounts of Light. Baptism was not celebrated since initiation into the community occurred by accepting Mani's wisdom through preaching Hymn cycles extalling redeeming knowledge were sung to focus believers attention on the beauty of Paradise, where rescued souls dwelt.[39]

With respect to Mani's doctrine the future life we have somewhat fuller information. The division mankind into three classes, the Elect, the Hearers, and the wicked is here specially emphasized. The Elect immediately after death, ascend by means of 'the pillar of glory' to the moon, and thence are conveyed to paradise. Its body remains behind; whatever light-particles it still contains will be drawn out of it by the forces of nature and gradually raised to the sun. The reminder of the body-now composed wholly of dark substance will be cast into hell.

Moreover, the Elect were indispensable to the salvation of the Hearers, who accordingly treated them with enormous reverance and awe. Each Monday the Hearers were obliged to confess to the Elect, whose superior illumination enables them to evaluate others' behaviour. Later at the seat of Judgement the Elect would be the Hearers advocates; there Jesus, Mithra or another of the saviours would separate all souls according to whether they deserved punishment or reward . Finally, the Elect served as copiers, preservers, and readers of books. All

Manichaeans greatly emphasized the importance of the written word in preserving Manis revelation.

Notwithstanding the rigorous life-style of the Elect, Manichaean Hearers were not subjected to any strict ascetic regimen. Anyone who felt love for the faith, though lacking the strength to practice rigid austerities, could become a Hearer if he was willing to protect the Church and succor the Elect. Hearers were supposed to "love each other like brothers and relatives" to fast, to pray and give alms, and if possible to "give a son to the Church" by converting a relative or buying a slave in order to "give him to righteousness". Like the Elect they had to fast every Ssunday "in accordance with Law and Ritual" and for an entire month each year between sunup and sundown. But even so common an ascetic regulation as the renunciation of meat-eating was not required of them. Hearers were, same as elect, also expected to observe the three "seals" on the mouth, hands and thoughts, which forbade impure speech and lies, evil deeds, and improper thoughts. It appears that these three prohibitions were borrowed from Buddhism. In another enumeration of commandments, the Hearers were enjoined to avoid (i) lying; (ii) false witness; (iii) Slander; (iv) sorcery; (v) taking life; (vi) cheating; (7) betraying a trust; (8) displeasing the sun-god and moon-god; (a) prostitution; and (10) injury to life otherwise they could marry and do the world's work.

The Hearers in the end must pass through a long process of purification and of wandering to and fro, before they join the Elect; while the souls of the wicked roam about the world, in a condition of hopeless misery, untill the final conflagration and are then consigned forever to the realm of darkness. There were rare exceptions, otherwise the Hearer's soul was subject to rebirth in this world ("transformation")—the form of which would depend upon its degree of perfection in the present life. So the souls of the Hearers after death do not ordinarily ascend directly to Paradise. Those Hearers who carefully observed the commandments of the faith and conscientiously served the Elect might themselves hope to become Elect in their next existence. Others might be reborn in the form of plants, which served the Elect as food; in this way their light-substance could ultimately win salvation. But those sinners (Non-Manichaeans) for whom there was no hope would be seized by the demons and tortured, then reborn in the bodies of animals. In the Manichaean view, however, this system of transmigration was merely another aspect of the inter-relatedness of the entire universe. In this way every human act formed part of the total cosmic process.

The Elect were not gained that status of Elect by birth but they were appointed by the "Father"—presumably meaning "our Father Mani" or his successors in the Church hierarchy. But apparently there was no initiation rite; the distinguishing mark of the Elect seems to have been chiefly their willingness to observe a rigid asceticism. The decision to assume this status might be the spontaneous consequence of inner illumination (gnosis), but could also be evoked by prayer, by studying the scriptures, or by direct revelation from one of the redeemers.

The connections of Mani with Shapur and the Parthian nobility suggests that he must have-his mission served a political as well as a religious purpose : namely, the reconciliation of the three great faiths of the Persian empire (Zorastrianism, Christianity, Buddhism). While the Church apparently had no sacraments, the Elect took ritual meals together.

Both Elect and Hearers participated in periodical religious festivals. Most important of these was the Feast of Bema (i.e. "throne feast")[40], Which was celebrated in the memory of Mani's martyrdom and death. The congregation addressed him as a divine being:

"We worship thee, the judge, the Paraclete,
we bless thy Bema [throne] whereon thou art seated.
We worship thee, the Paraclete,
We implore thee in the presence of thy Bema to forgive us our sins that we have committed during the year.

For there is none in this flesh that is free from sin in his heart."[41]

The Manichaean church was a missionary institution, and the Elect were its apostles. Mani himself had laid upon them the obligation of incessant wandering. Manichaeism was propogated self-consciously by missionaries who believed that their religion would ultimately conquer the entire world, despite their painful asceticism, the Manichaean Elect did not live in monastic seclusion. Mani had carefully explained to them that wisdom is "greater in my mouth, when I proclaim it, than when it is found in my heart." When a disciple once remarked that "seven angles are created through the fasting of a single Elect," Mani replied that fasting is certainly praiseworthy, but:

> "Greater is the fame, the victory and the goodness of him who preaches, in that he builds the church, than for the brother who retreats into himself, shuts himself up in himself, and builds himself [i.e. through asceticism and study]."[42]

In fact the Elect rejected most of the achievements, as well as the comforts and pleasures, of civilization. But they withdrew from the world only inwardly, not by avoiding contact with it. Their permanent obligation was to preach the faith in every corner of the earth; and they believed in the ultimate success of their efforts.

It was Manichaean doctrine which taught that the Church's final triumph would coincide with the end of the world. Just prior to that event, the scattered souls would assemble before the throne of the Father of Greatness to undergo a final judgement. A great fire would engulf the earth, lasting far 1468 years. In this conflagration the remaining light would be purified, while the souls of the wicked would be bound together with darkness into a great mass, or "lump". The earth would be destroyed; the realm of Darkness would sink into a cosmic moat and be covered by a gigantic stone. But whether Good and Evil would return entirely to their primal state of separation was a matter of dispute among the Manichaeans themselves. Through its association with Light, a nature contrary to itself, Darkness had been incurably poisoned. Never again would it be capable of attacking the Light-realm; its defeat was total and irrevocable.

Whatever the Manichaeans may have behaved as to the origin of the historical Jesus, the nature of His body, etc. it would certainly appear that they denied the fact of his crucifixion. Hence according to Augustine, they were in the habit of contrasting the unreal sufferings of Christ with the real sufferings of Mani, which they solemnly commemorated by an annual ceremony, Bema. That the Muhammadan writers say very little on this christological question may be due to the fact that here their own views happened to resemble those of the Manichaeans.[43]

As Syrian Christianity on the whole regarded Jesus as possessing a single nature-divine but not human similarly as a divine emanation in human form. According to the Kephalaia, far instance, Jesus came to earth as a spirit, " without body", and "assumed the form of a servant." In his light-essence he is identical with the human soul. His crucifixion has merely symbolic value: his passion consists in its the fact that even now his light-substance is dispersed throughout the plants, animals and human creatures of the whole world. Thus he is the suffering Jesus who is "hanged on every tree"—i.e. a redeemer in need of redemption. Within the Manichaean system, his character could scarcely be otherwise. Conversely, the Manichaean Jesus could not have a sinless bod; that would be a contradiction in terms. In any case, a human nature was in no way essential to the function of a saviour enlightening humankind as to its higher destiny.

But other saviours were equally essential to Manichaeism's all embracing theology : Mithra, Ohrmazd, Buddha, etc. In the Eastern forms of the faith Jesus was rarely mentioned : the saviour bore other names. One interesting fragment from Tun-huang in Central Asia speaks of Mani as the "Buddha of Light".

Implicitly referring to Gautama's life-story, the saviour in this text declares : "I shall manifest myself as the crown prince, leave family-life and enter the way, and be called Mani.[44]

As a major component of this faith, Indian religion unquestionably influenced the Hellenistic world. No doubt when Mani went to India, the framework of his thought was already Gnostic: his revelations were complete. But the mission to India could only have confirmed his world negating attitudes. Probably it was here that he found the model for his Elect, who practiced a degree of asceticism hitherto not known in the Hellenistic world to any great extent. His Elect-those filthy and ragged wanderers, with never-cut nails and wild hair, emaciated of body and pallid of countenance, oblivious to personal health or danger, and enduring the most fearful privations, but terribly in dread of sexuality and of doing harm to animals. Like Indian ascetics, the Manichaean Elect did not work, but spent their time praying and preaching, meditating and weeping over the world's sins. Possibly the conception of the Bodhisattva, the enlightened but compassionate holy man, attracted him also. The fact that Mani acknowledged the Buddha as one of his three spiritual predeccessors may well be due to his Indian journey.

The contribution of India to Manichaeism, finally, must be assessed in the context of all the other influences upon this syncretistic faith. Like Gnosis generally, Manichaeism shared the life-negating attitudes of Hinduism, Jainism and Buddhism. Its fundamental premise, like theirs, was that earthly existence is evil. Salvation was defined as liberation from this world—an aim essentially negative in character, though having a positive counterpart in the believer's expectation of ultimate bliss beyond the grave.[45]

Another obvious similarity between Manichaean and Indian ascetics concerns their extraordinary precautions not to harm animals and plants. The Elect's respect for animal and plant life came to expression in their prohibitions against sowing and reaping, milling or cooking-sins they regarded as no less serious than the murder of a human being. The life-style of Jain monks—cloths in front of their faces, sweeping the ground before them demonstrates a similarly extreme attitude. Like the Jains, Manichaeans were told that:

> "It is proper for a person to look at the ground when travelling along a road, in order not to step upon the cross of Light with one's feet and ruin the plants. In principle the same goes for the snake, that one does not step on it and kill it with the feet."'[46]

Hindus and Buddhists, on the whole, seem likewise to have forbidden the killing or eating of animals. All these prohibitions had a similar intellectual justification—namely, that the identical soul is present within animals, plants and human beings. The Manichaean was concerned not to harm the light substance which inhabits all forms of life. Hindus, Jains and Buddhists, feared to injure a soul which might reside in a human body in its next incarnation.

In Manichaeism, as in Buddhism, the central position in the religious life was held by an order of ascetics : Manichaean Elect; Budhist monks. The Manichaean division between Elect and Hearers paralleled almost exactly the Buddhist distinction between monks and laymen. In both cases the ascetics conformed most nearly to the ideals of the faith, while laymen were expected to support them through almsgiving. Like the Manichaeans, Buddhist monks regarded manual work with distaste, indeed as a positive hindrance to meditation. They spent most of the year in wandering and subsisted by begging.

In the ideal of the missionary-monk appears another Manichaean Indian similarity. Like the Manichaean Elect, some Indian ascetic orders required that their members lead a vagrant life. This was partly a method of chastisement for the wanderers themselves, who had no fixed place of residence and never knew the source of their next meal, but also a most effective means of publicity. By means of his personal austerites—often performed in public—the ascetic unfailingly demonstrated his conviction that bodily comforts and pleasures count for nothing, and that true happiness lies in another, non-material sphere. Among the Indian religious, Mahayana Buddhism showed particular concern for the spiritual welfare of ordinary folk. Its ideal was the Bodhisattva—the holy ascetic whose merits entitled him to Nirvana, but who postponed this apatheasis in order to communicate his own enlightment to others. By their self-inflicted hardships, the Manichaean Elect similarly bore witness to a profound inward detachment from earthly enjoyments. Like the Bodhisattvas, they remained in close contact with the world at large in order better to propagate their message of salvation.

Buddhist asceticism, however, was comparatively moderate in nature : renunciation rather than self-mortification. By contrast, the Manichaean Elect-resembled Indian ascetics of the more extreme variety. They permitted their laymen to commit sins in order themselves to remain pure, much like those Indian Jains who were forbidden to cook, but willingly drank the water which laymen had used for cooking. Like some types of Hindu ascetics, the Elect engaged in practices of which the inevitable results was the destruction of physical health. Continuous standing on one leg, or with one arm upraised, or squatting on one's heels indefinitely, lying on ground burning hot from the sun, or on beds of thorns or ashes, rigorous fasting even when food was available—all these naturally led to the loss of the use of the limbs, production of sores, and encouragement of disease. The Manichaean Elect resembled those holy men described in Indian texts as wild-looking creatures with long matted hair and uncut nails, covered from head to foot with filth. By contrast, Gautama had insisted on cleanliness : the three items which Buddhist monks carried on their wanderings were a razor, a comb and a begging-bowl. Finally, the Elect rivalled some of the extreme Indian ascetics in their apparent search for self-destruction, i.e. their refusal to take the slightest precautions against danger from man or beast. Indian literature, too describes how certain ascetics walked into fires, threw themselves from pricipices, or fasted mercilessly in the conviction that this would give them secure entrance to the world of Brahman.

One of the major attractions of Manichaeism, as of the major Indian religions, was that it regarded human and physical nature as forming a cosmic unity. For Manichaeans the entire cosmic process held religious meaning, as an aspect of the struggle to liberate Light from Darkness. The identity of animal souls, plant souls and human souls, together with the possibility of transmigration into any of these forms, served to bind the universe together. A similar link appears in the Hindu and Jain concepts of metempsychosis. Buddhism offers a variation on the same theme, accepting metempsychosis but denying the existence of souls. Curiously, even the manichaean notion of the soul's passage via the moon and sun to the Paradise of Light Finds a counterpart in Indian texts. According to several Upanishadic passages, the perfectly liberated atman (soul) follows "the way of the gods" via the moon and stars, from which it will never again return to earth. But the unfreed atman takes the "way of the Fathers", from which it must descend again into on earthly body.

Texts from Turfan in Central Asia specifically interpret the Manichaean message in Buddhist terminology. Transmigration (i.e. "reforging") of souls is compared to the Buddhist Concept of the flow of Existence, *samsara*; the ascent of the soul to the Paradise of Light is described as an escape from *samsara* into *Nirvana.*

A whole series of documents from Turfan is entitled "Parinirvana Hymns". The death of Mani is described thus :

"It was a day of sorrow and an hour of lament as the envoy of Light (Mani) entered Nirvana."[47] Another possible reminiscence of Buddhism appears in the Manichaean Throne Feast. Central to the entire cremony was the empty throne which symbolized Mani's teaching. In similar fashion Buddhist are depicted the presence of the Buddha by the symbol of a vacant throne.

The organization of the Manichaean Church was almost certainly indebted to Buddhists models. The hierarchical structure of the two institutions was similar; likewise their emphasis on missionary activity and the high status given to monks (Elect) as against laymen. However, metempychosis was certainly a familiar doctrine to Mani before he ever saw India; it was typical of Gnosis. Mani's concept of the soul's path after death could have been borrowed from the older Upanishadic view that the soul must follow either the "way of the Gods" or the "way of the fathers"—i.e. either to Paradise or to another earthly life.[48] In particular, he did not adopt the comparatively mild Buddhist form of asceticism, but a much more extreme type: possibly from the Jains or from various Hindu ascetics.

It is likely that Indians were among the first Manichaeans. In India Mani began his mission; according to the Kephalaia, he made "a good selection" of converts there. It would have been utterly natural for some of these believers to accompany their master back to Persia, and to assist him in future disseminating their shared revelation. Quite possibly Indian converts formed the nucleus of the new Manichaean Church, thus providing a model for all of those who later aspired to Elect status. In final reckoning, the ascetic example probably constituted India's most important influence upon Manichaeism. The Elect who resembled them became the vanguard of the Manichaean Church, the truest embodiment of its doctrines. It was they, the ascetic missionaries, who were responsible for Manichaeism's astonishingly rapid and widespread diffusion. Certainly their examples was a potent one within the Hellenistic world, and even beyond it in the form of medieval heresies. But their probable influence upon Christian monasticism denotes an even profounder effect of India upon Europe.

REFERENCES

1. Bevan, A.A., "Manichaeism in *ERE,* Ed. James Hastings, 1980,Vol. 8. p. 394.

2. Cunningham, Agnes, " Manichaeism" in *Elwell Evangelical Dictionary.*
3. Radhakrishnan, S., *Eastern Religions and Western Thoughts*, 1939, New Delhi, p. 190.
4. *Ibid.*, p.190.
5. Bevan, A. A., " Manichaeism" in *ERE*, Ed. James Hastings, Vol. 18. pp. 396-367.
6. Hoffecker, W.A., "Mani", *Elwell Evangelical Dictionary.*
7. Sedlar, *op. cit.*, p. 209.
8. Sedlar,*op. cit.* p.166.
9. Sedlar, *op. cit*,p. 210; *Elwell Evangelical Dictionary.*
10. *Ibid.*, p. 210.
11. *Ibid*, pp. 292-293.
12. *Ibid.*, p. 213.
13. Hoffecker, W.A., *Elwell Evangelical Dictionary.*
14. *ERE*, Vol. 8. *op. cit.*, p.397.
15. Sedlar *op. cit.*, p. 203.
16. Boyce, Mary, *The Manichaean Hymn-Cycles in Parthian*, London, 1954, p. 87.
17. *Ibid.*, p. 93.
18. Sedlar, *op. cit.*, p. 214.
19. Bevan, A. A., *op. cit.,ERE*, Vol. 8, p. 397.
20. Cunningham, Agnes, *Elwell Evangelical Dictionary.*"Manichaeism", Trans. Charles Kesler, London, 1965, pp. 43-44.
21. Windengren, *Mani and Manichaeism,*
22. *Fihrist*, quoted in *ERE*, vol. 8. op. cit., p.397.
23. Sedlar, *op.cit.*, p215.
24. Widengren, *Mani*, *op. cit.*, pp. 55-56.
25. Bevan, A. A., *ERE, op. cit.*, 397.
26. Sedlar, *op. cit.*, p. 317.
27. *ERE, op.cit.*, p.398.
28. Sedlar, *op. cit.*, p. 217.
29. Bevan, A. A., *op. cit.*, p. 399.
30. *Elwell Evangelical Dictionary*, *op. cit.*
31. A.A. Bevan, *op. cit.*, p. 399.
32. Sedlar *op. cit.*, p. 218.
33. *ERE, op. cit.*, p. 399.
34. Sedlar, *op. cit.*, p. 219.
35. *Ibid.*, p. 219
36. Sedlar, *op. cit.*, p. 219.
37. *ERE*, *op. cit.*, p. 399.
38. *Ibid*, p. 399.
39. G. Widengren, "Mani and manichaeism" *op. cit.*, p. 52.

40. Sedlar, *op. cit.*, p. 222.
41. *Ibid,* p. 222.
42. Sedlar, *op. cit.*, p. 222.
43. *ERE.*, *op. cit.*, p. 398.
44. Haloun, G. and Henning, W.B., " The Compendium of the Doctrines and Styles of the Teaching of Mani, The Buddha of Light,. AM, 1952, pp. 189. 190. 192.
45. Sedlar, *op. cit.*, p. 227.
46. *Kephalaia*, Trans. ed. Hans J. Polotsky, vol. I. of MHSMB, Stuttgart, 1940, p. 208.
47. Sedlar, *op. cit.*, p. 230.
48. *Kausitaki* I. 1-4; VI. 2.2. & VI 2.15.16; *Chandogya* V. 101-9, *Upanisads*, Trans., Radhakrishnan, S. as *The Principal Upanisads*, London, 1953. pp. 753-57, 309-10, 314-15, 431-34.

MONASTIC TRADITIONS: ANCIENT INDIA & ANCIENT GREECE

The word 'monasticism' is derived from the Greek word "monos" means 'alone', 'solitary'.[1] These words indicated the idea of solitude, of isolation. This solitude must not, however, be interpreted as implying absolute isolation—such as that of the hermit in the desert. As we shall see, the term 'monk' has come to be applied to men living the same life in common—a life in which they are indeed separated from the world, but not from one another. Strictly speaking the term, 'monasticism', should be reserved for the form of religious life led by those who, having separated themselves entirely from the world, live in solitude—as, in fact, the etymology of the words 'monk', 'monastery', etc., clearly indicates.[2]

Monasticism is the religious practice of renouncing all worldly pursuits in order to fully devote one's life to spiritual work.[3] Monasticism (Greek word monos means 'single') usually refers to the way of life- communitarian or solitary-adopted by those individuals, male or female, who have elected to pursue an ideal of perfection or a higher level of religious experience through leaving the world. Monastic orders historically have been organized around a rule or a teacher, the activities of the members being closely regulated in accordance with the rule adopted.[4] Those pursuing a monastic life are usually called*monks* or *brothers* (male), and *nuns* or *sisters* (female). Both monks and nuns may also be called *monastics*.[5]

Technically, monasticism embraces both the life of the hermit, characterized by varying degrees of extreme solitude, and the life of the cenobite, that is, the monk living in a community offering a limited amount of solitude. Monasticism always entails Asceticism, or the practice of disciplined self-denial. This asceticism may include fasting, silence, a prohibition against personal ownership, and an acceptance of bodily discomfort. Almost always it includes poverty, celibacy, and obedience to a spiritual leader.[6] The goal of such practices is usually a more intense relationship with God, some type of personal enlightenment, or the service of God through prayer, meditation, or good works such as teaching or nursing.

The practice is ancient forms of monasticism existed in India almost 10 centuries before Christ. It can be found in some form among most developed religions : Hinduism, Buddhism, Jainism, Taoism, the Sufi branch of Islam, and Christianity. In ancient times among the Hindus, the laws of Manu provide that, after the rearing of a family, members of the three upper castes may retire to a hermit life and seek truth in contemplation.[7] Buddha created a monastic order, for which he drew up a set of rules that contain many analogies with the rules that were later instituted by Christian religious orders.[8] Among the Greeks the members of the Orphic brotherhood and the followers of Pythagoras showed marked tendencies toward the practice of monasticism. Among the Jews the communities of the Essenes had many of the characteristics of religious orders. Later, among the followers of Islam, some communities of Sufis settled in Monasteries as early as the 8th century A.D.[9]

There were only two Jewish groups—the Essenes and Therapeutae—engaged in any form of organized asceticism.

The Essenes may be regarded as one of the most striking examples of monastic life outside of Christianity. Those of the Essenes who inhabited the monastery at Qumran near the Dead Sea appear to have lived in ascetic style, practicing chastity, poverty and obedience. Whether they be looked on as a sect, as a tribe or as a religious community, the Essenes (150 B.C.) offer all the principal characteristics of the cenobitic life—

community of goods, practice of poverty and martification, prayer and work, meals and religious exercise in common, silence, celibacy, etc.[10] But the majority of Essenes were townsmen rather than monks, though all of them observed strict canons of piety, especially as regards the Sabbath. Apparently some of them, though not all, renounced marriage![11] The Qumran monastery was destroyed during the Roman-Jewish war of 66-70 A.D., and the fate of the Essenes thereafter is uncertain. It is unlikely that they had any impact upon Christian monasticism, which began only in the late 3rd century.[12] Although there is no direct relationship between them, it is nevertheless true that both Essenian and Christian asceticism derived much of their practice from the same source, viz. the Jewish religion.[13]

The Therapeutae were contemporary with the Essenes. They abandoned families and possessions in order to live in ascetic seclusion far from the noise and commotion of cities.[14] Philon of Alexandria is our sole witness to their very existence. He describes them as passessed by desire for the mystic vision[15] and as cenobites, leading a life almost identical with that of the Christian cenobites.[16] They resided in a monastic community near Lake Mureotis in Egypt, where each of them lived alone in a makeshift, unembellished hut placed some distance from all the others.[17] Renunciation of the world, prayer, life in common in real monasteries, vigils, chants carried out by alternate choirs, the practice of fasting and other mortification—such are the chief characteristics of the life of Therapeutae.

Their dietary regime was austere : they never ate before sunset, and then only spring water and bread flavoured with salt or hyssop,[18] costly dishes they rejected as promoting sexual desire; wine ''acts like a drug producing fally'; animal flesh they avoided for reasons unspecified.[19] Women shared in their fellowship, though according to Philon these were mostly "aged virgins." In order to preserve "the modesty becoming to the female sex,"[20] at the general assemblies of the sect, men and women were separated by a partition five or six feet high.

Nevertheles they do not seem to have exercised any direct influence on Christian monasticism.

The Nazirites were men who lived an austere life, abstained from wine and all fermented liquors, never cut their hair, avoided serupulously all legal impurities, and took a vow to consecrate their lives to God. The "Nazirite" vow of sexual abstinence, though of limited duration, found little favour with the rabbis; some of them considered it positively objectionable. They had certain practices in common with the monks, although their ideal was not the same.

Some regard the Rechabites as forming 'a sort of religious order, analogous to the Nazarites', and St. Jerome himself saw in them the precursors of the monks. But such analogies should not be pressed too far.[21] The Rechabites were distinguished by certain special observances, such as abstinences from wine, the prohibition against building houses, and the obligation to live in tents, but it is difficult to see in them anything more than a tribe of Bedawi such as still exist in these days and observe the customs of their ancestors with such zeal.

The two unique contributions which Indian civilization has made to the common stock of culture are "Asceticism" and "Monasticism". Asceticism concerns the theory and practice of individual conduct. Monastic organization is a special aspect of social organization in general. As an individual practice asceticism gets modified to some extent when it brings together more individuals than one. Two or three ascetics living together or moving together demonstrate that the ascetic ideal of complete withdrawal is already partially defeated. A kind of living together habitation of these ascetics forms a monastic centre. There were rules to regulate life at the centre. Monastic life leads to the endeavour of creating social organisation peculiarly fitted for the ascetic life. So asceticism leading in its growth to monastic life creates the paradoxical phenomenon of social organization for those who not only negatived but also renounced social connection and individual wants.[22]

The main contribution of Buddha to asceticism in general

and Indian asceticism in particular is the organization of monastic order. The tradition of the individual ascetic mendicant had become so deeply rooted in Indian culture that though a number of ascetic sects arose soon after Buddha's time, as their names indicate they were not organised in centres. As we know from Hiuen Tsang's description of Northern India, even so late as the beginning of the 7th century A.D., the two Saiva ascetic sects that were prominent at that time do not appear to have had distinct monastic centres comparable to the Buddhist 'Vihara's. The ascetics of the sects used to live in local temples. The first monastic organization of Hindu ascetics historically dates from the 8th or the 9th century A.D. when Samkaracarya accomplished his great work. He founded four religious centres in four places of India, and either established or reorganized ten orders of Saiva ascetics. Asceticism under Samkaracarya's aegis took a further step in organizational technique.

Christian asceticism is known to have begun in Egypt about the 3rd or the 4th century A.D., and is associated with St. Anthony. It is believed that about the end of the 3rd century Anthony's life as a solitary ascetic was brought to an end by a number of disciples gathering round him. So he becomes the father of Christian monasticism. It was this type of monastic life that prevailed in Egypt upto the middle of the 5th century A.D. All later Christian asceticism and monasticism is traceable to it.

It is a travesty of truth that all the poor, destitute, criminal persons and others wounded in battles must have found avasas, viharas, samghas or asramas as their ultimate resort.[23] Leaders of the innovating sects of the sixth century B.C. unequivoccally condemned casteism. Jainism and Buddhism embraced within their folds persons irrespective of caste, creed and colour. Caste did no more pose an impossable bar to the realisation of the supreme reality. The Buddha had the message to the poor and destitute that how a Buddhist monk could get his food readily without much toil and hardship.[24] This shows how the Buddha trapped the sentiments of people slashed by object poverty towards his fold. In *Vinaya Pitaka* one finds a mention of Upali whose poor parents thought of his monkhood which guranteed livelihood without menial work.[25]

Thus in the last half of the first millenium B.C., the monks differentiating themselves from the wanderers of forest - dwellers developed a system to such an extent that settled life throughout the year at a monastery became the rule of the religious life among them.[26] But Buddhism took the lead to form such monastic establishments to which other sects added their own monasteries later on. The *Jataka* sories speak that the period witnessed an unprecedented wave of asceticism. The poor, the tramps and casteless lots easily flocked together under the banner of such establishments. Initially the runaway slaves, the savage tribesmen, the escaped criminals, the chronically ills and the indebted as well as aboriginal Nagas were denied admission. But in the post-Maurya period when there was a tremendous pressure on economy and the standard of life deteriorated, there was no other go for these poor lots except coming into the fold of monasteries. At this period as it was a great credit for every sect to attract as many followers as they could, so there was a flood of false ascetics and tramps to such orders.

From ancient times the legal tradition recognized the power of properly constituted groups to formulate their own laws.[27] These groups included merchant guilds, trade associations, castes and, more importantly for our study, ascetic communities.[28] One title of law deals with violations of corporate law, and it was the king's duty to respect those special laws and to enforce them on the members of the respective groups.[29] The references to ascetic communities within this context, however, use the term pasanda, a term that usually refers to the so-called heretical sects, such as the Buddhist and the Jain.[30] It is unclear whether Brahmanical monastic communities also enjoyed such corporate privileges, but it seems likely that they did. One problem in incorporating those groups into dharmasastric rules is that the legal fiction of the itinerant lifestyle of renouncers was maintained within the dharmasastric tradition. The existence of monasteries (*Matha*) is never recognized within Brahmanical *dharma*, and references to *mathas* are extremely rare even in texts dealing specifically with the renouncer's *dharma*. The laws of brahmanical renouncers, furthermore, were part of *dharma* and were theoretically located in the vedas and smritis and not in private corporations. The fact, however, was that different Brahmanical monastic groups, such as the Sri-Vaisnavas and the Samkara *mathas*, had distinctive rules and practices.[31] The enforcement of these rules, in all likelihood, fell within the same title of law as other corporate bodies.

Indeed, in modern times heads of some of the leading monasteries, especially the Samkaracaryas, "have been in the habit of assuming to themselves jurisdiction over persons professing to follow their dogmas in ecclesiastical matters such as prescribing penances for lapses, settling disputes between castes, and deciding upon questions of outcasting"[32]. It is likely, as Kane[33] has shown, that monastic leaders may have played a similar, although more restricted , role even in medieval times.

P.V. Kane states[34] about the right of monasteries and religious institution of giving justice regarding spiritual and religious matters. He states, according to the theory of Dharmasastra, the king is not only the head of the civil administration and the fountain of justice, but he is also the final controlling authority in preserving religious and spiritual institutions, he is to see that people follow the dharma, to punish them for breaches of the religious and spiritual codes and to see to the administration to them of appropriate penances. In short, he is also the Defender of the Faith. But he regulated spiritual and religious matters not by his arbitrary authority but on the advice of his *purohita* and ministers and after taking the opinion of the assemblies (*parisad*) of learned men. Whenever difficult questions arose about the validity of anything from the religious point of view or about penances for lapses, or about excommunicating or outcasting a man, the opinion of the assembly of learned men was sought. Therefore, detailed rules are laid down in the Dharmasutras and Smrtis about the constitution of parisads. A few words must be said about the parisads and about the claims of the Samkaracaryas (the modern heads of *mathas*) to regulate religious matters affecting their followers.

During the time of the Maratha domination learned Brahmanas of holy places like Paithan, Nasik and Karad were consulted in religious matters by the king or his minister, that the holders of 'gadi' of Samkaracarya and other seats were also rarely consulted in these matters and that it is only after the advent of the British rule that the Samkaracaryas have began to claim almost exclusive jurisdiction in ecclesiastic matters and in restoring men to their castes or excommunicating them for lapses. It can be stated that both the learned Brahmanas at holy places like Karad and the Samkaracaryas claim the exclusive right in these matters by reason of immemorial usage.[35]

The above brief account will show that for hundreds of years even before the first Samkaracarya flourished, it was the privilege of the assembly of learned Brahmanas to decide doubtful points of religious conduct and prescribe penances for lapses, that the same privilege continued undisturbed till the advent of the British rule, that rarely the heads of the*mathas*, by virtue of their eminent position, their supposed detachment from and renunciation of worldly affairs and their reputation as ascetics, were asked to decide doubtful points of religious and theological importance, that it is only during the last few decades that such heads began to claim exclusive jurisdiction in such matters.

Both Buddhism and Brahmanism passess institutions that have certain characteristics analogous to those of Christian monasticism. In the sacred books of the Hindus mention is made of hermits forming colonies and dedicating their lives to the study of the Vedas and to the contemplation of Brahman. They are vegetarians, and practise martification in all its forms.

While in Brahmanism the monastic life has preserved its eremitic character, in Buddhism we find it, on the contrary, in the cenobitic form. The monks live together in monasteries, in the practice of poverty- as mendicants, in fact—and celibacy. Such monasteries are still to be found in Japan, Korea, China, India and Ceylon.

The Sangha, democratic order of Buddhist monks and nuns, was founded by Gautama Buddha during his lifetime of missionary work over 2500 years ago. Established to preserve the doctrine and discipline now known as Buddhism, they are a living example for the laity.[36] A monk, known as a *Bhikku* in Pali, firstly ordains as a *Samanera* (novice) for a year or untill the ripe age of 20. If deemed acceptable and able by the order, he then receives full ordination and now lives by the 227 monastic rules, called the patimokkha, which are stated in the *Tripitaka*. Buddhist nuns or Bhikkhuni adhere to 311 rules of discipline. Monastics eat one meal at noon and fast untill sunrise the following day. Between midday and the next day, a strict life of celibacy, scripture study, chanting, meditation and occasional cleaning forms most of the duties. It is necessary for not only monks but the laity to practice with intuitive insight, in a state of mindfulness and concentration, here and now, to benefit from the experience. Only then is Enlightenment possible.

The distinction between Sangha and lay persons has always been important and forms the *Purusa,* Buddhist community. Here, monastics teach and counsel the laity at request while laymen and laywomen offer donations for their future support. This interconnectedness serves as a marriage and has sustained Buddhism to this day. A. Hilgenfeld and other writers have tried to establish the influence of these institutions on Christian monasticism. But it is easy to show, with the advance of scholarship, that it is the contrary that is true and that certain practices of Buddhist monasticism owe their inspiration to Christian influence.[37]

Monasticism in Christianity is a family of similar traditions that began to develop early in the history of the Christian Church, modelled upon scriptural examples and ideals, but not mandated as an institution by the scriptures. While most people think of Christian or Catholic monks or nuns as "Something to do with living in a Mmonastery", from the Church's point of view the focus has nothing to do with living in a Monastery or performing any specific activity, rather the focus is on a ideal called the religious life, also called the state of perfection. This idea is expressed everywhere that the things of God are sought above all other things, as seen for exmple in the *philokalia*, a book of monastic writings. In other words, a monk or nun is a person who has vowed to follow not only the comandments of the Church, but also the counsels (e.g., vows of poverty, chastity and obedience). The words of Jesus which are the cornerstone for this ideal are "be ye perfect like your heavenly father is perfect".[38]

Christian cenobitic monasticism as it is mainly known in the West started in Egypt. Originally, all Christian monks were hermits, and especially in the Middle East this continued to be very common untill the decline of Syrian Christianity in the late Middle ages.

The first Christian hermits seem to have established theselves on the shores of the Red Sea, where in pre-Christian times the therapeutae, an order of Jewish ascetics, had been established. Not long afterword the desert regions of Upper Egypt became a retreat for those who fled from the persecutions of the Christians so frequent in the Roman Empire during the 3rd century, and for those who found the vices of the world intolerable. The earliest form of Christian monaticism was, probably, that of the anchorites or hermits; a later development is found in the pillar saints, called stylites, who spent most of their time on the tops of pillars in order to separate themselves from the world and to mortify the flesh. After a time, however, the necessities of the religious life itself led to modifications. In order to combine the personal seclusion of individuals with the common exercise of religious duties, the early hermits had an aggregation of separate cells called laura, to which they could retire after their communal duties had been discharged. From the union of the common life with personnal salitude is derived the name cenobite (Greek Koinos bios,"Common life") by which a certain class of monks is distinguished.[39]

Saint Anthony, the Great was connected with the first Egyptian hermits; Saint Pachomius (d. 346), with the first communities of cenobites in Egypt. Saint Basil, the Great (*fl.* 379), Bishop of Caesarea, placed monasticism in an uran context by introducing charitable service as a work discipline.[40]

St. Anthony, who embraced solitude, established himself at Alexandria, and the fame of his sanctity, as well as his gentleness and learning, drew many disciples to him. Most of his followers accompanied him when he retired to the desert. One of his disciples, St. Pachomius who established a great monastery on an island in the Nile River, is regarded as the founder of the cenobitic manner of living. Pachomius drew up for his subjects a monastic rule, the first regulations of the kind on record. Many thousands of disciples flocked to him, and he founded several other monasteries for men and one for women under the direction of his sister. All of these houses recognized the authority of a single superior, an abbot or archimandrite. They constitute type of the religious order. The cenobitic the original form of monasticism was first introduced into the West at Rome and in Northern Italy by St. Athanasius, in Central North Africa by St. Augustine, and in Gayl by St. Martin of Tours. The religious revival effected by St. Benedict of Nursia early in the 6th century gave western monasticism its permanent form.[41]

Mar Awgin founded a monaster on Mt. Izla above Niribis in Mesopotamia (350), and from his monastery the cenobitic tradition spread in Mesopatamia, Persia, Armenia, Georgia and even India and China. St. Sabbas, the Sanctified organized the monks of the Judean Desert in a monastery close to Bethlehaem (483), and this is considered the mother of all monasteries of the Eastern Orthodox. Churches. St. Benedict of Nursi founded the monastery of Monte Cassino in Italy (529), which was the seed of Roman Catholic monasticism in general, and of the order of Benedict in particular.[42]

Mohammadanism has given birth to several 'religious orders' the chief of which are the Quadiri, the Maulavi, the Baqtashi, the Rufai, etc. The monks are called Dervishe "poor"; they live together 20, 30, or 40 at a time, in a monastery under a head (Shaikh).[43] Dervishes believe that love is a projection of the essence of God to the universal. Many of the dervishes are medicant asectics who have taken the vow of poverty. Though some of them are beggars by choice, others work in common professions; Egyptian Qadirities, for example are fishermen.

The dervishes wear a long robe of coarse stuff. Reception into their order is preceded by a time of probation. As regards their religious practices, these Mohammadan monks have prayers, sacred dances, and sometimes penances, such as the privation of sleep, immobility (ensured by betters on the fect), fasting, and solitude. Many of them are also mendicants.[44] Whirling dance, which is the practice of the Mevlevi sect inTurkey, is just one of the physical methods to try to reach religious ecstasy(Majdhb) and connection with Allah, Rifgites, also called the hawling dervishes cut themselves with knives, handle red-hot iron and eat hot coals are live serpents, depending on the subsect[45]. Other brotherhoods and subgroups chant verses of Koran, play drums or dance vigorously in groups, all according to their specific traditions. Each brotherhoods uses its own grab and methods of acceptance and initiation, which may be rather severe[46].

Some of the orders claims to go back to the time of the Prophet himself, although he had said, "In Islam there are no monks", and although no mention of the monastic life is to be found in the *Quran*. Even during the lifetime of Muhammad, however, the sufis gave themselves up to certain practice of monasticism and lived together in community. Abu Bakr an Ali, contemporaries of the Prophet, formed with his approval, communities of the same kind.[47] Other orders were founded on the same model in Egypt, Arabis, Persia and Turkey. There are also various dervish brotherhoods who trace their origins from various Muslim saints and teachers, especially Ali and Abu Bakr. They live in monastic conditions. Superficially similar to Christian monk brotherhoods. Various sects and subsects have appeared and disappeared over the centuries.[48]

The monastic institutions of the Jain in some respects hold an intermediate position between those of the Hindu and the Buddhists. Their rule and order are more definitely framed than the former, but are less exacting than the Buddhist and allow more freedom to the individual. As in Buddhism also, the existing system or practice of the Brahman monks or asetics formed the model on which the founder of the Jain faith ordered his own community. Mahavira himself is said to have had a following of fourteen or fifteen thousand monks, and more than twice that number of nuns. Over the monastic schools into which the community was divided were placed eleven chief disciples, or *ganadharas*, or twelve if Gosala be reckoned, who proved himself the unworthy rival and opponent of his master.[49]

Jainism has two branches, each has a slightly different take on monasticism. Digambara monks do not wear clothing; however, they do not consider themselves to be nude—they are wearing the environment. Digambaras believe that practice represents a refusal to give into the body's demand comfort and private property—only Digmabara ascetics are required to forsake clothing. Digmabara ascetics have only two possessions: a peacock feather broom and a water gourd. They also believe that women are unable to obtain moksha. As a result, of the around 6000 Jain nuns, barely 100 are Digambaras. The Shvetambaras are the other main Jainist sect. Shvetambaras, unlike Digambaras, neither believe that women ascetics must practice nudity, nor do they believe that are unable to obtain moksha. Shvetambaras are commonly seen wearing face masks so that they do not accidentally breath in and kill small creatures.[50]

By the Indian life has ever been regarded as essentially evil, and relief from the burden and sorrow of existence as the chief and final goal. In many forms of Indian doctrine, especially the Buddhist' but also in that of Hindu Leaders and teacher before Gautama, this end was to be achieved only in and through a monastic dedication and life. It was impossible for the layman, distracted by the cares and encumbered by the possessions of the world, to secure salvation. Emancipated from these he was free to devote himself to the highest aim and to win his way to deliverance (Moksha).

In Hinduism, monastic tradition varies somewhat from sect to sect. Historically this path has been open to males only, but some traditions now accept female renunciates as well. Hindu monks are called sadhus and in most traditions are easily recognized by their saffron robes. Vaisnava monks shave their heads excepts for a small patch on the back of the head, while Saivite monks in most traditions let their hair and beard grow uncut. A sadhu's vow of renunciation typically forbids him from: owning personal property apart from a bowl, a cup, two sets of clothing and medical aides such as eyeglasses; having any contact with, looking at, thinking of or even being in the present of women; eating for pleasure; possessing or even touching money or valuables in any way, shape or form; maintaining personal relationships.

Apparently the habits and methods of the monastic life have undergone little change or development since the earliest ages. The mendicant or wandering ascetic, rather than the resident community of monks, has been the characteristic features of Indian religious life: and the monasteries have served in a greater degree as lodging-or rest houses than for fixed and permanent habitation. The earliest delineations of Indian social and religious life present the same features as are seen in modern times—a large drifting population of mendicants and ascetics, who find only a temporary home in the monasteries, and after a longer or shorter stay move on entirely as their own inclination prompts.

The habit of monasticism owes it origin, it has been said, to the natural tendencies of mankind towards mysticism and asceticism. These are developed, set in order and satisfied, in the rule an restraint of the monastic life. In India, more perhaps than elsewhere, the practice is of very great antiquity; and the motives and instincts suggested, although true in general of the rise and history of Indian monasticism, in two respects at least render an insufficient account of the causes at work. In the routine existence of the monasteries, as for as this is distinct from the solitary or wandering life of the hermits and ascetics, mystical devotion has played but a small part. Mysticism in India has shunned companionship. The mystic aim has been the chosen and cherished pursuit of the lonely ascetic.

It has been stated by P. V. Kane[51] that the ascetic should wonder alone because it was the ideal of the Hindu ascetic. A ascetic should always wander alone without a companion, as by so doing he will be free from attachments and the pangs of separation." Daksa[52] emphasizes this point very well 'the real ascetic always stays alone; if two stay together, they form a pair; if three stay together they are like a village and if more (than three stay together) then it becomes like a town. An ascetic should not form a pair or a village or a town; by so doing he swerves from his *dharma*, since (if two or more stay together) they begin to exchange news about the ruling prince, about the alms obtained and by close contact, sentiments of affection, jealousy or wickedness arise between them. Bad ascetics engage in many activities viz. expounding (texts) for securing money or honour and also gathering pupils round them. There are only four proper actions for an ascetic and no fifth viz. contemptation, purity, begging, always staying alone.[53]

Some characteristics of ascetics have been stated in some other texts also. The *Jabalopanisad*[54] describes the state of paramahans as at great length. They are sages like Samvartaka, Aruni, Svetaketu, Durvasas, Rbhu, Nidagha, Jadabharata, Dattatreya, Raivataka; they do not exhibit any visible signs of their order or any visible rules of conduct; though they are really not mad they behave like one mad; they go out for alms only for keeping body and soul together; they are unaffected by acquisition or absence (of alms), they have no house but wander about and stay in a temple or on a heap of grass, on an ant-hill, or at the foot of a tree or on a river bank or in a cave, they have attachment for nothing, they are centred in contemplation of the one spirit.[55]

The ascetic motive or ideal, has been overwhelmingly predominant among the causes that have urged such great numbers of Indian men and women at all times to adopt the monastic robes and manner of life. Another motive, however, exercised a powerful influence in determining the choice of the monastic profession. This was the Indian view of life as a whole. In Indian tradition the life's final goal was moksha and which can be achieved only in and through a monastic dedication and life.

Another respect in which historically Indian monasticism in general has been distinguished from Buddhist or Christian is the deficiency of co-ordination or of a central control. The ideal of the Indian monk or ascetic is not and never has been a fixed residence and occupation, but rather freedom to wander at pleasure, to visit the various sacred places and shrines, and to dispose his manner of life and his time independently in all respects as seemed best to himself. In India monasteries have served in a greater degree as lodging or resthouses than for fixed and permanent habitation.[56]

According to Hindu regulation of the four asramas every Brahman toward the close of his life must renounce the world and adopt the homeless life and the ascetic garb. So it was clear that no low-caste or out-caste man could become a monk, but only the 'twice-born'. In practice, of course, the wandering population is recruited from all castes; and many follow the life as an easy and convenient mode of gaining a subsistence without trouble to themselves.[57] The ancient Indian custom, familiar to Indian thought and in the closest harmony with Indian ideals, formed the model for the great Buddhist and Jain communities of monks, and gave to them precept and habit and rule. Only in organisation did the daughter communities go for beyond anything that was developed in Hinduism. Here the preference for an independent and self-regulated life proved itself the stronger, and broke away from all attempts at a settled and established order or government.

Now we would see some features of Indian monasteries or 'maths'. The Hindu maths or monasteries, are invariably of small size, providing accomodation for only a few inmates. Except at the important pilgrim centres, where durable buildings of brick are found, they are often little more than a collection of huts or cells ranged around a central court-yard. Permanent quarters are provided for the *mahant*, or presiding abbot, of the monestary and his resident students. The remaining buildings are occupied at the periodical festivals by the members of the order to which the monastery belongs. Attached are a temple or shrine for the service of the diety, and in the larger monasteries at least a separate *dharmasala,* or rest-house, for the accommodation of travellers. The term *matha* appears to have been originally applied to the solitary hut of the religious recluse, and then to similar dwellings of the communities of hermits living together in the forest in the practice of austerities. An attractive description is given in Kalidas's *Sakuntala* about such a woodland hermitage.[58]

The *maths* exist in considerable numbers all over India, but the inmates for the most part live a retired life, keeping to themselves, and both they and their homes are little known to outsiders. Each sect or monastic order has its own *maths*, that of the founder of the order being regarded as the chief. There is however, no central control, nor any interference in the management or affairs of another monastery.

It was an act of religious merit to erect a monastery for the service of the monks and wandering ascetics. Pious Hindus have been exceedingly liberal in their bequests for religious and charitable purpose, sometimes devoting considerable property towards the establishment and maintenance of temples with their connected monasteries and rest-houses. The religious merit acquired by the construction of a temple and its dedication to the worship of particular divinities is extolled in numerous sacred texts :

"*Agni purana*" : 'Of those persons who are ever contemplating the construction of a temple for Hari, the sins of a previous hundred births are destroyed.'[59]

"*Vishnu Purana*": 'A man attains the regions presided over by that deity whose temple he erects.'

"*Skanda Purana*": ' On beginning the construction of a temple for Krishna, the sins committed in seven births are annihilated, and the ancestors rescued from hell'.[60]

"*Vamana Purana*" : 'The establisher of a temple for Vishnu procures the salvation of himself and of eight generations above his grandfather!'[61]

In most instances an endowment for the upkeep of the monastery is provided either at the time of erection or by subsequent grant, and this is increased from time to time by the gifts of patrons who endeavour thus to secure merits for themselves.[62] The individual monk is bound by a vow of poverty, but the monasteries often become exceedinly wealthy in revenue and lands. Since the monks themselves do no manual labour, nor indeed work of any kind, the lands are usually formed out to Hindu lay-proprietors.

H.H. Wilson states[63], "The *mathas,* asthals, or *akharas,* the residences of the monastic communities of Hindus, are scattered over the whole country. They vary in structure and extent, according to the property of which the proprietors are possessed, but the generally comprehended a set of huts or chambers for the *Mahant* or superior and his permanent pupils; a temple sacred to the diety whom they worship, or the*samadh,* or shrine of the founder of the sect, or some eminent teacher; and a *dharmsala,* one or more sheds or buildings for the accommodation of the mendicants or travellers who are constantly visiting the math.

The oversight of the monastery and the responsibility for

entertainig itinerant monks or strangers are in the hands of a presiding elder or abbot (*mathadhipati*). There were a number of disciples who gathered around him to follow his instructions. There is, however, no definite or fixed hierarchy or gradation of office. The inmates of the monastery are free to come or go at their own will, and neither their movements nor their actions are in any way controlled. They must observe the vow of poverty, depend entirely upon the bounty of others for their daily sustenance and must wear the monastic garb. Apart from these simple conditions they do as they please. It vary from sect to sect that what should be the actual possessions which the monk or sannyasin carries with him. The essentials are the robes and a begging bowl; to which are usually added a staff, water-pot, and rosary, a strainer, a pair of sandals, the materials for smoking and betel-chewing, and perhaps one or more vessels for carrying or cooking food.[64]

There is considerable differences between the sects in respect of the degree of ascetic self-denial or actual discomfort and pain which they voluntarily endure. Saivite monks are, as a rule, more extreme in their manner of life and austerities. The Vaisnavites allow themselves greater liberty and seldom, if ever, inflict upon themselves the prolonged bodily tortures by which the others seek to gain notariety or accumulate merit.

In the popular work known as *Pancatantra,* ascribable to a period not latter than the 4th or the 5th century A.D., for the first time we get references to the settled abode of an ascetic. Asceticism had developed into an institution and individual ascetic into the counterparts of '*kulapatis*' of more ancient date. The abode in which an ascetic resided and received disciplines, evidently to be initiated into asceticism, is called a '*matha*' , an abode or settlement[65]. In one of the contexts in which the word '*matha*' is used in the pancatantra[66], it occurs as the second part of the compound '*vaidy matha*' 'vidhyamatha', as both the word and the context of its use show, was a college or an institution where instruction or rather knowldege was imparted. One '*Vidhya matha*'—the one referred to in the text was situated in the region of Kanauj- was not necessarily run by one individual. The other *mathas* mentioned in three different conections, are quite explicitly institutions run by individual ascetics.[67] In two of these placesthe word *matha* combines with *ayantana*, which too means an abode, to form the compound *mathayatana* The expression *Mathayatana* means a monastic centre or a convent, emphasizing the fact of its being a settled place. It could be by itself in a secluded spot or in a town attached to a temple of Mahadeva or 'Siva'. It is noteworthy that the latter type, which gets its epigraphical notice in the 11th century, and has continued to be the preponderent form ever since in the South of Tamilnad, mentioned, in this popular book of the 5th century, was located in the town of Mahilaropa, i.e. modern Mylapore, near Madras.

The abode was not only to be an important person, to be the owner or to be in charge of a convent, but also to undertake very heavy responsibility. The worries and cares of running or keeping a monastic entre, *matha*, were "enough to lead one to hell in three days." It is doubly interesting that the third reference to a *matha* of an ascetic[68] pl aces it in the famous city of Ujjain and mentions the ascetic by name as Bhairavananda. Ananda-ending names of ascetics are thus clearly older than 'Samkaracarya's endeavour of formal organisation by about four centuries. This raises the probability of the monastic orders being older than Samkaracarya who may have to be looked upon as a renovator only and not the original formulator of the orders.[69]

The teaching activity of the monasteries was in the Upanisadic age are the sweet concern of individual ascetics. Hiuen Tsang[70] has something to say about such individual teachers though he does not describe them as ascetics. He states, "there are some, deeply versed in antiquity, who devote themselves to elegant studies, and live apart from the world, and retain the simplicity of their character. These rise above mundane present, and are insensible to renown as to the contempt of the world. Their name having spread afar, the rulers appreciate them highly, but are unable to draw them to the court. The chief of the country honours them on account of their (mental) gifts and the people exalt their fame and render them universal homage. This is the reason of their devoting themselves to their studies with ardour and resolution, without any sense of fatigue. They search for wisdom, relying on their own resources. Although they are possessed of large wealth, yet they will wander here and there to seek their subsistence. There are others who, whilst attaching value to letters, will yet without shame consume their fortunes in wandering about for pleasure, neglecting their duties. They squander their substance in costly food and clothing. Having no virtuous principle, and no desire to study, they are brought to disgrace, and their infamy is widely circulated."

This practice is attested in sanskrit literature about two generations before Hiuen Tsang. Dandin in his *Dasakumaracarita*[71] referes to an ascetic named Vamadeva, residing and having pupils in the Vindhya forest. Dandin calls him 'Topodhana', 'one whose wealth is austerity'. Another ascetic who had established a reputation for 'divine sight' is referred to as 'Maharsi' and 'Bhagavan' Marici. He had his establishment just outside Campa, the capital of Bengal of that time.[72]

Samkaracarya while giving the monastic interpretation of the *Brahmasutra* carved out a working compromise between renouncing this world and carrying on its routine duties. The path of knowledge as the method of salvation would necessitate renouncing the world. That was one way of Brahma-realization. The path of mundane duty rightly performed, Samkaracarya preached , effects the same salvation but in a deferred manner. The generality of mankind would do well to follow that path. Thus he preached against indiscriminate Samnyasa and stemmed it in one way.

Samkaracarya, himself a 'naisthika brahmacari', life -long celibate, could hardly be expected to have his favourite disciples from among householders. He seems always to have been on the move and his favourite disciples could not but be 'naisthika brahmacaris' like himself. We know the names of at least four of them. For the consolidation and spread of his religio-philosopical ideas he established four centres. What determined the choice of these we do not know exactly in respect of all of them. Dwarka and Puri were evidently famous centres of pilgrimage. But Badri, or rather Jyoti, was not so well-known a centre. We remember the observation of Hiuen Tsang about Haradwar being the most famous centre of his time. And Haradwar is situated only a few miles down the road which connects Badri with the plains. Prayag was another religious centre; and to judge by the magnificence of its temples and the large number of resident ascetics, Banaras, as described by Hiuen Tsang, was still another. But none of these was selected for basing the monastic centres. Sringeri was selected perhaps because of Samkaracarya's personal experiences and also owing to the centres of kapalika and kalamukha sects being in the nearby region. These four centres were placed under the charge of the four disciples. And they were entrusted with the responsibility of religio-philosophical affairs of their specified regions. With due deference to the great vision of the philosopher, it must be pointed out that Badri was too inconvenient a place to supervise and control the religious affairs of the major and important portion of northern India coming under its charge.

We have come to know that the educational arrangement prevalent in northern India in the times preceding Samkaracarya. There is no evidence to show that these temples served as educational centres. The situation in South India was the same. Nor was there any Buddhist educational institution of note. Under these circumstances the emergence of temple-colleges, whether meant for householders or for ascetics or for both, about the beginning of the 10th century A.D., must be attributed to the impetus given by Samkaracarya's organizational activity. It may be thus justified to credit Samkaracarya with having comprehended the duty of educational activity in the routine life of the pontiffs of the monastic centres and their disciples.

Pious devotees bestowed considerable donations on these *mathas*. In course of time these *mathas* went on increasing and huge properties came to be under the control of the pontiffs of these several *mathas*. There arose ten orders of advaita sanyasins alone[73] viz. Tirtha, Asrama, Vana, Aranya, Giri, Parvata, Sagara, Saraswati, Bharati and Puri. These ten orders are said to be the pupils in succession of the four disciples of Samkara. The several *mathas* at Sringeri, Kanci, Kumbhakonam, Kudalgi, Sankesvara, Sivaganga have been quarrelling among themselves as to their jurisdictions[74] and their rights to claim monetary payments from the people and to exercise spiritual authority in matters of expiations, excommunication etc.

According to the biographers of Samkaracarya, Samkaracarya in the short span of his life put through an amazing amount of organizational work which is functioning even to-day. Samkaracarya, to whom is attributed the final defeat of Buddhism. In India, was not slow to perceive the imperative need for monastic centres. He selected four places in four different quarters, namely Badri in the north, Dwarka in the west, Sringeri in the south and Puri in the east, for establishing monastic centres. The names of these monastic centres by which they are known are Jyoti or Joshi, Sarada, Sringeri and Govardhan respectively.

Samkaracarya's first disciples, whom he admitted to samnaysa, were Padmapada, Hastamalaka, Suresvara and Totaka. Of these, the first had two pupils, Tirtha and Asrama; the second, Vana and Aranya; the third had three, Saraswati, Puri and Bharati; and the fourth also three, Giri, Parvata and Sagara. The ten orders of Dasanamis are, according to this account, to be traced for their appelations to the names of the disciples of Samkaracarya's own disciples.[75] It is not possible at this stage to ascertain what truth, if any, is contained in this account.

At the monastic centres, besides the Samnyasis proper there

are other, generally younger, ascetics, whose task it is to render personal service to the senior and aged Samnyasis as well as to the centre as a whole. They are called Brahmacaris. And each centre has its own specific name for its Brahmacaris. They are Ananda, Swarupa, Caitanya and Prakash respectively.

Each one of the four monastic centres has its own special tutelary male and female deities. Joshi centre of Badri has Narayana and Purnagiri as its tutelary deities. It is interesting to note that the Dasanamis generally greet each other with the expression 'Namo Narayanaya', 'bow to Narayana'. Some use a different greeting formula, namely 'Namah Sivaya', 'bow to Siva'. The female diety of this centre is know as Purnagiri, a rather unfamiliar goddess. Siddhesvara and Bhadrakali preside over the Sarda centre at Dwarka. Both these are well-known forms of Siva and Parvati respectively. Kamaksi is the tutelary female deity of Sringeri centre. Oral accounts identify her with Sarada. Jugannatha, a form of Vishnu, for which Puri has been famous for all these ages, is naturally the tutelary deity of its manastic centre. The female deity presiding there, is Vimala. We may note here that though the Dasanami Samnyasis, who are follwers of the monastic Vedanta of Samkaracarya, accept for worship various aspects of the diety in more or less human forms, in theory they are expected to meditate on the formless Supreme Soul. It is characteristic of Hindu religious synthesis, that even Samkaracarya, the great logician and metaphysician that he was, saw good reason to permit and even to prescribe anthropomorphic worship as a step towards final spiritual realization.

Each one of the centres has its own sacred place and sacred waters. Badarikasrma and the river Alaknanada serve the northern centre. Dwaraka is naturally the sacred place of the Sarda centre of the west. For the sacred waters somehow this centre has been assigned the far off Gomati river Sringeri was chosen by Samkaracarya because of its beautiful situation on the Tungabhadra river. The Tungabhadra naturally figures as its sacred waters. The sacred place assigned to this centre lies further south Ramesvaram, the southernmost extermity of India is the choice. The town of Puri, commonly known as Jagannathpuri, is the sacred place for the fourth centre with the appellation of Purushottama, an epithet which is comonly applied to Vishnu. Its sacred waters are the ocean.

In religious terminology the abbot or the original Mahanta of Joshi centre was Totaka, Suresvara, Hastamalaka and Padmapada being those of Sarda, Sringeri and Govardhana centres respectively.

The four *Vedas* are distributed among the four centres. The *Atharvaveda*, which is generally relegated to an inferior position and excluded from the sacrosanct triad of the other three Vedas, becomes the particular concern of the Joshi centre. Sarada centre has to take care of the Samveda. To Sringeri is assigned the Yajurveda. The Rgveda, which is not only the oldest but is also the fundamental basis for the Yajurveda and Samveda, is assigned to the Govardhan centre. We have not been able to get any enlightenment on the rationale of this assignment.

A monastic centre, after all, stood for its philosophy and its inculcation among its inmates. And the centres being founded by Samkaracarya could have only one philosophy, that of Advaita Vedanta or pure monism. The four centres were assigned special aphorisms as their symbols of philosophical quintesence. The inmates were to realize Brahma through and as that formula. The inmates of Jyotirmatha realize Brahma with the formula, 'Ayam Atma Brahma', 'This self is Brahma'. The samnyasis of Sarada Matha use the famous sentence, 'Tat Tvum Asi', 'That is Thou', in which the term Brahma does not occur, as their motto. The Sringeri Matha relies on a little more egoistic expression of the same truth for its guiding symbol. It runs 'Aham Brahma Asmi', 'I am Brahma'. The motto of the Govardhana Matha, which is 'Prajnanam Brahma', 'True Knowledge is Brahma' is the most impersonal and abstract. These formulae technically known as Mahavakyas, aphorisms, occur, all the four of them together in one sentence in the *Hayagrivopanisad*. But there is a slight variation. Instead of 'Ayam

Atma Brahma' we have in the *Upanisad* the sentence 'Ayam Atma Antaryami Amartah' 'this self is the deathless controller.'

A samnyasi of whatever order was easily distinguished from Vaishnava ascetics by the colour of his garment which used to be that of Ochre. It was in reference to this colour of their garment that all kinds of Saiva ascetics or Samnyasis were designated as 'Lal Padris', red monks. The Vaishnava Bairagis used to wear white garments and were generally designated as 'Sita padris', white monks, the sanskrit word 'sita' meaning white. Among all principal types of ascetics there is a section which goes naked or used to go naked. Naturally they were not so easily distinguishable, one from the other, the Samyansi from the Bairagi. Their distinctness could be made out only by the 'tilak'-mark on their forehead. The majority of Samnyasis except the Jogis wear a cut and stitched garment. Only a minority sticks to unstitched piece and objects doctrinally to the use of stitched garment. Those of the Samnyasis who can managae to obtain it carry a tiger's or panther's skin on their shoulders which provides them with a convenient seat whenever necessary.

The English writers[76] on the subject mention that the Dasanamis wear a necklace-rosary of Rudraksha seeds consisting of 32 or 64 beads.[77] All Samnyasis wear their forehead 'tilak'-mark of the horizontal variety. Almost all of them use ashes for making it.[78] Samnyasis carry a Kamandalu', bowl, in their hand which is expected to be in shape nearly elliptic and broad rather than vertical and long.

A Dasnami may live at one place or may go on wandering. His choice is not conditioned by weather. He is not required like the Buddha 'Bhikshu' of old or the Jain Sadhu of to-day to remain at one place during the four months of the rainy season. If he chooses to stay at one place, then a Dasanami lives in a monastery generally blonging to the Dasanami school. If he goes on his wanderings, he is generally expected not to stop at one place for more than three days. On such wanderings a Samnyasi may resort to any 'saiva monastery', if one exists at his visiting place. Otherwise he has to beg for his food. On occassions of religious significance, when ascetics are expected to visit certain places both to discharge their own religious duty as well as to remind the lay public of an important aspect of their religion, they generally go in company, in tens and twenties. Religious-minded individuals of charitable disposition have founded special rest-houses called Dharmasalas and Annachatras, where such ascetics get shelter and at meal times are given appropriate food. At the place of pilgrimage, the local Saiva monasteries are always ready to cater with much enthusiasm for their religiously bent quests.

At the temple of the monastery, those who stay at the monastery generally carry on the usual worship of the deity at the temple of the monastery. With the help of their Rudraksha rosary, they mutter their motter or the great sentence or some other sacred formula. Some of them practise a little 'yoga' through much more of it is theoretically expect. One form of 'yoga' known as Hathayoga is properly speaking forbidden to Dasanamis, yet the contortions and postures referred to above, which ascetics resort to at places of pilgrimage, are nothing but an aspect of that 'yoga'. Some of them read some religious literature. Generally one of the senior resident ascetics daily gives a religious discourse or conducts a divine service . Senior ascetics of the Paramahamsa stage are almost always well-versed in philosophical literature and are expected to carry on disputations and to preach and teach.

In the ownership of the establishment generally there is some property. Some of the establishments are so rich that their management and atmosphere is not very dissimilar to that of a state. The head looks upon it as his duty not only to provide the usual amenities for its inmates but is also very enthusiastic and eager to offer the same to visiting Samnyasis. Most of these establishments or Sthanas engage in teaching activities especially in Sanskrit language and in religio-philosophical literature in that language or in the vernacular. They also feed civilian visitors and beggars if they happen to arrive at meal time. Hospitality, in fact, is one of their distinguishing marks.

The monastic order in Budhism, as instituted by Gautama Buddha himself, was not essentially a new creation in India, but was derived from ancient Hindu usage and practice, separation from the world, in the solitary existence of a hermit or ascetic or in regulated communities, had been almost from time immemorial a characteristic feature of Indian life. In adopting the principle of monastic a rule and self-discipline as the basis of his religious system, and defining this as the sole way of religious attainment, the Buddha presented to his hearers no new doctrine or ideal, but urged and enforced a duty familiar to them from the teaching of their own sacred books. The distinctive feature of the Buddhist order, in which it was differentiated from its prodecessors, and to which, in large part at least, it owed its wide extension and success was the removal of all restrictions of caste.

Membership of the order was open to all from the highest to the lowest, without distinction of race or birth. All alike were bound by the vow of poverty, relinquished all personal or individual possession of worldy goods, and sought in Meditation and spiritual endeavour that deliverance from the bonds of existance and misery which the Buddha taught, could never be achieved in the turmoil and distraction of a life in the world. To indicate, therefore, the life of renunciation and strenuous pursuit of the highest aim to which they pledge themselves the monks were known as *bhiksus,*'beggars' *sramans* or *sramaneras,* 'endeavourers; the latter term being given to the novices or junior monks, and sthaviras, 'elders,' to those who were the senior or ruling members in the monasteries. The community of monks as a whole was known as the *sangha* or order, and with the Buddha himself and the *Dharma,* the sacred rule or law, formed a Buddhist triad, each member of which was idealized and invested with a sacred character, and ultimately became the object of a definite worship. On the sculptures the sangha is represented as is man holding a lotus in his hand, the symbol of stainless purity.

In the beginning and intention the monasteries were not the established homes of the monks. To the latter no permanent abodes were assigned, but they were to follow the wandering life of an ascetic or beggar, dependent for their livelihood upon the gifts of the laity, their only shelter the trees of the forest, or booths constructed of leaves and branches. Only during *Vassa (Varsa),* the rainy season, they were free to remain in a definite place or a permanent building. For the early Buddhist monks, caves, either natural or artificially excavated in the rock, seem to have been among the favourite dwelling-places. The more elaborate and permanent dwellings were, in the first instance, apparently always the gifts of wealthy laymen, who desired in this way to do honour to Gautama himself or to the order which he had founded. A usual name for the larger monasteries was *sangharama,* the abode or delight of the sangha; and the term *vihara* was employed also to denote the temple where the images were enshrined in a building which, in the great monasteries at least, was usually distinct from the main hall.[79]

According to tradition a great gathering of monks met at the Magadhan capital of Rajagraha soon after the Buddha's death. At this council Upali, one of the chief disciplies, recited the *vinaya pitaka,* or rules of the order (Sangha), as he recalled having heard the Buddha give them.[80] Soon after the Buddha's death many communities of monks gave up the practice of constant travel except in the rainy season, and settled permanently on the outskirts of towns and villages, often near the local caityas. With time many of these little monasteris grew in size and importance,[81] By Asoka's time India was covered with *viharas,* which were both monasteries and temples.

According to Hsuan Tsang, in the 7th century, in many places great monasteries were in ruins and places of pilgrimage almost deserted. But the faith was still important, and had thousands of monks and many prosperous monasteris. Chief of these was Nalanda, which, under the patronage of kings of Pala line, remained a centre of Buddhist-piety and learning until the Muslim invasion.[82]

It became necessary moreover, at an early date to place restrictions upon the absolute freedom of enterance into the order. Such restrictions took the form of the prohibition of admission to those suffering from any mental or bodily defect, as the blind or lame, and to the vicious in habit or life, gamblers and those involved in debt. Membership of the Buddhist order was not restricted by caste, but slaves, soldiers, debtors and other persons under obligation or in tutelage might not enter it without the permission of their superior. Novices might be admitted from the age of eight upwards, but they could not only qualify for full membership of the Order after a long course of study, at the minimum age of twenty.

The earliest ceremony of admission to the monastic order appears to have been as simple as possible, and confined to a recital of the 'three refuge formula', together with a declaration on the part of the applicant of his desire to become a monk. The rites of admission were simple, involving putting on the three yellow or orange robes of the order, ceremonially shaving the head, and pronouncing the three Jewels and the 'Ten Precepts'. These "three jewels' form the basic profession of faith of Buddhism, and which every Buddhist, both monastic and lay, repeats to this day : "I go for refuge to the Buddha; I go for refuge to the doctrine (*Dharma*); I go for refuge to the Order (Sangha)."[83] The "Ten Precepts" form a sort of Buddhist decalogue :

1. "I accept the precept to refrain from harming living beings.
2. "I accept the precept to refrain from taking what is not given.
3. "I accept the precept to refrain from evil behaviour in passion.
4. "I accept the precept to refrain from sura, meraya and majja (alcoholic drinks) which cause carelessness.
5. "I accept the precept to refrain from false speech.
6. "I accept the precept to refrain from eating at farbidden

times (i.e. after midday).

7. "I accept the precept to refrain from dancing, singing, music and dramatic performances.
8. "I accept the precept to refrain from the use of garlands, perfumes, unguents and jewellery.
9. "I accept the precept to refrain from the use of a high or broad bed."
10. "I accept the precept to refrain from receiving gold and silver."[84]

These precepts were not lifelong vows, but earnest resolves. They were repeated regularly, and if any monk felt that he could no longer honestly maintain them he might leave the order quiet freely, though public opinion tended to frown on the backslider. The vows were aften taken for a definite duration only, as is still done in Burma, where boys on leaving school often spend some months in a monastery in preparation for adult life. In this the Buddhist order sharply contrasts with Christian monasticism.

On admission, the candidate provided himself with the usual almsbowl and the appropriate three vestments which constituted almost his sole possessions. The colour of the robes seems to have been originally dull red or reddish-yellow, as worn by most of the Hindu ascetics, but varies at the present time in differnt countries ; in the south it is usually yellow. Strictly a monk might own only eight "requisities"—threee robes, a waistcloth, an alms-bowl, a razor, a needle, and a cloth to stain his drinking-water, the last in order to ensure that no living creature should inadvertently be destroyed by him when drinking. In fact he often owned much more than this by the convenient fiction, not unknown in some Christian religious communities, that his property belonged to the order, from which he had it on loan.

The monk had to beg his food from door to door every morning, taking it back to his monastery for his midday meal. As the monasteries become wealthy, however, the begging round was after reduced to a mere formality, or dropped altogether. The daily routine of monastic life admitted of little variation. The day began early with recitation and prayers, followed by the regular round for alms. Whatever was bestowed they were to accept with gratitude; if no gift were offered, they were to pass on to the another house without showing resentment. On their return a simple noon-day meal was followed by rest and meditation, the day closing with service and recitation in the temple or half of the monastery.

In most of the monasteries regular instruction was given to the *sramaneras*, or junior monks, and an elementary education was thus available for the entire male population. There were no public services, however, within the monasteries, nor any worship in the usual sense of the term. Only in *Vassa* did the monks ordinarily engage in preaching, or place themselves at the service of the laity for the reading of the scriptures or prayer. Twice a month at the new and full moons on the *upastha* days, the days of abstinence and fasting, the pratimoksa or confesson of sin, was to be formally recited at a full chapter of the monks.

If a monk do any fault and his fault was serious his case was referred to a committee of elders, which might impose penance or expel him from the order. The ceremony concluded with the preaching of sermons, to which the pious layfolk of the vicinity listened.

The daily life of the monk was chiefly spent in study and religious exercises, but he was expected to take his share in the work of the monstery, cleaning his cell, and sweeping the courtyard and the monastic buildings, while the elder monks devoted much of their time to teaching the novices. Among the most important of the monks spiritual exercises were the four sublime Moods (*Brahma-vihara*), in which siting quietly cross-legged, he endeavoured to fill his mind with the four cardinal virtues of Buddhism—love, pity, joy, and serenity—and to consider all living beings in the light of these virtues. A fifth moods was that of impurity, in which he considered all the vileness and horror of the world and of the life of the flesh. For those more advanced in sanctity there were more advanced meditation, which brought the monk very near to the realization of Nirvana.

While the Buddhist monk resembled his Christian counterpart in his vows of chastity and poverty, he took no vow of obedience. Each novice or junior monk had his preceptor, and was expected to treat him with great respect, but the monk was essentially a free member of a community of free men.

There was no central authority to regulate the many monasteries and enforce uniformity; each was a law unto itself, guided only by the precepts of the master as it had received them, and as it interpreted them. The constitution of the monastery had elements of democracy about it. The chief monk, or abbot, was not appointed from above or nominated by his predecessor, but held office by the suffrage of all the monks in the monastic parish. The day-to-day business of the monastery was managed by a committee of elder monks and important discisions, such as the admission or expulsion of members could be made by the committee and not by the chief. Important business was discussed at meetings of the whole monastery.

In intention and practice, therefore, the Sangha formed a brotherhood, within which no distinction was made of rank or birth; age, learning, and seniority formed the only title to authority and respect. the control of the monasteries was in the hands of the *sthaviras*, The eleders or senior monks. The *upadhayayas* or *acharyas* were ordained members of the fraternity of some years' standing, qualified by character and learning to give instruction and to conduct the recitations and prayers. The novices or junior monks were required to devote themselves to study, to perform the necessary services of the monastery buildings, to wait upon the senior monks, and sometimes to attend them, when they moved abroad. All alike pledged themselves to obey the rules and discipline of the order.

There were, however, no irrevocable vows. The monk was free at any time without blame to discard his robes and return to the world. In this way in some Buddhist countries the entire male population passed through the monastery schools, and for a longer or shorter period wore the yellow vestments. By this return to the world the monk definitely desisted from his endeavour to secure for himself deliverance from suffering and misery; for only within the order, according to the teaching of the Buddha, was salvation to be attained. Lay breathren also (*upasaka*,'worshipper,' 'servant') were admitted to the monastery as labourers and servants, and upon them a less strict discipline and obligation were imposed. Nothing further probably was required of them than to recite the 'Three-refuge formula.' they took no part in the regular life of the monastery, did not join in the daily itinerancy for alms, and were in all matters under the direction of the monks. The outside laity also were accustomed to visit the monasteries to make offerings at the shrines.

All classes of the community, kings, princes, merchants and craftsmen, made donations to the Order, which are recorded in numerous inscriptions. Though the individual monk was bound by his vows to own no property except bare necessities, and to touch no silver or gold, the monasteries grew rich on the alms of the faithful. The revenues of whole villages were alienated to them by pious kings, and even the individual monks began to take their vows of poverty lightly, for more than one inscription records donations made to the Order by ordained members of it. The rules of extreme poverty incumbent upon the monks individually did not extend to the monasteries in their corporate capacity. These might be and often were powerful and wealthy corporations, possessed of great resources, and wielding a corresponding influence in the neighbouring districts. Their property consisted for the most part of land and the revenues of estates or villages which had been granted to them in perpetuity by wealthy patrons, whose piety and liberality earned its recompense in the merit which thereby accured to the donor. Gifts in money as well as in kind were frequently bestowed. Sometimes also these donations took the form of the building and furnishing of monasteries for the use of the breathren. Such benefactious are recorded within the lifetime of Gautama himself. He gave his premission for the dedication of the estate and buildings, expressed his pleasure at the meritorious service of his followers, and prophesied of the future good which would be their's as a certain reward.

Apparently only with much reluctance did the Buddha consent to the establishment of an order of nuns (*bhiksunis,* Pali *bhikkhunis*). The traditional account relates that at the thrice-repeated request of Maha Prajapati, Gautama's aunt and nurse, strongly support by Ananda, the Buddha gave his permission for women to 'go out from the household life and enter the homeless state under the doctrine and discipline proclaimed by the Tathagata.' The concessions, however, would prove disastrous, so Gautama prophesied, to the prosperity and duration of the faith which he taught; the pure religion and the good law would endure only for five hundred years instead of a thousand. On the same occasion he prescribed the obligations and duties of the *bhikksunis* contained in 'Eight Chief Rules' to which they were bound in strict obedience. The regulations involved subservience to and dependence upon the order of monks in all respects. A nun even of a hundred years' standing was to rise and respectfully salute even the youngest monk, nor was a nun to venture to admonish a monk, though she must submit to receive admonition from him. Further a nun may not keep *vassa* in a district in which no monk is resident. It is probable that the ordination of womens as *bhikkhunis* and the establishment of nunneries are in reality due to a later age than that of the founder of Buddhism. The institution has never become popular or gained a strong hold in any Buddhist country; and the number of the nuns has always been small relatively to the number of monks.

The origins of early Christian monasticism are not clearly known and are, therefore, subject to controversy. Some scholars believe that the monastic movement was prompted by Late Jewish communal and ascetic ideals, such as those of the Essenes. Still others speculate that Manichaean and similar forms of dualism inspired extremes of asceticism within the

Christian family. However, the first Christian commentators on monasticism believed that the movement had truly gospel origins.

Christian monastics drew their spiritual strength from Christ's emphasis on poverty and on the "narrow way" to salvation. Early monastics believed that Paul preferred celibacy to marriage. Indeed, the first nuns seem to have been widows of the late Roman period who decided not to remarry. From one point of view, the decision of some Christians to live separate from the community, both physically and spiritually, was regrettable. From another, the commitment and service of the monastics made them the most valued people in early medieval society.

Deprived of the supervision of Christ the Christian communiites had to organise themselves. They had no formal bond of union. Each assembly regulated its own affairs. No central authority claimed control over the rest. As the generations of disciples succeeded each other, and the applicants for admission increased, it became necessary to regulate the conditions of entry. Not many wise after flesh at first presented themselves, not many mighty, not many noble. The philasophic observer of later days might scoff at the believers as ignorant and stupid and low; he knew little or nothing of the long and serious discipline which often preceded baptism, or the watchfulness with which the members of doubtful professions, the soldiers, the actor, the schoolmaster who must teach the stories of the gods, were all regarded. As the vivid spiritual energies of the first days declined, the travelling apostles and prophets became fewer and fewer and at last disappeared. The spontaneity of the early ministry gradually faded away. The need of organisation grew more and more accute as the expectation of the Lord's appearance with the angelic host slowly gave place to the perception that the Church must adapt itself to permanent conditions in the social order. Its worship must be duly directed; its teaching systematised; its business arrangements safeguarded; its charities properly administered;

its hospitalities adequately discharged. Within a century after the death of Jesus, Ignatius, the Bishop of Antioch, on his way to martyrdom at Rome, still sees the world hastening to its end, and proclaims a threefold ministry within the Church of bishops, priests and deacons, as part of the divine ordinance in the great conflict between the power of satan and the immeasurable design of God. The development of these three orders takes place at different rates in different localities, but little by little through mutual intercours practice is unified. Confessors, readers, widows, virgins, form specific groups with their own duties and privileges, but there is as yet no dual standard of conduct such as that between the secular disciple and the Buddhist monk. The difference between the layman and the 'religious' will appear at a later day. Meantime Christian thinkers like Irenaeus appealed to the continuity of history from creation to the Gospel; the Church was the heir of prophecy, and over the separate congregations from east to west, from Mesopotamia to Gaul, arose a vision of a spiritual Church created before sun and moon, a virgin daughter of light, to which each earthly assembly belonged in mystical fellowship, the ideal impersonation of God's saving purpose for mankind.[85]

The monastery represented a community. No work done within it or by it, whether manual or intellectual, was directed to an end outside its walls. This is not to say that the monsatery would not give relief to the people in the neighbourhood who asked for it, but that its primary concern was with itself and not with others. Only with the emergence of a more complex society did there arise divisions and specializations in monastic life, of choir monks and lay brethren, of contemplative groups and of active ones. The sphere of work of the new orders of friars lay normally outside the convent. They established themselves in the poorest localities of the growing towns and thus brought religion to the outcasts of society. In doing so, they not only supplied a need which the then existing clergy did not satisfy, but also, assimilating themselves to the conditions of the surrounding life, created a fraternal feeling in the hearts of the destitude.[86]

The first monks of whom we have a good record represent an extreme phase in the evolution of monasticism. These are the so-called desert fathers, hermits, living in the eremitical style in the deserts of Egypt, Syria, and Palestine. Enraged by sin and fearful of damnation, they left the towns for a solitary struggle against temptation. Some, like Simeon Stylities live very exotic lives and became tourist attractions. More typical, however, was Anthony of Egypt (C. 250-356), whose commitment to salvation led him back to the community to evangelize unbelievers. His extreme asceticism deeply touched the sensibilities of the age.

The question for the desert fathers was one of the lonely, individual struggle against the devil as opposed to the obvious support that came from living in some sort of community. Pachomius (C. 290-346), an Egyptian monk, preferred the latter. He wrote a rule of life for monks in which he emphasized organization and the rule of elder monks over the newly professed. The rule became popular, and the movement toward communal life was ensured.

To the idea of community Basil the Great (C. 330-79) added another element. In his writings, and especially in his commentaries on the scriptures, this father of Eastern monasticism defined a theory of Christian humanism which he felt was binding on the monasteries. According to Basil, monastics were bound to consider their duty to the whole of Christian society. They should care for orphans, feed the poor, maintain hospitals, educate children, even provide work for the unemployed.

During the fourth through the sixth centuries monasticism spread throughout the Christian world. From Asia Minor to Britain its ideal flourished. However, the Celtic monks tended to espouse the old eremitical tradition, whereas latin monasticism, under the great rule of Benedict of Nursia (C. 480-547), codified itself into a permanent, organized communal form. To the old promises of poverty, chastity, and obedience to Christ the Benedictines added stability. Monks could no longer driff about from monastery to monastery but were bound to one for life. The essence of Benedict's rule is its sensible approach to Christian living. It forbade excess and provided practical advice for every aspect of monastery life. It gave an elaborate description of the role of each person in the community from the abbot, who represented Christ in the community, to the lowliest postulant. For this reason, the Benedictine Rule became the standard in western Europe. Because of their devotion to the rule, monks came to be known as the "regular" clergy, from the Latin regua "rule".

The great work of the monasteries of th Middle Ages was the Opus Dei, the work of God, prayer and praise to the Almighty throught the day and night. This "work" was organized the offices of the monatic day. These varried somewhat according to place and season, but generally vigils, lauds, terce, sext, vespers and compline were chanted throught christendom. In addition, monks and nuns performed physical labour, provided charitable services, and kept learning alive. They studied and copied the scriptures and the writings of the church fathers as well as classical philosophy and literature.

In the monastic hands writing became an art. The monasteries had a monopoly on education untill the evolution of the cathedral school and the university in the High Middle Ages.

Early madieval monasticism may have reached its height in the foundation of the Abbey of Cluny in Burgundy in the tenth century. Cluny set a new standard of liturgical splendor. It also sought to escape corruption by establishing its independence from the feudal system in which all medieval institutions were rooted. Cluny and its "Daughters" (houses which it founded and disciplined) exercised enormous spiritual authority in the eleventh century. Though it is no longer draw direct connections between the cluniac reform movement and reform papacy of Grgoary VII (1073-85), both represent institutional responses to the rapid changes in medieval society.

By 1100, monasticism was on the defensive. It was no longer clear that monastic service to God and society was commensurate with the praise and gifts which society had lavished on the monasteries. Great donations and other forms of wealth made monks rich at a time when other medieval institutions were assuming society duties formerly the responsibility of the monasteries. The popularity of the monasteries attracted less than devout postulants, and the aristocracy used the great houses as a repository for spinster daughters and younger sons. Yet even as monasticism approached its crisis, new reformed orders appeared. The Cistercians, under their most influential leader Bernard of Clairvaux, sought a new life of evangelical purity. They confined membership to adults, simplified services, abandoned all feudal obligations, and tried to restore the comtemplative life. The Carthusians tried to recapture the old cremitical spirit of the desert fathers. They retreated from society and became an important feature of the medieval frontier, cutting down forest and opening new ground for agriculture.

Christian monasticism possesses certain characteristics all of which are not equally essential, but which, nevertheless, when taken together, are necessary to constitute a monk.

The first monks, after the example of the Christian ascetics, practised poverty, chastity, and humility—virtues which, along with obedience, soon came to be regarded as essential to the monastic life. They practised chastity under form of complete celibacy and perfect continence. The practice of obedience consisted in following in the footsteps of Jesus Christ, recognizing Him as their master and in submission to those who represent him here below. In the case of the cenobites this obedience was the result of their very life itself. The moment that many monks united to live together, they were oliged to adopt a rule of life which would be the same for all, and to submit to the authority of a head. Schenoudi of Atripe obliged his monks to make a profession of obedience to the Rule of the monastery. This profession was a written and signed engagement and was preserved in the archives of the monastery. The greater number of monasteries had the same custom under one form or another. These virtues were taught and practised by all the early monks, and , as soon as monastic customs began to be drawn up and codified, we find severe laws laid down to ensure their practice.

Mortification is essential to the practice of asceticism; it takes the form of the renunciation of the pleasures of sense (chastity, celibacy, fasting, etc.); work, silence, prayer even, may all be considered forms of mortification. As in all schools of asceticism (Neo Platonist, Buddhist, etc.), fasting is considered one of the essential exercise of the Christian 'athlete'; Jesus taught it to its disciples and practised it himself. Fasting was regarded by the monks as one of the most efficacious of all exercise of mortification. There is, in fact, no monastic Rule in which restraint in matters of food and drink is not arranged for. It is chiefly in the monasteries of the East (Syria, Palestine, Asia Minar) that one comes across extraordinary forms of mortification; though these must be regarded as exceptional cases, they cannot be passed over in silence. There were, first of all the Stylites and the Dendrites, who condemned themselves to perpetual immobility, the former on their coloumns, the latter on the branch of a tree.

Already in the East, during the 4th cent., it was an established principle that the monk should live by the labour of his hands. The work of the monk was of two kinds : (a) manual, and (b) intellectual. The manual labour of the early monks consisted chiefly in the weaving of mats or the cultivation of the soil. These occupation had as their principal motive not so much interest or gain as mortification in addition to all the mortifications already forming part of their existence, and especially the avoidance of idleness. In the case of the monks of the west this manual work was carried out in so orderly and methodical a manner that is resulted in the clearing of a large part of the waste land of Europe. The various arts and crafts had also their place in monastic activity, but in the West rather than in the East. A monastery came, in course of time, to form a little city in itself. Founded as most monasteries then were, far from the towns and centres of worldly activity, they were obliged to provide for themselves, and besides cultivating the soil, the monks had to give themselves to the exercise of the various trades necessary for their wants- e.g., baking, carpentry, weaving, etc. The intellectual work of the monks consisted chiefly in the *Lectio divina,* i.e. the reading and study of the sacred scriptures and other holy writings. In the West this part of the monastic curriculum underwent a great development. More and more time was given to intellectual work. The monks, especially in the East, retired from the world into salitude, there to lead lives of prayer and labour apart from all intercourse with it. They took part in the external ministry of the Church only on rare occasions and by force of special circumstances. In the West, the monks were led in time to take up in certain countries. They thus became missionaries, and had, in fact, a large part in bringing about the conversion of Europe.

A considerable part of his time was always devoted to prayer. In substance this prayer consisted in meditation on, or recitation of, the Psalter, which was distributed according to the days of the week or the hours of each day. It was oragnized more methodically when regular monasteries began to be established in greater numbers. Silence, recommended by philosophers as a necessary condition for meditation or intellectual research, was one of the practices most rigourously enforced in the monastic life. In the case of hermits, living in complete isolation, silence was practically absolute, and rare were the occasions on which they could indulge in conversation. They did, however, occassionally visit one another, and sometimes returned to their monasteries for a certain length of time. For the cenobites talking was naturally of more frequent occurrence, but severe regulations were established on this point in the greater number of monasteries.

Solitude, as in the case of silence, was interpreted in a more or less wide sense. For the anchorites, hermits, and Stylites, living in their caves, in their tombs, or on their pillars, solitude was complete and absolute. For the cenobites it consisted rather in their separation from the world, is the practice of silence, and in certain restraints. The monastery was enclosed by walls; one gate alone gave access to it. Communication with the outside world was subject to strict contrate, and, to render the necessity less frequent, the monastery, like a little city, was to be self-contained. There were exercised all the different trades and crafts demanded by the needs of the community. It is this need of solitude that may be said to have given to monastic architecture its principal characteristics and the disposition of its various parts.

Stability, i.e. the engagement undertaken by a monk to remain all his life in the same monastery, was only an accidental condition of the monastic state, and was not established everywhere. In certain regions a monk could pass from one monastery to another. The abuse of this custom, as seen in the wandering monks and other considerations as well, led to the establishment of stability as a law of the monastic state, which little by little became general.

The hermits and anchorites lived separate and alone in the desert; hence they were their own masters. Sometimes colonies of hermits were formed under the direction of a head, to whom the others rendered obedience. Again, we find hermits living near a monastery of cenobites, to which they were obliged to return at certain times, generally on Saturday and Sunday and on feastdays. With regard to the monastic hierarchy and the organization of authority among the cenobites, great variation is to be observed in primitive ages. At the head of the monastery was a superior, at once spiritual father and temporal administrator, who was known by the various titles of archimandrite, hegumenos, abbot prepositus, or provost, etc. The community was governed by this superior, sometimes with the help of an assistant and other officials who fulfilled various charges. He was generally assisted also by a council composed of the older members of the community (*senioree*). The office of the seniors, who were nominated by the superior himself, expired at the end of the year. The government of these monastic societies was a monarchy rather than an oligarchy; often it was even an absolute monarchy. The cellarer, the official who had charge of the stores of the monastery, had, as a rule, very wide powers over the temporal affairs of the monastery.

The monasteries thus constituted usually enjoyed complete autonomy. In the West it was not till the monasteries time of St. Benedict of Aniane that the idea of grouping together under a central authority was actually realized. For example, St. Basil in his Rule, which was the Law everywhere in the East, contents himself with giving a few general principles as to be choice of the superior and the exercise of authority. In certain monastic colonies, too, the organization was very rudimentary in character. Nevertheless, even in the early age of monasticism, we have instances of the attempt to group certain monasteries together under a central authority. Pachomius, e.g. formed his monasteries into a real 'congregation'. He assembled the superiors together four times a year. In these assemblies the interest and affairs of the various communities were discussed and settled. Pachomius himself nominated the superiors of the different houses, and a 'procurator-genral' for the whole confederation. Tabenna, the head-house of this congregation, was an almost military organization. At an early period the Rules, or consititutions, of the various monasteries came to be written down. A great number of these exist, some of which can be safely attributed to the most ancient masters of the monastic life.

It seems that there was originally no special dress for monks. The only rule on this point seems to have been that the monk in his character of ascetic should, like certain ancient philosophers, show in his costume the outward sign of the poverty and humility of his state of life and of his detachment from the things of this world. Even St. Benedict, at a time when monasticism already had customs and traditions both numerous and of long established date, does not seem to have given much importance to the form, colour or quality of the habit worn by his monks.[87]

The hermits ('desert') lived in solitude in the desert; St. John the Baptist, and later St. Paul the Hermit and St. Anthony, were the first of these. Anachorites or anchorites ('retreate') title is synonymous with the hermits, and indicates those monks who practised the solitary life. This form of the monastic life is the most ancient; it spread, first of all, in Egypt, then in Palestine and Syria, through the whole of the Eastern world, and , finally, in the West. Recluses and Stylites must be classed with hermits and anchorites. They may be regarded as exceptional cases because of their relatively small number. The former lived enclosed in cells, sometimes completely walled up and communicating with the exterior only by means of a small window. The latter, who are found almost exclusively in the East, lived on the top of a pillar, more or less elevated from the ground[88]. Dendrites ("Tree') lived in trees, Cenobite ('One who lives in common with ohers') was the general term for all monks living together in community. During the primitive period the comparative advantages and excellence of the solitary and cenobitic forms of monastic life formed the subject of frequent discussions. St. Basil strongly maintains his preference for the cenobitic life over the eremitic life, and his preference is shared by St. Benedict. The Sarabaites and the Gyrovagi were regarded as an evil kind of monks. The first , mentioned by St. Jerome under Their Syriae name of 'Remoboth', lived together in tows and threes in a monastery, in order to live a life without either rule or law, following no other rule than that of their own will or caprice. The Gyrovagi or Circumcelliones ('vagabonds') went from monastery to monastery, demanding a lodging for a few days, and scandalizing all true Christians by their excesses. Catenati, as the name indicates, these monks loaded themselves with chains. They took no care of their bodies, allowed their hair and beards to grow neglected and untrimmed, went barefooted, and wore a black cloak. Apatactities ('to renounce') formed a class intermediary between the earlier ascetics and the monks properly so called, they are found in Jerusalem, in the East, and in Asia Minor. Some of them followed the example of the Gyrovagi, and spent their life wandering about, and some fell into the heresy of the Encratites.[89]

Asceticism as a well-developed theory and systematic practice appears very much earlier in India than in the Greek world. By contrast with India, an organized asceticism appeared quite late in the history of Christianity- not until the end of the 3rd and beginning of the 4th centuries. The early Church gave little encouragement either to anchoritism (the solitary religious life) or to monasticism. Thus in Christianity, as apposed to the Brahminism, Jainism, Buddhism, or Bhakti-religious of India, asceticism was not inherent. This circumstance inevitably raises questions as to the reasons for the eventual development of ascetic practices within Christianity.[90]

The likelihood that the Manichaean example influenced Christian asceticism is far greater than the reverse case. The Manichaean Elect provided a model of ascetic practice which bore many affinities to Christian monasticism—and for the most part antedated it in time. The elect were the elite of their Church; laymen catered to their needs. Their cruel fasts, refusal to wash, and bodily moritfications undoubtedly carried enormous propaganda value. The fact that they were required to be vagrant preachers rather than monatery-dwellers rendered their example a very obvious one. Certainly many Christians of the 3rd and 4th centuries were familiar with their way of life. Chronology points in the same direction. Mani preached in the mid-3rd century A.D.; Christian anchoritism (the hermit's life) reputedly was founded by Antonius in Egypt in the latter years of the 3rd century. The alleged father of Christian cenobitism (Communal monasticism) was Pachomios, who formulated the first definite monastic rule of life in the early 4th century. Conceivably both these forms of Christian asceticism were in existence somewhat prior to the earliest historical mention of them. Nonetheless it is reasonable to assume that Christian monasticism—which only gradually overcome the opposition of important Christian theologians- arose at least partly in imitaion of Manichaean practice.

Bardaisan reports that the ascetics, however, have expressly chosen their status. Anyone wishing to join them must announce his intention to the ruler of his native place, then abondon the city and all his property. He will not return his wife and children, or pay any further attention to them. The ascetics live outside the city and spend their days in pious conversation. They residue in houses and temples (i.e. monasteries) built for them by the king, and of which they are stewards. Like the Brahmins they eat rice, bread, fruits and herbs; all are unmarried and without possessions. They willingly await-death, sometimes seeking it out when they are neither ill nor oppressed. Both Brahmins and ascetics are greatly respected by other Indians. The king himself visits the holy men; in times of danger he asks for their prayer and their advice.

Christian monasticism grew and took institutional form in order to provide a supportive setting for those who wished to take vows of poverty and chastity, who valued the love of Christ which surpasses the love of women. As a later development, Christian monasticism is not explicitly regulated by scripture. It has taken a wide variety of forms, from solitary hermits and begging mendicants to orders dedicated to nursing, teaching, scholarship and other form of service to the world.

The oldest form of Christian monastic tradition was anchoritism. The ascetic hermits generally lived in total salitude in the desert or wild steppe or in mountains or caves, thought occasionally two or three of them lived together. Not uncommon was the practice of spiritual marriage, whereby a monk and a nun lived together in the joint practice of austerities but without physical contact. The life of these anchorities was primitive in the extreme, and intentionally so. They rejected all food produced by work, accepting only the wild fruits and herbs provided by nature. Fire they considered the devil's handiwork: they refused to use it for light, warmth or cooking. Their garments were rough hair irritating to the skin. Believing that a life close to nature is an aid to repentance, they became the companion of wild animals, themselves wild looking and filthy. Prayer, hymn-singing and meditation filled their days.[91]

The monks actively sought physical suffering, since they regarded mortification of the body as nourishment for the soul. Eating and drinking they reduced to the limit of bodily endurance. At times they fasted completely for many days in sucession. They slept on bare ground, and slept little, keeping constant vigils. Moreover, they invented many harsh and unusual forms of austerity. Some of the monks assumed awkward physical positions which they maintained for long periods of time, or stood immoveable for hours praying in the rain, wind or snow. Others actively sought their own destruction, especially if they felt their ascetic resolution to be weakening : they took no precautions against wild animals or shakes, or threw themselves from precipices.

Toward the end of the 4th century the individualist asceticism of the anchorites gradually became rarer. Ascetic impulses came increasingly to be expressed through the communal life of monasteries, where monks were subject to rules and bishops supervised their activities. Small and crude monastic establishments grew in size, acquiring fields, orchards and gardens, inasmuch as an entire community of monk could not be supported solely on the charity of surrounding villages. Often the presence of monks near a town was considered lucky, and the towns-people helped to erect a building for them.

The original foundation of a monastery frequently came about when a widely known anchorite was joined in his solitude by a few disciples, and the anchorite failed to send them away. This happened with the monk. Juliana Saba (d. 366/67AD), for instance, who was famous enough to have the date of his death recorded in the official chronicle of Edessa. According to his contemporary St. Ephraim, Juliana was known to the "whole world". This outstanding anchorite inhabited a cave in the vicinity of Edessa, where the practiced severe mortification, including long rigils and severe fasts. He undertook extensive journeys into the desert to pray, sometimes permitting a single disciple to follow him at a distance and in silence. Gradually a group of admirers gathered around his cave, and Juliana organised a rudimentary form of common life for them. The group began the morning by singing hymns and praying together. Then all went into the desert two by two for prayer and worship; at evening they returned , ending the day with common prayer. The fame of Juliana Saba led other monks to follow his example. Ephraim compared his role in the organization of monasteries to a huge censer that spread incense throught the entire country around Edessa.[92]

The reputed founder of Christian anchoritism, Antonius, was first active in Egypt Ca. 280-90 A.D. But in 306 A.D. one of his disciples visited western Syria, i.e the intermediate region between Egypt and Mesopotamia, and reported that monasticism was as yet unknown there. Moreover, its origin in eastern Syria and Mesopotamia seem to date back to the end of the 3rd century, leaving insufficient time for it to have spread from Egypt. Thus it appears that monasticism arose spontaneously and independently in Egypt and in Syria-Mesopotamia.

The profound difference in character between Syrian and Egyptian monasticism further underlines the likelihood of an independent origin. The Greek-influeneced monasticism of Egypt and Palestine was less individualistic, more moderate in its asceticism, and thus less tolerant of extremes of physical mortification than its counterpart in interior of Syria and Mesopotamia. In Egypt Pachomios (d. 346 A.D.) who created the first rule of life for cenobites, objected strongly to ascetic excesses. He held that monks should not decide for themselves how to spend their time, or invent their own forms of penance, but instead must follow the regulations of the community. Basileios (329-379 A.D.), Bishop of Caesarea in Asia minor and known as the father of Greek monasticism, regarded cenobitism as the only truly Christian form of the monastic life. The reasons he set out in his "Great Rule". An anchorite cannot fulfill all of Christ's commandments, since he is unable to do good works or love his neighbour. Moreover, the stimulating effect of human society is denied him; he is exposed to spiritual dangers, especially pride; and solitude is contrary to nature.

As a natural consequence of such attitudes, asceticism in the Greek-speaking monastries of Egypt and Palestine was on the whole restrained in character. The monks were expected to control their sensuality, without recourse to extreme measures. Their leaders forbade any extraordinary physical mortifications, pointing out that men could not possibly behave like angels, who have no bodies. Greek monks did not observe liturgical fasts with the same painful rigour as the Syrians. Ordinarily they cooked their meals; vegetarianism and eating food raw were not regarded as virtues. In Greek monasticism, endless wandering or total seclusion in cave or cell were both relatively rare. Extremes of bodily morification were on the whole equated with vanity and boasting.[93]

Certainly Christian monasticism cannot have developed solely out of Christian and Judaic precedents, though there were conveniently available once the Church wished to use them. Despite the ascetic exmaples within its own tradition (e.g. John, the Baptist, the Virgin Mary, Jesus, Paul) the Church failed to develop any organized forms of ascetic life or an orthodox ascetic theology until the late 3rd and the 4th century (although Clemens and Origens early in the 3rd century provided some elements of the latter). The earliest Christian anchorites attracted mockery and insults; the Church was not sure whether to consider them true Christians. In Christianity it was new when monks came to be esteemed above laymen; when the highest ideal of Christian life became meditation and prayer rather than work; when mortification of the body was sought and admired; and the desert anchorites and stylities won tremendous fame. The solitary existence of desert hermits was considered superior even to the communal life of monks. Clearly such attitudes were extreme by comparison with the only moderately ascetic teachings of the Jesus or Paul or the practices of the ealiest Christian communities.[94]

The ascetic features of the new universalist religious constituted a major part of their attractiveness. Gnosticism and its offshoot, Manichaeim, taught an ethic of withdrawal from the world, renunciation of its pleasures, and meditation upon spiritual themes. Christianity in the course of the 4th century greatly strengthened its originally ascetic character Mithraism, which was popular among Roman soldiers, laid great stress on such non-materialist virtues as truth-telling, fidelity to contracts, loyaity to comrades, and fraternity. The God Mithra himself was allegedly chaste and encouraged continence in his worshippers, though the attitude of this religion promoted action rather than contemplation. Thus monasticism, which is asceticism in an organized and systematized form, was unquestionably a pervasive phenomenon of the age. Its rise reflected an altered popular mood, the reasons for which can in part be surmised.

To some extent, of course, 4th-century Christian monasticism developed naturally out of its own antecedents. Among its precursors were the Christian or Gnostic-Christian ascetic sects of the 2nd century: the Murkionities, Montanists, Encratites and Bardaisanities.Indeed, individual examples of Christians who enchewed marriage and every physical luxury in order better to commune with God date back to the earliest years of this religion. Nor did an organized Christian monasticism come suddenly into existence through the acts of a few inspired founders, despite the Church tradition that Antonius and Pachomios were its originators. Already in the period 250-270 A.D., Church historians noted the presence of Christian hermits in Egypt who resided on the outskirts of towns, farerunners of the later desert anchorites. Both Antonius and Pachomios were disciples of ascetic teachers like these. Yet apart from these individual antecedents, 4th century Christian monasticism was part of a broadly-based historical phenomenon which reached across doctrinal differences. Even if Christianity had disappeared utterly, an organised asceticism in some form would almost certainly have played a vital role in the life of the Hellenistic world, albeit under the aegis of Manichaeism or some other monostheistic and other worldly faith.[95]

Even apart from Mani's known connection with India, this affinity creates a strong presumption that he was influenced by Indian prototypes when he defined a suitable life-style for his elitie order of Elect. Thereby some of the more obvious aspects of Indian asceticism passed by way of Manichaeism into Christianity, particularly into the Christianity of Syria and Mesopotamia, where Manichaeism enjoyed greater influence than elsewhere. The relatively modest asceticism of the Greek-speaking monks betrays fewer manichaean features; in the Latin speaking West, monasticism took root even more slowly. Nonetheless, all forms of Christian monasticism were interconnected. The monks visited, imitated and learned from one another. Thus by this long chain of influences, Indian asceticism left its mark on the religious style of innumerable Christians who had never heard of India.

It is natural to compare and contrast the monastic principles and life of Buddhism with those of the Christian orders of the early and middle age in Europe. There are many similarities in general features of discipline and government. All communities vowed to poverty and a celibate life, whether Hindu, Muhammadan, Buddhist, or Christian, almost of necessity organize themselves on somewhat similar lines. The essentially distinctive features of Buddhist monasticism would seem to be two : (1) the practice of literal mendicancy which takes the form of a daily round, equipped with staff and begging-bowl, to receive whatever portions of food the charity of the householders may bestow. In the countries where the Mahayana type of Buddhism has prevailed this custom is not and probably never has been obligatory or usual. It forms a distinct and characteristic element, however, of early Buddhist rule and observance. (2) According to Buddhist teaching, salvation is to be found only within the limits of the order. The layman can achieve his own deliverance only if and when he dons the robe of the monk, and takes upon himself the monastic vows. He must seek refuge from the world in a life of retirement, meditation and self-denial, for not otherwise can the fetters of Karma be broken and *nirvana* gained. In Buddhist polity and doctrine, therefore, the order holds a pre-eminent place distinct from and above that which it occupies in any other great religious system.[96]

The two most powerful elements in the shaping of classical Christian thought were Christian monasticism and the early (fourth century) Christian Fathers. The origin of Christian monasticism is often traced only to the deserts of Egypt. But Antonine and Pachomian monasticism, which spread to Syria and Palestine, has no older ancestry. The influence of Buddhist monks and Chaldean mystics on the Jewish monasticism of the Qumran communities, two centuries prior to and after Christ, needs further study. The legend of Barlaam and Joasaph, traditionally attributed to St. John of Damascus, is a patently Christianised Buddhist story that was adapted from Indian-Buddhist sources to glorify Christian monasticism. The story concerns Joasaph, the son of an Indian king, who was converted from Buddhism to Christianity. It is now well-established that the original, which lacks the conversion ingredient, is Buddhist.[97]

Buddhist monks travelled all over the world, especially during the reign of the Indian Emperor Asoka (269-232 B.C.) Buddhism spread to central Asia, to Tibet, Mongolia and China, as well as to the West. One of the Greek kings of the Punjab Menander was a Buddhist. It was about this time. (First century A.D.) that the Greeks entered the spice trade, and travel between India and Greece became regular. Many Buddhists and Brahmans travelled to Rome and Alexandrea. Professor Emile Brehier of the Sarbonne has suggested that the Indian element was a catalyst in the culture of Alexandria, and gave rise to the mystical element in Neo-platonism.[98]

According to Professor Brehier's statement[99], Plotinus (A.D. 205-270), who taught in Alexandria and Rome, has two central ideas : (1) the intelligibility of the universe; the human minds capacity to penetrate beyond appearance and to know reality in its undifferentiated oneness : (2) The total union of beings with the One and the overcoming of duality. It is this latter concept that the west has termed 'mystiacism'. Brehier argues that it was the contact with Indian thought that transformed the Socratic Pythgorean and Stoic notions of the inner logos of the cosmos and the unity that stems from it, into the nation of a 'mystical union of the All with the One. So this thought that all should be united with one is main concept of Plotinus idea. Clearly this thought has no antecedent, in either Helllenic or Egyptian. Philosophy. It is pure Vedanta. The*Atma* (individual Soul) has only to shed its *avidya* (nescience) to realise its identity with the*Paramatma* (Supreme soul). On what basis did Plotinus develop this idea? Did he have any direct contact with Indian thought? This answer has been given by his contemporary, classmate and biographer, the Syrian Porphyry. Porphyry, a strong anti-Christian, was a great admirer and devotee of Plotinus. The matter of Indian origin has been thoroughly researched by Professor Willy Theiler and others![100]

Ammonius Saccas[101], the teacher of both Plotinus and Origen, strangely refused to put anything in writing—a practice reminiscent of the Indian oral tradition. He was almost certainly a vedantin, but not necessarily an Indian. The idea which Plotinus acquired from him was that of the union of Many with the One (or the realisation of their given unity). Plotinus also had a great desire to go to India, and Porphyry directly attributes this desire to Ammonius. When Plotinus returned from Persia, without succeeding in his plans go to India, he set up his own school in Rome in A.D. 244. What we today call 'western mysticism' thus has its major source in the *Upanisads* and in Hindu teachers who came West.[103]

The form in which Western Christianity absorbed contemplation notion can be traced directly from Plotinus, and possibilty the middle Plotonists. In Plotonists contemplation by used as a way to reconciling the individual soul with the

One, definitely has its source in the Indian tradition when we consider the relevance of Ammonius Saccus and his Hindu and Buddhist connections.[104]

Augustine introduced to Christianity the idea that the human soul turn away from sensible things to achieve a union with God. Although the form in which the idea was applied in Western mysticism is not Indian , it definitely has an Indian heritage. Over the ages, the Indian perception has played a large part in the shapping of Western classical mysticism.[105]

REFERENCES

1. Gaden, A.S., "Monasticism" in *ERE,* ed. James Hastings, p. 782.
2. *Ibid,*p. 781.
3. Encyclopedia Monasticism.
4. Marshall, C.T., "Monasticism" *Elwell Evangelical Dictionary.*
5. Encyclopedia Monasticism.
6. Workman, H.B., *The Evolution of the Monastic Ideal,* 1913.
7. Miller, D.M., and Wertz, D.C., *Hindu Monastic Life,* 1976.
8. Dumoulin, H., and Maraldo, J.C. eds., *Buddhism in the Modern World,* 1976.
9. Trimingham, J.S., *The Sufi Order in Islam,* 1971.
10. *ERE,* p. 782.
11. Judaeus, Philo, " Hypothetica"; XI. 1 Philo (Loeb) IX, 437; Josephus, "Jewish War", II. 24 (Loeb) II 371.
12. Sedlar, J.W., *India and the Greek World,* 1981, Totowa, p. 236.
13. *ERE, op. cit.*, p. 782.
14. Philo, "The Contemplative Life" 18-19, in *Philo* (Loeb) 125.
15. *Ibid.*, 11-12 (Loeb) 119.
16. *ERE, op. cit.*, p. 782.
17. Philo, " The Contemplative Life", *op. cit.*, 21-22, 24-38 (Loeb), IX, 125, 127, 135.
18. Philo, " The Contemplative Life, " 34, 37; 73 (Loeb) IX, 133, 135, 159.
19. *Ibid.*, 73-74 (Loeb), 159.
20. *Ibid.*, 68 32-33 (Loeb) 155, 131-33.
21. *ERE, op. cit.*, p. 782.
22. Ghurye, G.S., *Indian Sadhus,* p. 1.
23. Annals, 1988 ABORI, Vol. 69, p. 274, Evolution of the Institution of Beggary in Ancient India" by Acharya, Subrata Kumar.
24. Wagle, Narendra, *Society at the Time of Buddha,* p.155.
25. *Ibid.*, p. 41.

26. Dutta, Sukumar, *Monasticism in India,* Ch. i, Vol. II, p. 584
27. For a Detailed Study of Corporate Law, see Kane, *History of Dharamshastra,* 1974, II, 66-69; 1973, III, 158-60, 486-89.
28. Olivelle, Patrick, *The Asrama System,* p. 209.
29. Narada Smriti, 10.1-7.
30. Olivelle, Patrick, *op. cit.,* p. 209.
31. See for example Olivell 1986-87.
32. Kane, P.V., *op. cit.*, 1974, II. 2, p. 965-66.
33. *Ibid.,* p. 965.
34. *Ibid.,* p. 967.
35. *Ibid.,* p. 971.
36. Johnston, William M., (ed.) *Encyclopedia of Monasticism*, 2 Vols., Chicogo, 2000.
37. *ERE , op. cit.*, p. 782.
38. Johnston, William M. (ed.) *Encyclopedia of Monasticism*, 2 Vols. Chicago, 2000.
39. Johnston, William M., *op. cit.*
40. Knowles, D., *Christian Monasticism,* 1969; T. Merton, *The Monastic Journey*, ed. by P. Hart, 1977.
41. Butter, E.C., *Benedictine Monachism*; Chadwick, O., *Western Asceticism*; Knowles, D., *Christian Monasticism.*
42. Johnston, *op. cit.*
43. Heimbucher, 1, 51, t; "Dervish", in *Kath Lexicon*, iii 1527.
44. *ERE, op. cit.*, p. 783.
45. Johnston, *op. cit.*,
46. *ERE, op. cit.*
47. Heimbucher, *op. cit.*
48. Johnston, *op. cit.*
49. *ERE, op. cit.*, p. 804.
50. Johnston, *op. cit.*,
51. Kane, P.V., *History of Dharmashastra*, Vol. II., part 2, p. 933.
52. Daksha, VII, pp. 34-38 quoted by Apararka, p. 952.
53. Kane, P.V., *op. cit.*, p. 933.
54. *Jabalopanisad,* 6.
55. Kane, P.V., *op. cit.*, p. 941.
56. *ERE, op. cit.*, p. 803.
57. Oman, J.C., *Mystic, Ascetic and Saints of India*, p. 262.
58. *Ibid.*, p. 248.
59. Oman, J.C., *op. cit.*, p. 249.
60. *Ibid.*, p. 250
61. *Ibid.,* p. 250.
62. *ERE, op. cit.*, p. 803.

63. Wilson, H. H., *Sketch of the Religious Sects of the Hindus*, p. 33.
64. *ERE, op. cit.*, p. 804.
65. Ghurye, G.S., *op. cit.*, p. 42.
66. *Pancatantra*, V. 4.
67. *Ibid.*, I, 4, & II, I.
68. *Ibid.*, V, 2.
69. Ghurye, *op. cit.*, p. 42.
70. Beal, *Buddhist Records of the Western World* ,Vol. I, pp. 79, 80, 1884,
71. Dandin, *Dasakumaracharita,* pp 13, 23.
72. *Ibid.*, pp. 78, 90, 135.
73. Wilson, H.H., " Religious Sects of the Hindus" in *Works,* Vol. I, 1861, p. 202; Dr. Farquhar, *Outlines of the Religious Literature of India*, 1920, p.174.
74. Rajvade, Kanda 21 (In Marathi) Letter No. 190, p. 240.
75. Wilson, H.H., *Hindu Religion*, p. 130.
76. Russell and Hira Lal, the Tribes and Castes of the Central Provinces of India, Vol. III., 1916, p. 152.; *ERE* "Asceticism" II, p. 92.
77. Ghurye, *op. cit.,* p. 91.
78. *Ibid.,* p. 90.
79. *ERE, op. cit.*, p. 797.
80. Basham, A.L., *The Wonder That was India*, 1954, N. Delhi , London, p. 261.
81. *Ibid.*, p. 262.
82. *Ibid.*, p. 265.
83. Bhasham, *op. cit.*, p. 273.
84. Basham, A.L., *op. cit.*, p. 281.
85. Carpenter, J.E., *Buddhism and Christianity*, 1988, New Delhi, pp. 81-84.
86. Ghurye, G.S., *op. cit*, pp. 7-8.
87. St. Benedict, *Regula*, Ch. IV.
88. Clay, R.M., *'The Hermit and Anchorites of England'*, in *The Antiquary's Book*, London, 1914.
89. ERE, *op. cit.,* p. 797.
90. Sedlar, *op. cit.*, p. 235.
91. Sedlar, *op.cit.*, p. 247.
92. Ibid, p. 248.
93. Sedlar, *op. cit.*, p. 249.
94. *Ibid.,* p. 295.
95. Sedlar, *op. cit.*, 299.
96. ERE, *op. cit.*, p. 802.
97. *Oxford Dictionary of the Christian Church*, London, 1958.
98. Emile, Brehier, *La philosophie de plotin*, Intro, pp. XVIII-XIX.
99. Gregorios, Paul, 'The Monastic Tradition' in *India and Greece Connections*

and Parallels, Marg Publication, pp. 29-34.

100. Theiler, Willy, *For Schangan Zum Neoplatonismus: Quellen und studien zur Geschichte, der Philosophie.*

102. In detail see Chapter, Neoplatonism.

103. Gregorios, Paul, *op. cit.*, p. 31.

104. *Ibid.*, p. 32.

105. Gregorios, Paul, *op. cit.*, p. 32.

CONCULSION : THE PICTURE WHOLE

There were many forms of asceticism which were present in ancient India and ancient Greece. Some of them which were common in both the countries are "austerity, chastity, celibacy, wandering, fasting, abstinence from eating meat, etc. It was a source for them who wished to liberate from the wheel of birth, or the transmigration of souls. Asceticism is a unique feature of Indian society. And when we investigate we come to know that it was also present in the ancient Greek civilization in many forms.

It has been discussed that how the contacts of two great civilizations were possible in ancient time. These facts bear testimony to the fact that an interchange of the philosophical ideas was possible from both the sides.

J.W. Sedlar states the very generalized resemblance between the Brahman of the *Upanisads* and the arche of the Greeks testifies rather to the universality of human experience than to any likelihood of direct Indian Influence upon Greece. But when we study about the contacts we come to the conclusion that it was the emergence of Achaemanian Empire, of which the Greeks living in the colonized cities of Ionia and the Indians living in the region around Indus were integral parts, we have the first definite proof of Greeks knowledge of India. With Alexander's expedition began the important stage of Greek writings on India. He had been a disciple of the great master of knowledge and among the officers who acompanied him to India, some were distinguished for their literary and scientific achievements. Alexander's companions were the first Westerners to encounter the Indian sages, thus establishing the tradition of recognizing

India's fame as a land of philosophers. There are two topics in which one is very important where Onesikritos statements have been recorded in considerable details, that is his meeting with Gymnosophists.

Giving an account of this meeting Onesikritos stated that he had seen fifteen ascetics in different postures—standing, sitting or lying naked motionless and enduring the unbearable heat of the sun. One of these Sophists was Kalanos who later accompanied the king as far as Persia and died in accordance with his ancestral custom, being placed upon a pyre and burned. The oldest and wisest among them according to Onesikritos was Mandanis.

Who were the Gymnosophists or naked sages of Taxila? Their ideas and teachings, as known to us through Onesikritos, are common in Indian thought. So far as their ascetic practices are concerned, there were many sects then in India performing such practices.[1] The nakedness too, although more prominent among the Jainas, was not restricted to them. The Vatarasana Muni mentioned in the *Rgveda* lived naked.[2] Besides Jainas, the *Uttaradhyayanasutra* also mentioned the naked sects of Mrgacarika, Uddandaka, and the Ajivikas[3]. Vassiliades thinks that it is more likely that the naked ascetics formed a part of an early sect of Saiva Nagas. In the *Jabala Upanisad (6)* the ascetic is advised to live naked as he was born and the *Paramahamsa Upanisad* (2 and 4) mentions space to be the clothing of the Paramahamsas.[4]

The Achaemenian Empire, from 6th century BC to the 4th Century BC had made possible the exchange of ideas between diverse types of Indian and Greek people. There were soldiers, traders, sailors and persons in administrative services, and also philosophers and ascetic wanderers who came in contact with one another. A group of Indian philosophers is said to have visited Athens, where they had met Sokrates. They asked him the object of his philosophy, 'An enquiry into human affairs', he told them. The Indian burst into laughter. 'How' asked the leading sage, 'can a man understand human affairs if he is ignorant of divine.[5] The Greek philosophy was born not in the Athens of Sokrates, the intellectual capital of Classical Greece, but on the coast of Asia Minor in Ionia, where the Achaemanian empire had enabled its Ionian Greek subjects to come in contact with developed civilizations of the Orient. The results of these contacts were spectacular, particularly in the domain of philosophy.

While analyzing the similar Indian and Greek philosophical ideas, some scholars take them up as a parallel development.[6] The others recognize the Indian influence.[7] The doctrine of metempsychosis unquestionably provides more specific analogy causing scholars to speculate that the idea as it occured in Greece, was ultimately derived from India. The causal link between a person's current social status and his good or evil deeds in a previous birth, is found only in India and Greece. In Greece, the doctrine is said to have been propounded by philosophers such as Orpheus, Pherekydes, Pythagoras and Empedocles, but is not directly attested by any source before Plato. Nonetheless the doctrine was not widely held there, whereas it is undoubtedly a prominent concept in Indian thought. The ancient Greeks too were agreed upon the point that Pythagorism was an idea alien to their land. But from where it had come, they were not sure. In the beginning Egypt was thought to be its source[8], but after Alexander when India came to be known as the land of philosophers, it was also recognized as the source of Pythagorism.[9]

Onesikritos' mention of Pythagoras, Sokrates and Diogenes, as having views similar to those of Indians, is fairly evident. Pythagorism's closeness to Indian ideas is well-known. The metempsychosis, the doctrine of five elements, the character of his religio-philosophical fraternity, mystical speculation, vegetarianism, prohibition of eating beans, and the pythagorean theorm, are the doctrines attributed to Pythagoras. These appear to be completely Indian.[10] The life of Sokrates also was like that of Indian ascetics, an example of self-discipline, voluntary hardship. The emphasis of Indian sophists on hardship as a means of strengthening the understanding; the remark that "the best house is that which requires the least repairs" and self tortuous asceticism practised by the naked sages of Taxila, are the features which are also present in Greece Philosophy.

We may say that Pythagoras himself taught transmigration, and may also be safely credited with the complex of ideas with which transmigration is bound up: the doctrine that the human soul is immortal, that it owes its immortality to its essential kinship with the divine universal soul, and that it may hope to return to its divine source when purified. This circumstance has naturally suggested the possibility that the ideas of ethical metempsychosis originated in India and spread thence to Greece. The fairly exceptional occurrence of this idea in Greece, combined with the Greeks' own conviction that it was a foreign concept, clearly suggests that metempsychosis was not native to Greece.[11]

We may conclude about Pythagoras in the words of Rawlinson, 'It is more likely that Pythagoras was influenced by India than by Egypt. Almost all the theories, religious, philosophical and mathematical taught by the Pythagoreans, were known in India in the sixth century B.C., and the Pythagoreans, like the Jains and Buddhists, refrained from the destruction of life and eating meat and regarded, certain vegetables such as beans as taboo.'[12]

There are many resemblances between Gnosticism and the ideas of the *Upanisads* mainly the Brahman atman doctrine. The Gnostic light-spark (or pneuma) and the*Upanisadic* atman are both defined as the inmost-self of the human being. They are similarly treated as identical in substance with the Supreme Power of the universe, i.e. with the Gnostic God or the *Upanisadic* Brahman. Each light-spark constitutes a portion of the heavenly light; each atman is in essence identical with Brahman, the World-Self. With this all, in both Gnosticism and the *Upanisads*, knowledge of this identity is similar to salvation.

According to Sedlar, there is a great likelihood for Gnostic system to have been influenced by Samkhya, he adds that no single Indian system can be considered as its complete counterpart, rather it has analogies with many, namely, *Upanishads, Bhagvad-Gita, Samkhya* and *Buddhism*.

The view of Gnosticism about coming of the soul on this earth has been defined in the "Purush" and "Prakriti" of Samkhya. "Purush" is pure consciousness and after assimilating with "prakriti" and matter has forgotten its divine origin. 'Purusha' is tied in flatters of earthly allurements from where it can be free through yoga, meditation and intelligence of knowledge.

In the light of the above study we see that there were vivid similarities in the philosophy ivolved between the ancient India and Greece. There were great similarities between Samkhya one of the six Orthodox philosophies of India and the Gnosticism of Greece. "Purush" in Samkhya in India and "pneuma" is Gnosticism of Greece are the similar terms. Both are of the opinion that the soul comes to the earth from almighty and getting influenced by the worldly allurements it forgets that it is the part of the divine and at the end it becomes one with Him. The soul can go back to the divine through the medium of intelligence and knowledge after being detached from this world and yoga is the other medium of it.

Rawlinson states that Gnosticism, a far more serious and noble creed, together with its later offshoots, shows traces of both Hindus and Zarathustrian influence. Its doctrine of the plurality of heavens is essentialy Indian : its "three qualities" resemble the "three gunas" of the Samkhya system.[13]

So there are the countless similarities which gives an idea that there was a possibility of Indian influence upon Gnosticism. In chronological order all the major Indian systems were more ancient. The *Upanisads* and the *Bhagavad Gita*, Buddhism, Jainism and probably Samkhya all arose in India long before Gnosticism took form in the Hellenistic world. Unfortunately, there is little direct evidence for Indian influence upon any of the Gnostic sects. We can trace the Indian-Gnostic connection mainly upon the striking similarities between the two, and on this possibility that Indian religious ideas might had accompanied Indian merchants, ambassadors and holy men into the Hellenistic world.

The cradle of Neoplatonism was not the quiet university town of Athens, but the great manufacturing city of Alexandria which was at that time not only a great intellectual centre but also the place where East and West rubbed their shoulders, where the wisdom of Asia was in high repute and where men of wisdom like Philostratus expressed the highest veneration for the learning of the Indians and even went to India to consult the Brahamanas.

Like the Upanisadic philosophy, Neoplatonism believes in the technique of entering into spiritual consciousness. Through meditation we can free the soul from its subjection to the body and attain union with the Divine. In order to attain this union we must strip everything of the body until the vision is attained. We must abstract from the body, from the soul, from sense perceptions, appetites and emotions, and from even the intellect with its duality. Then the soul touches and gazes on the supreme light. In this account we may see a replica of the Indian theory of contemplation.

In the presence of these historical data we may conclude that Indian thought might have played a great part in the development of the doctrines of Neoplatonism, and that Neoplatonism might be the result of the religious syncretism which arose from the conquests of Alexander the Great and the undertakings of the Roman Empire.

So we may say that some of the fundmental doctrines of Neoplatonism which have striking similarities with the doctrines of Indian philosophy were well-established in the *Upanisads* at least in the 6th century B.C.—long before the rise of Neoplatonism.

The teachings of Manichaeism can be explained in this way that was a most important example of Gnosticism. Central in the Manichaean teaching was dualism, that the world itself, and all creatures, was part of a battle between the good, represented by God, and the bad, the darkness, represented by a power driven by envy and lust.

As a major component of this faith, Indian religion unquestionably influenced the Hellenistic world. No doubt when Mani went to India, the frame-work of his thought was already Gnostic; his revelations were complete. But the mission to India could only have confirmed his world negating attitudes. Probably it was here that he found the model for his Elect, who practiced a degree of asceticism till than not known in the Hellenistic world to any great extent. His elect, those filthy and ragged wanders, with never-cut nails and wild hair, emanciated of body and pallid of countenance, oblivious to personal health or danger, and enduring the most fearful privations, but terribly in dread of sexuality and of doing harm to animals. Like Indian ascetics, the Manichaean, Elect did not work, but spent their time praying and preaching, meditating and weeping over the world's sins. Possibly the conception of the Bodhisattva, the enlightened but compassionate holy man, attracted him also. The fact that Mani acknowledged the Buddha as one of his three spiritual predecessors may well be due to his Indian journey.

The organization of the Manichaean Church was almost certainly indebted to Buddhists models. The hierarchical structure of the two institutions was similar; likewise their emphasis on missionary activity and the high status given to monks (Elect) as against laymen. However metempsychosis was certainly a familar doctrine to Mani before he ever saw India; it was typical of Gnosis. Mani's concept of the soul's path after death could have been borrowed from the older Upanishadic view that the soul must follow either the "way of the Gods" or the "way of the fathers"—i.e. either to Paradise or to another earthly life. In particular, he did not adopt the comparatively mild Buddhist form of asceticism, but a much more extreme type : possibly from the Jains or from various

Hindu ascetics.

Even apart from Mani's known connection with India, this affinity creates a strong presumption that he was influenced by Indian prototypes when he defined a suitable life-style for his elite order of Elect. Thereby some of the more obvious aspects of Indian asceticism passed by way of Manichaeism into Christianity, particularly into the Christianity of Syria and Mesopotamia, where Manichaeism enjoyed greater influence than elsewhere. The relatively modest asceticism of the Greek speaking monks betrays fewer Manichaean features; in the Latin-speaking West, Monasticism took root even more slowly. Nonetheless, all forms of Christian monasticism were interconnected. The monks visited, imitated and learned from one another. Thus by this long chain of influences, Indian asceticism left its mark on the religious style of innumerable Christians who had never heard of India.

Asceticism as a well-developed theory and systematic practice appears very much earlier in India than in the Greek world. By contrast with India, an organized asceticism appeared quite late in the history of Christianity—not until the end of the 3rd and beginning of the 4th centuries. The early Church gave little encouragement either to anchoritism (the solitary religious life) or to monasticism. Thus in Christianity, as apposed to the Brahminism, Jainism, Buddhism or Bhakti-religions of India, asceticism was not inherent. These circumstances inevitably raise questions as to the reasons for the eventual development of ascetic practices within Christianity. In Christian Monasticism the monks actively sought physical suffering since they regarded mortification of the body as nourishment for the soul. Eating and drinking they reduced to the limit of bodily endurance. At times they fasted completely for many days in succession. They slept on bare ground, and slept little, keeping constant vigils. Moreover, they invented many hars hand unusual forms of austerity. Some of the monks assumed awkward physical positions which they maintained for long periods of time, or stood immoveable for hours praying in the rain, wind or snow. Others actively sought their own destruction, especially if they felt their ascetic resolution to be weakening : they took no precautions against wild animals or snakes, or threw themselves from precipices.

Both Buddhism and Brahmanism possessed institutions that have certain characteristics analogous to those of Christian monasticism. In the sacred books of the Hindus mention is made of hermits forming colonies and dedicating their lives to the study of the Vedas and to the contemplation of Brahman. They are vegetarians, and practise mortification in all its forms. While in Brahmanism the monastic life has preserved its eremitic character, in Buddhism we find it, on the contrary, in the cenobitic form. The monks live together in monasteries, in the state of poverty practicing celibacy as mendicants. Such monasteries are still to be found in Japan, Korea, China, India and Ceylon.

Here we may conclude in the light of the above study that in ancient times there were so many doctrines of various sects of Greece which were parallel or similar to doctrines of Indian religious sects and philosophy. Our study shows that religious sects in Greece were directly or indirectly influenced by India.

REFERENCES

1. Law, B.C., *India in Early Texts of Buddhism and Jainism,* London, 1940, p. 222.
2. Arora, U.P. "The Fragments of Onesikritos on India" An appraisal in *Indian Historical Review,* Vol. XXXII, No.1 (Jan. 2005), ICHR, New Delhi, 2005, p. 76.
3. *Ibid,* p. 76.
4. Vassiliades, Demetrios Th., *India and Greece Philosophical Understanding*, Delhi, 2000, p. 49.
5. Fernanado Tola and Carmen Dragonetti, "India and Greece Before Alexander", *ABORI,* Poona, 1986, Vol. 67 (1-4) pp. 159-194.
6. Sedlar, J.W., *India and Greek World*, Totowa, 1980, pp. 265.
7. *Ibid.*, p. 271.
8. Guthrie, W.K.C., *A History of Greek Philosophy*, Cambridge, 1962, Vol. 1, p. 163.
9. Sedlar, *op. cit.,* p. 31-32.

10. Schroeder, Leopld V., *Pythagoras und die Inder*, Leipsic, 1884; Garbe, R., *Philosophy of Ancient India*, Chicago, 1879; Radhakrishnan, S., *Eastern Religion, op. cit.* pp. 142-43; Tripathi, C. L., "The Influence of Indian Philosophy on Neoplatonism", *op. cit.* pp. 273-292.
11. Sedlar, *op. cit.*, p. 32.
12. Rawlinson, H. G., *Legacy of India*, p. 5.
13. Rawlinson, H.G., *Intercourse Between India and the Western World*, *op. cit.*, p. 177.

BIBLIOGRAPHY

DICTIONARIES & ENCYCLOPEDIAS

Dictionaries :

Classical Dictionary, Lempriere, London, 1984.
Dictionary of Philosophy and Psychology, James Mark, Baldwin, 1901.
Dictionary of Classical Mythology, Pierre Grimal, England, 1985.
Oxford Dictionary of the Christian Church; London, 1958.
Sanskrit-English Dictionary, Macdonell.
A Classical Dictionary of Hindu Mythology and Religion, Geography, History and Literature, Downson, John, New Delhi, 1973.
A Dictionery of Hinduism, Margaret and James Stutley, London, 1977.
Elwell Evangelical Dictionary. Trans. Charles Kesler, London, 1965.

ENCYCLOPEDIAS

Encyclopaedia of Religion and Ethics, Vol. IX, ed., James Hastings.
Encycclopaedia of the Upaniṣads, Subrahmaniam N.S., New Delhi, 1985.
The Encyclopedia of Religion, Ed. Mircea Eliade, New York, 1987.
Encyclopaedia Britannica, 11th edn. Professor, W. Bausset, "Gnosticism".
Encyclopaedia of Indian Mysticism, ed. Shantideva Sadhu, Delhi, 1999.
Encyclopaedia of Social Sciences.

Encyclopedia Monasticism, Ed. Johnston William, M. 2 Vols., Chicago, 2000.

Encyclopedia of Religions, Virgiliars, Newyork, 1945.

The Encyclopaedia of Philosophy, Vol. V., Paul Edwards.

ORIGINAL TEXTS

Indian, Greek & Others

Alberuni's India: Ed. Dr. Edward C. Sachau, New Delhi, 1964.

Atharva Veda: Trans. W.D. Whitney and Edited by C.R. Lamman, Cambridge, Mass, 1905 (Repr. Delhi. 1971).

Aristotle: Joeger, E.T., 1935.

Aṣtadhyāyī of Pāṇini: Nirnaya Sagar Press, Bombay, 1955 Ed. S.C. Vasu, Delhi, 1962.

Brhadāṛaṇyaka Upaniṣad: Ed. R. Roer, 1856-Trans. (Hindi) Samkara's Comm. Gita Press, Gorakhpur, 1968.

Brhatsamhita of Varahmihira: Ed. H. Kern, Calcutta, 1865 with Eng. Trans., Notes, Comments by M. Ramkrishna Bhatt, 2 Vols., Delhi, 1981.

Enneads, Plotinus, V.I. 3.

Fragmenta Historicorum Graecorum: Aristoxenos in C. Mueller, (in 5 Vols.) Vol. II Paris, 1841.

Geography, Strabo, Text and trans. Ed. by H.L. Jones, 8 Vol. Loeb Classical Library.

History of Alexander (Anabasis): Arrian, 2 Vol. Trans. Rev. E. Lliffe Robson, Loeb Classical Library.

Historia: Herodotus, Text with Eng. Trans. by A.D. Godley 4 Vols. Loeb. Classical Library.

Kephalaia: Trans. & Ed. Hans J. Paltsky, Vol. I of *MHSMB* Stuttgart, 1940. (Manichaische Handscriften dertaatichen Museen Berlin).

"Laws" ***Plato*** (Loeb).

Life of Plotinos, Porphyry in Kenneth Guthrie ed. Plotinos, *Complete Work,* London, 1918.

Mahābharata, Crit. Edn., Poona, 1927-66 Eng. Trans., M.N. Dutt, Calcutta, 1895-05. Hindi Trans., & Text., Gita Press, Gorakhpur.

Mahābhaṣya, Patanjali, Ed. F. Keilhorn (in 3 Vols.) Bombay, 1892-1909.

Maitri Upaniṣad: Ed. and Translated by E.B. Cowell, 1870.

Manu Smriti: Ed. V.N. Mandlik, Bombay, 1886, Tr. with notes, G.N. Jha, 5 Vols., Calcutta, 1922-29. Eng. Trans., G. Buhler, SBE XXV, Oxford 1886, (Rep. Delhi 1964).

Milinda Pañho: Nagsena, Eng. Trans. T.W. Rhys Devids. SBE Series, 2 Vol. Oxford, 1890-94 (Repr. Delhi, 1964).

Natural History, Pliny, Text and Trans. by Rackham and Others, 10 Vol., Loeb Classical Library.

Nāradā Smriti: With extracts from the comm. of Asahaya, Ed. J. Jolly, Calcutta, 1885. Trans. by J. Jolly, SBE, XXXIII, Oxford, 1889. (Repr. Delhi, 1964).

On Yaun Chwang's Travels in India, Thomas Watters, London, 1904-05.

On Abstinence from Animal Food, Porphyry, Trans. Thomas Taylor, Ed. Esme Wynne Tyson, London, 1965.

Philo Judeaus, "Hypothetica" ("Apologia, Pro Judaeis"), Trans. F.H. Colson in *Philo,* Loeb Library, Vol. IX., Cambridge Mass, 1960.

"Phaedo" in *Plato* (Loeb) 1.

Rāmāyaṇa: Crit. Edn. Borada, 1960, Gita Press Ed. (Hindi Trans.), Gorakhpur, Eng. Trans. by Har Prasad Sastri, London, 1962.

Ṛgveda: Text with Sayanas Commentary, Ed. by F. Max Mueller, 1980-92. Trans. K.F. Geldner, Cambridge, 1951.

Ṛgveda: *Hymns from the Vedas,* Bombay, 1966. Bose A.C., Tr.

Śatapaṭha Brāhmaṇa: Ed. with Sayana Comm. A. Weber, London, 1885. Eng. Trans. J. Eggeling. SBE. Vol. 12, 26, Oxford, 1882-1900.

Si-Yu-Ki: Buddhist Records of the Western World, Chinese Accounts of India, Ed. & Trans. by S. Beal, London, 1884 (Repr. Delhi, 1980).

The Attic Nights (Leeb): Aulus Gellius.

The Hymns of the Ṛgveda: Trans. Ralph T.H. Griffith, Benares,1897.

The Question of Milinds's: Trans. I. B. Harner in Vol. XXII of SBB, London, 1963.

The Contemplative Life, Philo Judueus, Trans. F.H. Calson in *Philo.,* Loeb Library, Cambridge Mass: Vol. IX, 1960.

The life of Apollonius of Tyana, Philostratus, Trans. F.C. Conybeare, Loeb Library, London, 1912, 2 Vols.

"The Frogs" in *Aristophanes* Verse Trans. by Benjamin Bickley Rogers, 3 Vols. Loeb Classical Dictionary.

The Laws of Manu trans. George Buhler, Oxford, 1886.

The Mahābhārata of Krishṇa-Dwaipāyana Vyasa, trans. Pratap Chandra Roy.

Vasudevāśrama Yatidharma Prakāśa, Olivelle Patrick, Ed. and trans. Delhi & Vienna, 1976-1977.

MONOGRAPHS & ARTICLES

Agarwal V.S., *India as Known to Pāṇini,* Varanasi, 1963.

Agarwal V.S., *Sparks from the Vedic Fire,* Varanasi, 1944.

Agarwal V.S., *Vedic Lectures,* Varanasi, 1963.

Agarwal V.S., *Shiva Mahādeva: The Grerat God,* Varanasi, 1966.

Altekar A.S., *Education in Ancient India,* Benares, 1944.

Armstrong A.H., "Plotinus and India",*Classical Quarterly,* 1936.

Arnaldo Mamiggliano,*Alien Wisdonn: The Limits of Hellenization,* Cambridge, 1976.

Arora U.P., *Motifs in Indian Mythology : Their Greeks and Other Parallels,* Delhi, 1981.

Arora U.P., *Greeks on India,* ISGARS, Bareilly, 1996.

Arora U.P.,"The Reliability of Megasthenes' India" in *Contact Between Cultures,* Vol. 2, South Asia, Selected Papers from 33rd International Congress of Asian and North African Studies, Toronto, Ed., K.I. Koppedrayer, New York & Queeston,1992.

Arora U.P., "The Folklore in Ancient Indian and Greek Literature" in *Essays on Indology, Polity and Administration-in Honour of Padmabuṣaṇ Shri R.K. Trivedi,* S.D. Trivdei (Ed.), Delhi, 1989.

Arora U.P., "Ancient India and Ancient Greece" in *Life Thought and Culture in India (600 B.C. to A.D. 300),* Ed. G.C. Pande in *History of Science, Philosophy and Culture in Indian Civilization,* Vol. 1, Part-2, New Delhi, 2001.

Arora U.P., "Form of State Power in Mauryan India–Megasthenses' Evidence" in *Facets of Indian History, Culture and Archaeology,* S.P. Gupta and K.S. Ramchandran (ed.). New Delhi, 1991.

Arora U.P., "The Fragments of Onesikritos on India" An Appraisal" in *Indian Hisstorical Review,* Ed. U.P. Arora, Vol. XXXII, No. 1 (Jan. 2005), ICHR, New Delhi, 2005.

Arora U.P., "Roman-Age Authors on Ancient India" *Yavanika No. 1- ISGARS,* Bareilly, 1991.

Ayar K. Narayanswami, *Thirty Minor Upanishads,* Delhi, 1987.

Banerjea R.D., *The Eastern Indian School of Medieval Sculpture,* Archaeological Survey of India, Delhi, 1933.

Banerjee G.N., *Hellenism Ancient India,* London, 1920.

Banerji Suresh Chandra, *Dharma Sutras,* Calcutta, 1962.

Barnett L.D., *Antiquities of India,* Calcutta, 1964.

Basak Radhagovinda, *Aśokan Incriptions,* Calcutta, 1959.

Basham A.L., *The Wonder That Was India,* London, New Delhi, 1954 (1981).

Beal S., *Si-Yu-ki, Buddhist Records of The Westen Worlds,* Vol. 1, London, 1884, (Repr. Delhi, Varanasi, 1980).

Benjamin Preciado-Solis, "Some Problems Concerning the Origin of Saṁnyāsa", *ABORI,* Poona, 1987.

Bernard Paul, "Ai Khanum on the Oxus : A Hellenistic City in Central Asia, "*Proceedings of the British Academy,* Vol. 53, London, 1967.

Bevean E., *House of Seleucuss,* Vol. 1, London, 1966.

Bhagat M.G., "Asceticism in The Purāṇas", "*Indica,* Journal of the Heras Institute of Indian History and Culture, Bombay, Vol. 12, 1975.

Bhandarkar R.G., *Early History of the Dekkan,* Bhartiya Publishing House, 1975.

Bhandarkar R.G., *Vaishnavism, Shaivism and Minor Religious System,* Varanasi, 1965.

Bhat M.S., *Vedic Tantrism,* Delhi, 1987.

Bharti Durgachaitanya, *Sanyāsa aur Sanyāsi,* Benares, 1949.

Bhattacharya, Art: The Background of Buddhist Philosophy, *Indo-Asian Culture,* July, 1952.

Bhattacharya N.N., *Tantric Buddhism,* New Delhi, 1999.

Bhattacharya N.N., *Ancient Indian Rituals and Their Social Contents,* Delhi, 1996.

Blumenthal H.J., *Plotinus' Psychology: His Doctrine of the Embodied Soul,* The Hague, 1971.

Bloomfield, *Religion of the Vedas.*

Bose, Nirmal Kumar, *Culture and Society in India,* Bombay, 1967.

Boyce Mary, *The Manichaean Hymn-cycles in Parthian,* London, 1954.

Brehier E., *La Philosophie de Plotin,* Paris, 1938, quoted in Staal, *Advaita and Neoplatonism.*

Brown T.S., *Onesicritus,* Berkeley, 1949.

Butter, E.C., *Benedictine Monachism.*

Carpenter J.E., *Buddhism and Christianity,* New Delhi, 1988.

Cartledge Paul, *Ancient Greece,* (Cambridge Illustrated History) Cambridge, 1998.

Chadwick Owen, *Western Asceticism,* London, 1958.

Chakrovarti Haripada, *Asceticisim in Ancient India,* Calcutta, 1973.

Chand, *Memoirs of Arch. Survey of India,* No. 1.

Chandra Lokesh, "The Sublime and the Infinite" in *India and Greece-Connection and Parallels,* S. Doshi (ed.), Marg. Pub. Bombay, 1985.

Chapekar Nalinee, *Ancient India and Ancient Greece,* Delhi, 1977.

Chatterjee Asim Kumar, *A Comprehensive History of Jainism,* Vol. 2, New Delhi, 2000.

Chattopadhyaya Shankar, *Evolution of Hindu Sects,* New Delhi, 1970.

Chattopadhyaya D.P., "Uddālaka Āruṇi : The Pioneer of Science". *Indian Historical Review,* ICHR, Vol. XIII, No. 12, New Delhi, (July 1986 Jan. 1987)

Clay R.M., "The Hermit and Anchorites of England" in *the*

Antiquary's Book, London, 1914.
Colebrook H.L., *Miscellanious Essays,* Vol. 1. London, 1873.
Compton Piers : *The Great Religious Orders,* 1931.
Conford F.M., "Mysticism and Science in Pythagorean Tradition", *Classical Quarterly,* 1922.
Coulton. G.C., *Five Centuries of Religions.*
Crooke W., *The Popular Religion and Folklore of Northern India,* New Delhi, 1968 (1896).
Cumon, *Lux Perpetua,* Paris, 1949.
Cunningham, Agnes, "Manichaeism" in *Elwell Evangelical Dictionary.*
Dasguptạ Surendranath, *A Study of Patanjali,* Delhi, 1920 (1989).
Davids Rhys T.W., *Indian Budhism,* Allahabad, 1972.
Detienne Marcel, *Les Jardins d' Adonis,* Paris, 1972.
Deussen Paul, *The Philosophy of the Upanishads,* Trans A.S. Geden, Edinburg, 1906.
Deussen Paul, *Sixty Upanishads of the Veda,* New Delhi, 1980.
Dimock Edward C., *The Place of the Hidden Moon,* Delhi, 1991.
Dikshit K.N., *Pre Historic Civlization of the Indus Valley,* Madras, 1793.
Diskshit Chintamani T.R., *The Saṁnyāsa Upanishad,* Madras, 1966.
Dodds, E.R., *Humanism and Technique in Greek Studies,* 1936.
Dumont Leuis, "Renunciation in Indian Religions" In *Religion, Politics and History in India,* Nouton, The Hague, 1970.
Dumoulin, H., and Maraldo, J.C. Eds., *Buddhism in the Modern World,* 1976.
Dunbabin T.J., *The Western Greeks,* Oxford, 1948.
Dupont Sommer, *The Essence Writings from Qumran,* Oxford, 1961.
Dutt Nalinaksha, *Early Monastic Buddhisim,* Calcutta, 1971.
Dutt Sukumar, *Buddhist Monks and Monasteries of India,* London, 1962.
Eliade, Mircea, Yoga, *Immortality and Freedoms,* Princeton, 1969.
Fernando Tola and Carmen Dragonetti, "India and Greece

before Alexander"., *ABORI,* Poona, 1986, Vol. 67.

Filliozat J., "Ancient India and Graeco Roman World" *Proceedings of the Fifth World Sanskrit Conference.*

Filliozat Jean, "Intercourse of India with the Roman Empire during the Opening Centuries of the Christian Era", *JIH,* Vol. XII, 1950.

Flaherty W. D. O., *Asceticism and Eroticism in the Mythology of Shive, Delhi*, 1973.

Flinders-Petrie, "Memphis and Its Foreigners" *in Scientific American Supplement,* 1904.

Frank Knight, G.A., *Nile and Jordan*, 1921.

Garbe Richard, *Philosophy of Ancient India,* Chicago, 1897.

Garber William, *The Mind of India,* New York, 1967.

Ghurye Govind S., *Cast and Race in India,* Bombay, 1953.

Ghurye Govind S., *Indian Sadhus,* Bombay, 1953.

Ghurye Govind S., *Vedic India,,* Bombay, 1979.

Ghose Shishir Kumar, *Lord Gaurang or Salvation for All,* Calcutta, 1897.

Gomperz, *Greek Thinkers,* Vol. 1, New York, 1953.

Gompopa, *Jewel Ornament of Liberation,* Trans, Guenther, Chap. 21, quoted in Walllis, *Neoplatonism.*

Gopal Lallanji, "Samkhya and Greek Pilosophy" in *Graeco-Indica India's Cultural Contacts with Greek World,* Ed. U.P. Arora, Delhi, 1991.

Gregorios Paul, "The Monastic Traditions" in *India and Greece Connections and Parallels,* Ed. S. Doshi, Marg Publication, Bombay, 1985.

Gupta Sunil, "List of Explored and Excavated Early Historic Sites in India Yielding Material Evidence of Indo-Roman Trade", *Yavanika, Journal of the Indian Society for Greek and Roman Studies,* No. 3, 1993.

Guthrie, W.K.C., *A History of Greek Philosophy,* Cambridge, 1962.

Haloun G. & Henning W.B., "The Compendium of the Docctrines and Styles of the Teaching of Mani, The Buddha of Light", *Asia Major,* 1952.

Hamilton, *Description of Hinduism,* London, 1820.

Hapkins F.W., *Religions of India,* New Delhi, 1970.

Hardman Oscar, *The Ideals of Asceticism: An Essay in the Comparative Study of Religion,* New York, 1924.

Hindu Manners, Customs and Ceremonies, New Delhi, 1973.

Inge, W.R., *The Platonic Tradition in English Religious Thought,* 1926.

Inge, W.R., Trans. *Philosophy of Plotinos,* Vol. II, 1918.

Jonas Hans, *The Gnostic Religion,* Boston, 1958.

Josephus Flavius, *The Jewish War,* Trans. H.S. J. Thackeray in *Josephus* Loeb Library, Cambridge Mass: 1927-28, Vol. 2-3.

Kane P.V., *History of Dharmashastra,* Poona, 1974.

Karttuen Klaus, *India and the Hellenistic World,* Helsinki 1997.

Kazanas N., "Advaita and Gnosticism" in *Indian Historical Review,* Ed. U.P. Arora, Vol. XXXII, No. 1 (Jan. 2005), ICHR, New Delhi, 2005.

Keith, A.B., "Pythogoras and Transmigration", *JRAS,* 1909.

Kennedy, "Buddhist Gnosticism", *JRAS,* 1902.

King, C.W., *The Gnoastics and Their Remains–Ancient and Mediaeval,* 2nd Ed. 1887.

Knowles, D., *Christian Monasticism,* 1969.

Larson Gerald James, *Sāṁkhya Kārika*, XXI in *Classical Sāṁkhya An Interpretation of Its History and Meaning,* Delhi, 1969.

Law, B.C., *India in Early Texts of Buddhism and Jainism,* London, 1940.

Law, N.N., *The Indian Historical Quarterly,* New Delhi, 1985.

Lawrence J. Hatab, "Plotinus and the Upanishads" In *Neoplatonism and Indian Thought,* Ed. by R. Baine Harris, Delhi, 1992.

Lohse, Bernhard, *Askese und Monchtum in der Antike und in der alten kirche,* Munich, 1969.

Majumdar R.C., *Classical Accounts of India*, Calcutta, 1960.

Marshall Sir John, *A Guide to Taxila,* Cambridge, 1951.

Marshall, *Journal of the Royal Asiatic Society,* 1909.

Masson J. Moussaieff, "The Psychology of the Ascetics",*Journal of Asian Studies,* August, 1976.

Mathew Black, *The Scrolls and Christain Origins,* New York, 1961.

Mc Crindle J.W., *Ancient India as Described by Ktesias the Knidian,* Calcutta, 1882.

Mc Crindle J.W., *Ancient India as Described by Megasthenes and Arrian,* Calcutta, 1877.

Mc Crindle J.W., *Ancient India as Described by Ptolemy,* Calcutta, *1885.*

Mc Crindle J.W., *Ancient India as Described in Classical Literature,* Westminster, 1901.

Mc Crindle J.W., *The Commerce and Navigation of the Erythraen Sea,* Calcutta, 1879.

Mc Crindle J.W., *The Invaison of India by Alexander, the Great,* Westminister, 1901.

Merton, T. *The Monastic Journey,* Ed. by P. Hart, 1977.

Miller David, M. and Dorothy C. Wertz., *Hindu Monastic Life: the Monks and Monasteries of Bhubaneswar,* Montreal, 1976.

Minar E.L. *Early Pythagorean Politics in Practise and Theory,* Baltimore, 1942.

Mitchiner John E., *Traditions of Seven Risis,* Delhi, 1992.

Mitchiner John E., "Rishihood and the Soma Cult" in*Proceedings of 29th All India Oriental Conference,* 1978.

Moor, *Hindu Pantheon,* London, 1810.

Narian A.K. *The Indo-Greeks,* Oxford, 1957.

Ojha K.C., *The History of Foreign Rule in Ancient India,* Allahabad, 1968.

Olivelle Patrick, *The Āśrama System,* New York, 1993.

Olivelle Patrick, "Contributions to the Semantic Development of Saṁnyāsa" *Journal of the American Oriental Society,* 1981.

Oman J.C., *Mystic Ascetic and Saints of India,* London, 1901.

Oman J.C., *The Great Indian Epics,* London, 1899.

Pande G.C., *Studies in the Origins of Buddhism,* New Delhi, 1957.

Paul Deussen, *The Philosophy of the Upanishads,* New Delhi, 1906, (1985).

Paul Dahlke, *Buddhist Essays,* New Delhi, 1978.

Paul. Y. Diana, *Women in Buddhism,* London, 1985.

Pearson, *Lost Histories of Alexander, the Great,* New York, 1960.

Puri B.N., *India Under the Kushanas,* Bombay, 1965.

Radhakrishnan S., *Eastern Relligions and Western Thoughts,* New Delhi, 1939.

Radhakrishnan S., *Indian Philoophy,* Vol. 1, New York, 1923.

Radhakrishnan S., *The Concept of Man,* Delhi, 1966 (1992).

Rawlinson H.G., "Indian in European Literature and Thought," in G.T. Garrati (Ed.), *The Legacy of India,* Oxford, 1937.

Rawlinson. H.G., *Intercourse Between Indian and the Western World from the Earliest Times to the Fall of Rome,* Cambridge, 1916.

Roychaudhari H.C., *Political History of Ancient India,* Calcutta, 1950.

Russell and Hira Lal, *The Tribes and Castes of the Central Provinces of India*, Vol. III, 1916.

Sabbatucci, *Saggio sul misticismo greco,* Rome, 1965.

Sankalia H.D., *Rāmayaṇa-Myth or Reality*, New Delhi, 1973.

Schroeder, *Pythagoras und dei inder,* Leipzig, 1884.

Sedlar Jean W., *India and The Greek World,* Totowa, 1980.

Sharma Har Dutta, *Contribution to the History of Brahamanical Ascetiscism,* Poona, 1939.

Sharma Rajendra Nath, *Ancient India According to Manu,* Delhi, 1980.

Shastri Ajay Mitra, " Yavanas in Western Indian Cave Inscription" *Yavankika,* No. 3, ISGARS, Bareilly, 1993.

Sholapurkar, *Saints and Sages of India*, Delhi, 1992.

Singhal D.P., *India and the World Civilization,* Delhi, 1972.

Smith H. Daniel and M. Narsimha Chary, *Hanbook of Hindu Gods, Goddesses and Saints,* Delhi, 1991.

Smith Vincent, *Early History of India,* Oxford, 1924.

Sorokin, *Social and Cultural Dynamics,* Vol. 1.

Sprockhoff Joachim Freidrich, *Samnyasa,* Wiesbaden, 1976.

Staal J.F., *Advaita and Neoplatonism,* Madras, 1961.

Stace T. Walter, *The Teachings of The Mystics,* New York, 1960.

Subrata Kumar Acharya, "Evolution of the Institution of Beggary in Ancient India", Vol. 69, *ABORI,* Poona, 1988.

Swain Word Joseph, *The Hellenic Origins of Christian Asceticism,* New York, 1916.

Tarn W.W., *Alexander, the Great,* Vol. II, Cambridge, 1950.

Tran W.W., *The Greeks in Bactria and India,* Cambridge, 1938 (1980).

Taylor E. Alfred, *Platonism and Its Influence,* New York, 1927.

Thapar Romila, *Ancient Indian Social History,* Hyderabad, 1984.

Thapliyal U.P., *Foreign Elements in Ancient Indian Society,* New Delhi, 1979.

Theiler Willy, *Far schangan zum Neoplatonismus. Qullen und studien zur Geschichte der philosphie, Berlin,* 1966.

Thomas J. Edward, *The History of Buddhist Thought,* Delhi, 1997 (1993).

Trimingham, J.S., *The Sufi Order in Islam,* 1971.

Tripathi, C.L., "Influence of Indian Philosophy", In *Neoplatonism and Indian Thought,* Ed. R. Baine Harris, Delhi, 1992.

Vassiliades. Demetrios Th., *The Greeks in India: A Survey in Philasophical Understanding,* Delhi, 2000.

Vassiliade, Dembtrios Th., "India and Greece : Early Philosophical Understanding", in *Indian Historical Review,* Vol. XXXII, No.1 (Jan. 2005), ICHR, New Delhi, 2005.

Velissaropoulas C. Dimitraos, "The Ancien Greek Knowledge of India Philosophy", *In Graecco Indica, India's Cultural Contacts with the Greek World,* Ed., U.P. Arora, Delhi, 1991.

Vidhyārthi P.B., *Early Indian Religious Thought,* New Delhi, 1976.

Wallis, R.T., *Neoplationsim*, London, Duckworth, 1972.

Ward William, *History Literature and Mythology of the Hindoos,* Delhi, 1985.

Weber Max, *Essays in Sociology,* Ed. Hans H. Gerth and C. Wright Mills, Oxford, 1958.

Wheeler M., *Indus Civilization,* Cambridge, 1953.

Wheeler Mortimer, *Flames Over Persepolis,* New York, 1968.

Whittaker, *Neo-Platonists,* Cambridge, 1918.

Widengreen G., *Mani and Manichaism,* Trans. Charles Kessler, London, 1965.

Williams M.M., *Hinduism,* Calcutta, 1951.

Wilson E., *Sacred Books of the East,* New Delhi, 1978.

Wilson H.H., *Sketch of Religious Sects of the Hindus,* New Delhi, 1977.

Wilson H.H., *The Religious Sects of the Hindus,* London 1904 (Originally Published, 1828, 1832)

Wilson, R. Mcl., *The Gnostic Problem,* London, 1958.

Winternitz, *Visvabharati Quarterly,* Feb. 1937.

Workman, H.B., *The Evolution of the Monastic Ideal,* 1913.

Zannas E. Lascarides, "The Hellenization of the East", *Proceedings of the Fifth World Sanskrit Conference.*

Zurcher, Dr.E., *Buddhism,* London, 1962.

INDEX